Theory and Practice of
Computation

Theory and Practice of
Computation

Proceedings of Workshop on Computation: Theory and Practice WCTP2016

The University of the Philippines Cebu, Cebu City, The Philippines
21 – 22 September 2016

Editors

Shin-ya Nishizaki
Tokyo Institute of Technology, Japan

Masayuki Numao
Osaka University, Japan

Jaime D L Caro
University of the Philippines Diliman, Philippines

Merlin Teodosia C Suarez
De La Salle University, Philippines

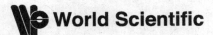
World Scientific

NEW JERSEY · LONDON · SINGAPORE · BEIJING · SHANGHAI · HONG KONG · TAIPEI · CHENNAI · TOKYO

Published by

World Scientific Publishing Co. Pte. Ltd.

5 Toh Tuck Link, Singapore 596224

USA office: 27 Warren Street, Suite 401-402, Hackensack, NJ 07601

UK office: 57 Shelton Street, Covent Garden, London WC2H 9HE

British Library Cataloguing-in-Publication Data
A catalogue record for this book is available from the British Library.

THEORY AND PRACTICE OF COMPUTATION
Proceedings of Workshop on Computation: Theory and Practice WCTP2016

ISBN 978-981-3234-06-2

Printed in Singapore

Preface

Computation should be a good blend of theory and practice. Researchers in the field should create algorithms to address real world problems putting equal weight to analysis and implementation. Experimentation and simulation can be viewed as yielding to refined theories or improved applications. WCTP 2016 is the sixth workshop organized by the Tokyo Institute of Technology, The Institute of Scientific and Industrial Research – Osaka University, University of the Philippines – Diliman and De La Salle University–Manila that is devoted to theoretical and practical approaches to computation. It aims to present the latest developments by theoreticians and practitioners in academe and industry working to address computational problems that can directly impact the way we live in society.

Following the success of WCTP 2011–2015, WCTP 2016 was held in the University of the Philippines Cebu, on September 21 and 22, 2016. This post-proceedings is the collection of the selected papers that were presented at WCTP 2016.

The program of WCTP 2016 consisted of selected research contributions. It included the most recent visions and researches of 6 talks in work-in-progress session, 18 contributions. We collected the original contributions after their presentation at the workshop and began a review procedure that resulted in the selection of the papers in this volume. They appear here in the final form.

WCTP 2016 required a lot of work that was heavily dependent on members of the program committee, and lastly, we owe a great debt of gratitude to the University of the Philippines Cebu, specifically, Ryan Ciriaco Dulaca, Julie Nieva Yuleta Orillo, Aileen Joan O. Vicente, and Robert Roxas, for organizing the workshop.

August, 2017

Shin-ya Nishizaki
Masayuki Numao
Jaime Caro
Merlin Teodosia Suarez

PROGRAM CO-CHAIRS

Shin-ya Nishizaki	Tokyo Insitute of Technology, Tokyo, Japan
Masayuki Numao	Osaka University, Osaka, Japan
Jaime Caro	Univeristy of the Philippines – Diliman, the Philippines
Merlin Teodosia Suarez	De La Salle Univeristy – Manila, the Philippines

PROGRAM COMMITTEES

Ken-ichi Fukui	– Osaka University, Japan
Satoshi Kurihara,	– The University of Electro-Communications, Japan
Koichi Moriyama,	– Nagoya Institute of Technology, Japan
Mitsuharu Yamamoto	– Chiba University, Japan
Hiroyuki Tominaga	– Kagawa University, Japan

Takuo Watanabe, Shigeki Hagihara, Masaya Shimakawa
　　　　　　　– Tokyo Institute of Technology, Japan

Raymund Sison, Jocelynn Cu, Gregory Cu, Rhia Trogo, Judith Azcarraga, Ethel Ong, Charibeth Cheng, Nelson Marcos, Rafael Cabredo, Joel Ilao
　　　　　　　– De La Salle University, the Philippines

Rommel Feria, Henry Adorna
　　　　　　　– University of the Philippines Diliman, the Philippines

Robert Roxas, Kurt Junshean Espinosa
　　　　　　　– University of the Philippines Cebu, the Philippines

John Paul Vergara, Mercedes Rodrigo
　　　　　　　– Ateneo De Manila University, the Philippines

Allan A. Sioson　　Ateneo de Naga University, the Philippines

GENERAL CO-CHAIRS

Hirofumi Hinode   Tokyo Tech Philippines Office, Tokyo Institute of Technology, Japan

Masayuki Numao   International Collaboration Center, The Institute of Scientific and Industrial Research, Osaka University, Japan

ORGANIZING COMMITTEES

Kurt Junshean Espinosa, Robert Roxas, Ryan Ciriaco Dulaca, Yuleta Orillo, Julie Nieva
– University of the Philippines Cebu

Contents

Preface   v

Committees   vii

CFRP: A Functional Reactive Programming Language for
Small-Scale Embedded Systems   1
  Suzuki, K., Nagayama, K., Sawada, K., Watanabe, T.

Discussion of LTL Subsets for Efficient Verification   14
  Shimakawa, M., Iwasaki, Y., Hagihara, S., Yonezaki, N.

First-class Environments in Categorical Combinators   28
  Joko, H., Nishizaki, S.

An Automated Way of Characterizing Protein Sequence
Entries Stored in a Database   44
  Pacilan, J. D., Alferez, K. P., Lao, D. M.

CALVIS: Educational Tool in Learning Intel x86-32
Instruction Set Architecture   59
  Alcalde, J. G., Chua, G., Demabildo, I. M., Ong, M. A.,
    Uy, R. L.

Assembly Optimization Loop Unroll Implementation for
RISC and CISC Processors and Metrics for Testing
Optimization Effectiveness   70
  Cempron, J. P., Gonzales, J. B., Hayakawa, Y., Salinas, C.,
    Uy, R. L.

Deployable Mobile Communication Infrastructure for
Emergency Services (DISTRESS)   83
    Chua, J. A., Go-Soco, J. P., Morano, I. S., Pequiras, K. D.,
    Ong, A. V.

Filmification: Visual Programming Environment -
Demonstrated Using Jacobi Relaxation Method as an Example   94
    Uriarte, B. D. C., Roxas, R. R.

Direction Tracking of a Single Moving Camera through
Periodic Image Stitching   106
    Ilao, J., Flores, F. K.

Score Transition of Card Game Strategy as Personal Progress
Situation in an Applied C Programming Exercise with a
Contest Style   120
    Hanakawa, N., Gemba, F., Tominaga, H.

A User Acceptance Test on ConnectUP: An Academic Social
Networking Application Developed Using University Ontology   132
    de Leon, R. P., Nazario, M., Solamo, Ma. R., Feria, R.

A Rule-Based Classification of ECG Rhythms Using Moving
First Derivative of the Signal   160
    Famador, S. M. W., Arellano, A. E. C., Pelayo, C. A.

Descriptive Academic Analytics System for the College of
Computer Studies of CIT University   172
    Cortez, B. M., Romana, C. L. C. S.

Emotion Analysis and Recognition of TAGLISHUANO
Online Customer Reviews   181
    Bucag, M. S. I., Feliscuzo, L. S.

Sentiment Analysis of Philippine National Elections 2016
Twitter Data   194
    Turla, Z. C., Caro, J.

Designing a Context-Based English Synonym Database   208
   Baclayon, J. M. C., Roxas, R. R.

A Study on Self-Organizing Maps and K-Means Clustering
on a Music Genre Dataset   219
   Azcarraga, A., Flores, F. K.

Music-emotion Recognition Based on Wearable Dry-electrode
Electroencephalogram   235
   Senachakr, P., Thammasan, N., Fukui, K., Numao, M.

Author index   245

CFRP: A Functional Reactive Programming Language for Small-Scale Embedded Systems

Kohei Suzuki*   Kanato Nagayama   Kensuke Sawada   Takuo Watanabe

Department of Computer Science, Tokyo Institute of Technology
W8-75, 2-12-1 Ookayama, Meguroku Tokyo 152-8552, Japan

Functional reactive programming (FRP) is a programming paradigm for reactive systems based on functional abstractions expressing time-varying values and events. In this paper, we present a strongly-typed pure FRP language named CFRP to show that FRP is beneficial for developing software for small-scale embedded systems. Although its design follows the tradition of signal-based FRP languages, our compiler can generate stand-alone C++ code that can be deployed effectively on resource-constrained microcontrollers. Through an example, we show that CFRP supports a declarative, modular and clean manner of developing small-scale embedded systems.

Keywords: Functional Reactive Programming; Functional Programming; Event System; Embedded Systems.

1. Introduction

A *reactive system* is a computational system that responds to external events. Embedded systems as well as interactive systems such as GUI/web applications, games are instances of reactive systems. In such systems, for example, sensor value changes, button presses, mouse movements and multi-touch gestures are all external events.

An important fact is that the arrival of events in a reactive system is asynchronous. Hence the arrival order of the events is not predictable in general. Thus, writing reactive behaviors in conventional sequential programming languages is not straightforward. In practice, *polling* and *callbacks* are commonly used patterns to deal with asynchronous events. However, they usually cut a control flow into multiple small pieces and thus are obstacles to modularity.

Functional reactive programming (FRP) is a programming paradigm for reactive systems based on functional (declarative) abstractions to express

---

*Currently with Cookpad Inc.

continuous *time-varying values* and events. Abstractions for time-varying values are significant because we often adopt continuously changing data as event sources. Environmental temperature and mouse position are examples of such data. Time-varying values provide natural ways to describe reactions to them. We can, of course, generalize the use of time-varying values to express discrete events.

FRP has been actively studied and recognized to be promising for various kinds of reactive applications such as animation[1], robots[2], and web/GUI applications[3, 4]. The applications to robots indicate that FRP might also be useful for other embedded systems. With a few exceptions, however, the majority of the FRP systems proposed so far are Haskell-based because of the flexible abstraction mechanisms provided by the language. Unfortunately, this fact has constrained the application areas of FRP. In particular, it is virtually impossible to use Haskell-based FRP systems on resource constrained platforms since current Haskell implementations require substantial runtime resources. Of course, advances in programming language studies and microprocessor technologies might allow using such heavy languages to program microcontrollers in the future. However, certain demands for small-scale, low-power and cost-effective devices should also remain.

To address this situation, we designed and implemented a new FRP language named CFRP that mainly targets small-scale embedded systems. The term small-scale here means that the target platform is not powerful enough to run conventional operating systems such as Linux. As in the existing FRP language such as Elm[4], CFRP employs signal types to represent time-varying values. Although the language design follows the tradition of previous FRP languages, the CFRP compiler generates standalone C++ code that can be deployed effectively on resource-constrained microcontrollers.

The rest of this paper is structured as follows. The next section, introduces the concept of FRP in embedded systems. In Section 3, we present the design of CFRP. Section 4 briefly describes the implementation of CFRP compiler and runtime system. We discuss related work in Section 5 and conclude in Section 6.

2. FRP for Embedded Systems

This section briefly introduces the notion of FRP using a simple embedded system example. We first present the example code in a procedural language and then show that FRP can simplify the same code.

```
1   // Setting up objects connected to external devices
2   TemperatureSensor tmp = new TemperatureSensor(...);
3   HumiditySensor hmd = new HumiditySensor(...);
4   AirConditioner ac = new AirConditioner(...);
5
6   // Main polling loop
7   while (true) {
8       float t = tmp.read();
9       float h = hmd.read();
10      // calculate current discomfort index
11      float di = t - 0.55 * (1 - 0.01 * h) * (t - 14.5);
12      // turns air-conditioner on if di > 24, off otherwise
13      ac.operate(di > 24);
14      sleep_ms(100);
15  }
```

Fig. 1.   Air-Conditioner Controller in a Procedural Language

2.1. *Example: Air-Conditioner Controller*

Fig. 1 shows a pseudo-code for a simple air-conditioner controller in a Java-like procedural language. The controller reads data from two environmental sensors (temperature and humidity) and turns an air-conditioner on or off according to the discomfort index[a] calculated from the sensor data. The objects tmp, hmd and ac have internal connections to the two sensors and the air-conditioner respectively. The method read returns the current sensor values, and the method operate turns the air-conditioner on (off) if its Boolean argument is true (false).

The main part of the code (lines 7–15) is a single polling loop that repeatedly reads data from the sensors, calculates the discomfort index and controls the air-conditioner. Such simple loop, however, does not work for complex reactive behaviors. For example, if we want to change the air-conditioner controller to read the sensor values at different timings, we usually need interrupts or threads to handle the I/Os separately. As a

[a]a.k.a. Temperature-Humidity index. About 50% of people feel uncomfortable if the value reaches 24.

result, the changed code becomes complicated with callbacks or concurrency controlling code.

2.2. *Air-Conditioner Controller in CFRP*

FRP can solve the problem discussed in the previous subsection by employing the notion of *time-varying values*. A time varying value abstracts a value that changes over time. In a reactive system, input events often refer to values sampled from continuously changing data, such as the sensor values in the above example. In a procedural code like Fig. 1, such values should be updated regularly by polling. Time-varying values provide natural representations for them.

```
1  -- Including C++ header files
2  %{
3  #include "sensors.h"
4  #include "ac_ctrl.h"
5  %}
6
7  -- Declaring identifiers connected to external devices
8  %input tmp :: Signal Float = sen_tmp;
9  %input hmd :: Signal Float = sen_hmd;
10 %import ac :: Signal Bool → Signal () = ctrl_ac;
11
12 -- Main expression
13 let di t h = t - 0.55 * (1 - 0.01 * h) * (t - 14.5) in
14 ac (lift1 (\x → x > 24) (lift2 di tmp hmd))
```

Fig. 2.   Air-Conditioner Controller in CFRP

Fig. 2 presents a CFRP code for the same example. Data types representing time-varying values are called *signals* in this language. For example, lines 8–10 in Fig. 2 declare that tmp and hmd are signals of floating-point numbers and ac is a function from Boolean signal to unit signal. These lines also associate the signals to C++ classes implementing connections to the external devices. For example, tmp is associated to C++ class sen_tmp that accesses the temperature sensor. The values of tmp and hmd change over time and represent the current environmental data measured by the sensors. The argument of the function ac is a Boolean signal that represents the current on/off status of the air-conditioner.

Lines 13 and 14 constitute the main part of the program. Line 13 defines a function named di that calculates the discomfort index. In line 14, the function ac is applied to a Boolean signal whose value is true if the discomfort index is more than 24 and false otherwise. The runtime system of CFRP continuously propagate the changes of tmp and hmd to all dependent signals. In this example, the argument of ac automatically changes according to the discomfort index calculated from the *current* values of tmp and hmd.

The CFRP program in Fig. 2 indicates that we do not have to describe explicit updates for the sensor values and the on/off status of the air-conditioner. Moreover, the code does not state update timings because any changes of each signal can be propagated regardless of other signals. Consequently, we do not need to modify the code if the two sensors should be read in different timings. In these senses, FRP supports a declarative and clean manner of describing reactive behaviors of embedded systems.

$Prog ::= Decl^*\ Exp$		*programs*
$Decl ::=$ **%input** $Id :: SvType = Cid;$		*input declarations*
$\vert$ **%import** $Id :: Type = Cid;$		*import declarations*
$Exp ::= Const$		*constants*
$\vert\ Id$		*identifiers*
$\vert\ \backslash Arg^+ \rightarrow Body$		*function abstractions*
$\vert\ Exp\ Exp$		*function applications*
$\vert\ Exp\ Op\ Exp$		*operator applications*
$\vert\ (Exp, \ldots, Exp)$		*tuples*
$\vert\ Exp.i$		*tuple elements* $(i = 1, 2, \ldots)$
$\vert$ **if** Exp **then** Exp **else** Exp		*conditional expressions*
$\vert$ **let** $Id = Exp$ **in** Exp		*let expressions*
$\vert$ **let** $Id\ Arg^+ = Body$ **in** Exp		
$Arg ::= Id \mid Id : FType$		*function arguments*
$Body ::= Exp \mid Clause^+$		*function bodies*
$Clause ::=$ '$\vert$' $Guard = Exp$		*guarded clauses*
$Guard ::= Exp \mid$ **otherwise**		*guards*

Fig. 3.   Syntax of CFRP

3. Design of CFRP

3.1. *Syntax*

Fig. 3 describes the syntax of CFRP. We here use a mixture of abstract and concrete syntax for explanation convenience. The notation X^* stands for zero or more repetitions of X and X^+ abbreviates XX^* as usual. The non-terminal symbol *Cid* refers to a C++ identifier and *Op* stands for a binary operator.

A CFRP program consists of zero or more declarations followed by a single expression. A declaration specifies the type of a CFRP identifier and associates it with a C++ identifier. An *input declaration* defines a signal value defined as a C++ object that expresses input from an external device, while an *import declaration* introduces a general reference to a C++ object.

The two input declarations in Fig. 2 (lines 8–9) associate `tmp` and `hmd` respectively with C++ identifiers `sen_tmp` and `sen_hmd` that implements inputs from the sensors. The C++ object referred as `ctrl_ac` implements a function that controls the air-conditioner. The import declaration in line 10 provides a connection between `ac` and the object.

3.2. *Signal Types*

Designing abstraction mechanisms for time-varying values is the central topic of FRP language design. As described in Section 2.2, CFRP provides *signal types* to express time-varying values. A time-varying value is conceptually equivalent to a function from (continuous) time to a certain type. Thus, it seems that we can define a signal type as

$$\textbf{Signal } \tau = \textit{Time} \rightarrow \tau$$

where *Time* and τ are the types of time and values changing over time. However, this naïve representation is known to be prone to unexpected memory grows (*space-leaks*) and unexpectedly long computations (*time-leaks*)[5]. For this reason, the majority of FRP languages and libraries proposed so far adopt different approaches.

For example, Yampa[2, 6] introduces *signal functions* that act as transformers of signals. A signal function type, denoted as $\textbf{SF } \tau_1 \ \tau_2$, is actually defined as an instance of *arrows*[7] instead of a usual function type $\textbf{Signal } \tau_1 \rightarrow \textbf{Signal } \tau_2$. This *arrowized* representation can effectively get rid of signal types and can avoid space-leaks.

Elm[4], an FRP language for programming client-side web applications, takes another approach. The language provides built-in signal types together with primitive functions that manipulate them. Using the notion of Yampa-flavored signal function, we can describe a signal type in Elm as

$$\texttt{Signal} \; \tau = \texttt{SF} \; World \; \tau$$

where *World* denotes the type of the states of the external world. Namely, through a data object of type **Signal** τ, we can observe the part of the external world as a time-varying value of type τ.

Both Elm-style FRP and Yampa-style (arrowized) FRP have the same expressibility[5, 8]. When compared to signal functions, signal types allow us to manipulate time-varying values more intuitively. Moreover, Elm-style FRP is free from space- and time-leaks thanks to introducing signals as built-in types.

$Type ::= FType \mid SType$		*types*
$BType ::= \texttt{()} \mid \texttt{Bool} \mid \texttt{Int} \mid \texttt{Float}$		*base types*
$VType ::= BType \mid (BType, \ldots, BType)$		*value types*
$FType ::= VType \mid FType \rightarrow FType$		*function types*
$SvType ::= \texttt{Signal} \; VType$		*value signal types*
$SType ::= SvType \mid AType \rightarrow SType$		*signal types*
$AType ::= VType \mid SvType$		*signal argument types*

Fig. 4. Type Expressions in CFRP

CFRP adopts the signal types similar to Elm. However, since CFRP is targeted at small-scale embedded systems, we designed its type system to restrict the runtime resource usage of a program.

Fig. 4 describes the type expressions in CFRP. We can find that type constructor **Signal** can only be applied to value types. This means that, in CFRP, time-varying values are limited to be base types or their tuples. Thus the size of any time-varying value can be determined at compile time.

Moreover, a function that returns signal type values cannot be an argument of other functions. It is easy to see that the syntax of type expressions (Fig. 4) and the syntax of expressions (Fig. 3) guarantee this property. The property states that the dependency relation between signal type data in a program does not change at runtime and hence the CFRP can adopt a simple memory management strategy.

3.3. *Primitive Functions for Signals*

Fig. 5 shows the primitive functions for signal types in CFRP. Note that τ_i $(i = 1, 2, \ldots)$ stand for value types (see Fig. 4) and k denotes a positive integer. In the concrete syntax, $\mathtt{lift}_k$ $(k = 1, 2, \ldots)$ are described as $\mathtt{lift1}$, $\mathtt{lift2}$, ... respectively.

$$\mathtt{lift}_k : (\tau_1 \to \cdots \to \tau_k \to \tau)$$
$$\to \mathbf{Signal}\ \tau_1 \to \cdots \to \mathbf{Signal}\ \tau_k \to \mathbf{Signal}\ \tau$$
$$\mathtt{foldp} : (\tau_1 \to \tau_2 \to \tau_2) \to \tau_2 \to \mathbf{Signal}\ \tau_1 \to \mathbf{Signal}\ \tau_2$$

Fig. 5.   Primitives for Signal Types

The function $\mathtt{lift}_k$ takes a k-ary non-signal function and convert it to a function that transform signals. Recall the example in Fig. 2. The type of sensor values tmp and hmd is **Signal Float** and the type of the function di (defined in line 13) is **Float** $\to$ **Float** $\to$ **Float**. To apply di to tmp and hmd to obtain a signal of discomfort index, we need to apply $\mathtt{lift2}$ to di first to get a function that transforms signals as

$\mathtt{lift2}$ di :: **Signal Float** $\to$ **Signal Float** $\to$ **Signal Float**.

Then we can apply this function to tmp and hmd to have the subexpression $\mathtt{lift2}$ di tmp hmd of type **Signal Float** (line 14 in Fig. 2) that represents the time-varying value of discomfort index. Similarly, we construct another signal-transforming function

$\mathtt{lift1}$ $(\backslash x \to x\ >\ 24)$ :: **Signal Float** $\to$ **Signal Bool**

to obtain a Boolean signal from the discomfort index signal. By applying ac to the result of this function, we can control the air-conditioner.

The other primitive function **foldp** allows us to describe history sensitive behaviors by providing accesses to past values of a signal. Below, we use the same example to explain the usage of this primitive.

In fact, the air-conditioner controller in Fig. 2 has a serious flaw. Let us consider a situation that the value of discomfort index drifts around the threshold (24). In such a case, the value of the Boolean signal given to the function ac may change at a fast rate, which results in quick changes of the on/off status that are hazardous to the air-conditioner.

```
12  -- Main expression
13  let di t h = t - 0.55 * (1 - 0.01 * h) * (t - 14.5) in
14  ac (foldp (\x s → if s then x >= 23.5 else x > 24.5)
15            False (lift2 di tmp hmd))
```

Fig. 6.   Air-Conditioner Controller with History-Sensitive Behavior

To avoid such situation, we add a history sensitive behavior (hysteresis) to the controller by replacing lines 12–14 in Fig. 2 with Fig. 6. In fact, we just replace **lift1** ($\x → x > 24$) with **foldp** ($\x s → \ldots$) False. The first argument of **foldp** is a function of type **Float** → **Bool** → **Bool**. The second (Boolean) argument of this function refers to the "previous" value of the Boolean signal that expresses the on/off status. The new program behaves as follows. If the air-conditioner is off, the discomfort index must be more than 24.5 to turn it on. If it is already on, the discomfort index must be less than 23.5 to turn it off. As a result, we can avoid the hazardous behavior (quick changes of the on/off status) explained above.

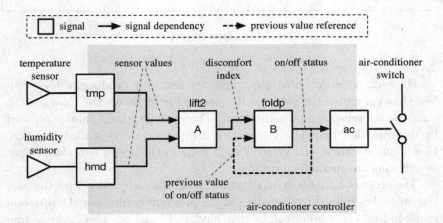

Fig. 7.   Program Graph of Fig. 6

4. Implementation

A CFRP program can be represented as a directed acyclic graph (DAG) called *program graph*. Fig. 7 show the program graph of Fig. 6. A node (square) stands for a signal, and a directed edge (solid arrow line) from a node to another node represents that the latter depends on the former. Nodes labeled A and B in Fig. 7 correspond to the function calls of **lift2** and **foldp** in Fig. 6 respectively. Edges from tmp and hmd to A represents that the values of signals tmp and hmd are required to compute the value of the expression **lift2** di tmp hmd.

```
1  class sen_tmp : public cfrp::node {
2  public:
3      sen_tmp() {}
4      virtual ~sen_tmp() {}
5      virtual cfrp::event process();
6      virtual void mark() const {};
7  private:
8      temp_sensor sen;
9  }
10
11 cfrp::event sen_tmp::process() {
12     return cfrp::event(true, cfrp::value(sen.read()));
13 }
```

Fig. 8. C++ Class for the Temperature Sensor Signal Node

For each node in a program graph, the compiler produces a C++ object that computes the value of the node. Fig. 8 shows the class for the temperature sensor signal node (tmp). The runtime system, also composed by the compiler, indefinitely repeats a computation cycle called *iteration*. In a single iteration, the value of each node in the graph is updated once by invoking the method process.

The order of updates in an iteration should be compatible with the partial order determined by the edges in the program graph. For the program graph in Fig. 7, the order can be tmp, hmd, A, B, and ac. The values of tmp and hmd are just taken from the sensors, while the values of other nodes are calculated using the values of the nodes on which they depend.

In CFRP, each node in a program graph corresponds to either an identifier introduced with a declaration or a call of primitive functions (**lift**$_k$ and **foldp**) described in Section 3.3. By the restrictions imposed by the syntax and the type system, the program graph does not change at runtime. Thus, it is enough for the compiler to generate the fixed size program graph as C++ code.

We implemented a compiler[b] that translates CFRP code into platform-independent C++ code. To demonstrate the benefits of FRP in the development of small-scale embedded systems, we used mbed LPC1768[c] (microcontroller board with 96MHz ARM Cortex-M3, 32KB RAM, 512KB FLASH) as a testing platform. We have tested some embedded applications including control programs for a small two-wheel robot[d].

Our compiler generates a C++ file from a CFRP file that contains a single CFRP program. The C++ objects and functions referred in the declarations of the program should be defined in separate C++ files. They are compiled and linked together with the generated C++ file to produce a stand-alone executable.

By using customized runtime classes, we can implement optimized behaviors suitable for embedded systems. For example, it is possible to define a *lazy node* as a C++ class, which can suppress unnecessary updates of node values. The lazy node is convenient in a situation that the value of a sensor is needed only when a certain condition holds. In addition, we can implement an interrupt handling using a special signal node and the customized runtime for it.

5. Related Work

5.1. *Elm*

Elm[4] is a purely functional language designed for client-side web programming. As discussed in Section 3.2, CFRP borrows the notion of built-in signal types from Elm. The crucial difference between the two language is in their runtime targets. Since CFRP is targeted at small-scale embedded systems, its compiler should generate memory efficient code. The carefully designed type system and other design choices enable our CFRP compiler to generate C++ code effectively deployable in microcontrollers with limited resource.

Recently, Elm adopted an abstraction mechanism named *subscription* and abandoned the signal-based FRP architecture[9]. The notion of subscription provides a sort of message based abstraction similar to the publish-subscribe architecture. Thus, the current version[e] of Elm is not an FRP language. We have not yet investigated that this abstraction is suitable

---

[b]https://github.com/psg-titech/cfrp
[c]https://developer.mbed.org/platforms/mbed-LPC1768/
[d]https://www.pololu.com/category/111/m3pi-robot
[e]0.17 and newer

for small-scale embedded systems. However, time-varying values can naturally express the external world of a computational system, and thus FRP provides a good way to developing embedded systems.

5.2. *Céu*

Céu[10] is an imperative programming language designed for small-scale embedded systems. The method of describing reactive behaviors in this language is completely different from that of FRP languages including CFRP. To describe reactive behaviors, Céu provides simple mechanisms for event handling and synchronous concurrent execution. The **await** statement plays roles of event handling and synchronization points as well as context-switching points. Using this statement and other language constructs, we can describe the reactive behaviors without bothered by callbacks and threads that might make the programming of embedded systems a complex task.

5.3. *Emfrp*

Emfrp[11] is another FRP language that is currently under active development in our research group. We designed the language also for small-scale embedded systems. The basic design of CFRP follows those of common functional languages such as ML and Haskell. For example, CFRP supports first-class anonymous functions as usual. In contrast, Emfrp throws them away to suppress dynamic memory allocations used to implement function closures. In addition, signal types are not first-class data in Emfrp. These somewhat rigorous restrictions make the amount of runtime memory consumption predictable. However, programmers who accustomed to popular functional languages will not have much trouble with CFRP because of its traditional language design.

6. Concluding Remarks

We have designed and implemented CFRP, a functional reactive programming language for small-scale embedded systems. The overall design of CFRP is similar to those of previous FRP languages. However, thanks to the syntax and type system, the compiler can generate efficient C++ code that is deployable on resource-constrained devices such as microcontrollers without conventional operating systems. Through an example, we showed that CFRP supports a declarative, modular and clean manner of describing reactive behaviors of embedded systems.

Acknowledgments

This work is supported in part by JSPS KAKENHI Grant No. 15K00089.

References

[1] C. Elliott and P. Hudak, Functional reactive animation, in *2nd ACM SIGPLAN International Conference on Functional Programming (ICFP 1997)*, (ACM, 1997).

[2] P. Hudak, A. Courtney, H. Nilsson and J. Peterson, Arrows, robots, and functional reactive programming, in *Advanced Functional Programming*, Lecture Notes in Computer Science Vol. 2638 (Springer-Verlag, 2003) pp. 159–187.

[3] L. A. Meyerovich, A. Guha, J. Baskin, G. H. Cooper, M. Greenberg and A. Bromfield, Flapjax: A programming language for Ajax applications, in *24th ACM SIGPLAN Conference on Object Oriented Programming Systems Languages and Applications (OOPSLA 2009)*, (ACM, 2009).

[4] E. Czaplicki and S. Chong, Asynchronous functional reactive programming for GUIs, in *34th ACM SIGPLAN Conference on Programming Language Design and Implementation (PLDI 2013)*, (ACM, 2013).

[5] E. Czaplicki, Elm: Concurrent FRP for functional GUI, Master's thesis, School of Engineering and Applied Sciences, Harvard University (Mar. 2012).

[6] A. Courtney, H. Nilsson and J. Peterson, The Yampa arcade, in *ACM SIGPLAN Workshop on Haskell (Haskell 2003)*, (ACM, 2003).

[7] J. Hughes, Generalising monads to arrows, *Science of Computer Programming* **37**, 67 (2000).

[8] C. McBride and R. Paterson, Applicative programming with effects, *Journal of Functional Programming* **18**, 1 (2008).

[9] E. Czaplicki, A farewell to FRP: Making signals unnecessary with the Elm architecture http://elm-lang.org/blog/farewell-to-frp (May, 2016).

[10] F. Sant'Anna, R. Ierusalimschy and N. Rodriguez, Structured synchronous reactive programming with Céu, in *14th International Conference on Modularity (Modularity 2015)*, (ACM, 2015).

[11] K. Sawada and T. Watanabe, Emfrp: A functional reactive programming language for small-scale embedded systems, in *Modularity 2016 Constrained and Reactive Objects Workshop (CROW 2016)*, (ACM, Mar. 2016).

Discussion of LTL Subsets for Efficient Verification

Masaya Shimakawa[1], Yuji Iwasaki[1], Shigeki Hagihara[1] and Naoki Yonezaki[2].

[1] *Department of Computer Science,*
Graduate School of Information Science and Engineering,
Tokyo Institute of Technology, Tokyo, Japan

[2] *The Open University of Japan, Chiba, Japan*

The verification of reactive system specifications can detect dangerous situations that may arise that were not anticipated while drawing up the specifications. However, such verification typically involves complex, intricate analyses. The most effective approach for avoiding this difficulty is to restrict the syntax of the specification language. In this paper, we discuss subsets of linear temporal logic (used in the formal specification description of reactive systems) in which the syntax is restricted to simplify the verification procedure.

Keywords: Linear Temporal Logic; ω-automata; Specification; Verification.

1. Introduction

Reactive systems are systems that interact with their environments. Many critical safety systems, such as those that control nuclear power plants or air traffic control systems, are considered reactive systems. Such systems should be designed to respond appropriately to any request from the environment at any time. We need to verify this property during the specification phase. If a situation that is not considered when describing the specifications exists, the developed system may become endangered. Therefore, it is important to verify that a specification does not contain such flaws.

In the verification of a reactive system specification, it is effective to describe the specifications in a formal language, such as linear temporal logic (LTL), or to check realizability.[1,2] Realizability is the property such that there exists a system model that satisfies given specifications in all situations. Realizability verification can detect dangerous situations, and a system model can be synthesized if the specification is realizable.[1]

However, such verification typically involves complex, intricate analyses. Therefore, realizability verification can be applied only to limited scale specifications. Realizability is checked as follows: we construct a deterministic

ω-automaton $\mathcal{D}$ that accepts behaviors that satisfy the specifications,[a] and then analyze the automaton $\mathcal{D}$. The construction uses Safra's determinization,[3] which is intricate. It is difficult to get an efficient implementation with it.

This difficulty can be avoided by restricting the syntax of the specification language. From a practical perspective, it is important to find subsets of the language in which specifications can be verified efficiently.

In this paper, we discuss subsets of LTL in which specifications can be translated into deterministic ω-automata by using the powerset determinization.[b] The powerset determinization is less expensive and simpler than Safra's determinization. While the worst number of states of deterministic automaton with Safra's determinization is $(12)^n n^{2n}$ (where n is the number of states of a non-deterministic automaton), that of the powerset determinization is 2^n. Moreover, the powerset determinization uses simple set operations only, while Safra's determinization needs operations of tree structures. Therefore, it is easy to get an efficient implementation.

The LTL subsets LTL^{safety}, $\mathrm{LTL}^{guarantee}$ (see Refs. 4, 5, etc.), and LTL^{det} (see Refs. 6 and 7) can be translated into deterministic ω-automata by using the powerset determinization. In this paper, we examine larger subsets of LTL.

The remainder of this paper is organized as follows. In Section 2, we introduce the concepts of LTL, ω-automata and outline a procedure for realizability checking. In Section 3, we describe already-known LTL subsets that can be translated into deterministic ω-automata by using the powerset determinization. In Section 4, we present ideas for new larger LTL subsets. In Section 5, we describe related works. We present our conclusion and future work in Section 6.

2. Preliminaries

2.1. *Linear Temporal Logic (LTL)*

The timing of input and output events is an essential element of a reactive system. A linear temporal logic (LTL) is a suitable language for describing the timing of events.[8] In this paper, we focus on an LTL with an 'until' operator and a 'release' operator.[c]

---

[a]ω-automata are automata that deal with infinite words.
[b]The powerset determinization is used in the determinization of finite state automata on finite words.
[c]In this paper, for the sake of simplicity, we do not deal with the 'next' operator.

Definition 2.1 (Syntax of LTL). *Let Prop be a finite set of atomic propositions. Formulas f in LTL are inductively defined as follows:*

$$f := p \mid \neg f \mid f \wedge f \mid f \vee f \mid f\mathbf{U}f \mid f\mathbf{R}f$$

where $p \in Prop$.

The notations $f_1 \to f_2$, $\mathbf{F}f$, and $\mathbf{G}f$ are abbreviations for $\neg f_1 \vee f_2$, $\top\mathbf{U}f$, $\bot\mathbf{R}f$, respectively. The operators $\mathbf{F}$ and $\mathbf{G}$ are dual, as are the operators $\mathbf{U}$ and $\mathbf{R}$. The notation $\mathbf{F}f$ means that 'f eventually holds', $\mathbf{G}f$ means that 'f always holds', and $f_1\mathbf{U}f_2$ means that 'f_1 always holds until f_2 holds'.

Definition 2.2 (Semantics of LTL). *Let $\Sigma \in 2^{Prop}$. A behavior $\sigma \in \Sigma^\omega$ is an infinite sequence over Σ. Let i be an index such that $i \geq 0$. The i-th set of a behavior σ is denoted by $\sigma[i]$. The i-th suffix of a behavior σ is denoted by $\sigma[i\ldots]$. When a behavior σ satisfies a formula f, we write $\sigma \models f$, and inductively define this relation as follows:*

- $\sigma \models p$ *iff* $p \in \sigma[0]$
- $\sigma \models \neg f$ *iff* $\sigma \not\models f$
- $\sigma \models f_1 \wedge f_2$ *iff* $\sigma \models f_1$ *and* $\sigma \models f_2$
- $\sigma \models f_1 \vee f_2$ *iff* $\sigma \models f_1$ *or* $\sigma \models f_2$
- $\sigma \models f_1\mathbf{U}f_2$ *iff* $\exists j \geq 0.((\sigma[j\ldots] \models f_2)$ *and* $\forall k(0 \leq k < j.\ \sigma[k\ldots] \models f_1))$
- $\sigma \models f_1\mathbf{R}f_2$ *iff* $\forall j \geq 0.((\sigma[j\ldots] \models f_2)$ *or* $\exists k(0 \leq k < j.\ \sigma[k\ldots] \models f_1))$

A formula is in negation normal form (nnf) if the negation operator $\neg$ only occurs immediately above atomic propositions. Every formula can be transformed into an equivalent formula in nnf by using the following equivalences: $\neg(f_1 \wedge f_2) \equiv (\neg f_1) \vee (\neg f_2)$, $\neg(f_1 \vee f_2) \equiv (\neg f_1) \wedge (\neg f_2)$, $\neg(f_1\mathbf{U}f_2) \equiv (\neg f_1)\mathbf{R}(\neg f_2)$ and $\neg(f_1\mathbf{R}f_2) \equiv (\neg f_1)\mathbf{U}(\neg f_2)$.

2.2. ω-automata

For analyzing LTL specifications, ω-automata, which deal with infinite words, are used. Here, we use Büchi automata and transition-based generalized co-Büchi automata, which are kinds of ω-automata.

Definition 2.3 (Büchi Automata). *A Büchi automaton (BA) is a tuple $\mathcal{A} = (\Sigma, Q, q_I, \delta, F)$, where Σ is an alphabet, Q is a finite set of states, q_I is an initial state, $\delta \subseteq Q \times \Sigma \times Q$ is a transition relation, and $F \subseteq Q$*

is a set of final states (an acceptance component). A run of $\mathcal{A}$ on an ω-word $\sigma = \sigma[0]\sigma[1]\ldots$ is an infinite sequence $\varrho = \varrho[0]\varrho[1]\ldots$ of states, where $\varrho[0] = q_I$ and $(\varrho[i], \sigma[i], \varrho[i+1]) \in \delta$ for all $i \geq 0$. We say that $\mathcal{A}$ accepts σ, if there is a run ϱ on σ such that $Inf(\varrho) \cap F \neq \emptyset$ holds, where $Inf(\varrho)$ is the set of states that occurs infinitely often in ϱ.

Definition 2.4 (Transition-based Generalized co-Büchi Automata).
A transition-based generalized co-Büchi automaton (TGCA) is a tuple $\mathcal{A} = (\Sigma, Q, q_I, \delta, \mathcal{F})$, where Σ, Q, q_I, and δ are defined as above for BA, and $\mathcal{F} = \{T_1, \ldots, T_n\}$ is a set of sets of final transitions (an acceptance component). A run of $\mathcal{A}$ on an ω-word $\sigma = \sigma[0]\sigma[1]\ldots$ is an infinite sequence $\varrho = (q_0, a_0, q_0')(q_1, a_1, q_1')\ldots$ of transitions, where $q_0 = q_I$ and $q_i' = q_{i+1}$ and $a_i = \sigma[i]$ for all $i \geq 0$. We say that $\mathcal{A}$ accepts σ if there is a run ϱ on σ such that $\exists T_i(Inf^t(\varrho) \cap T_i = \emptyset)$ holds, where $Inf^t(\varrho)$ is the set of transitions that occurs infinitely often in ϱ.

The set of ω-words accepted by BA (or TGCA) $\mathcal{A}$ is called the language accepted by $\mathcal{A}$, and is denoted by $L(\mathcal{A})$.

The notation $q \to^+ q'$ means that there exists a transition sequence $(q_0, a_0, q_0')(q_1, a_1, q_1')\ldots(q_{n-1}, a_{n-1}, q_{n-1}')$ such that $q_0 = q$, $q_{n-1}' = q'$, $q_i' = q_{i+1}$ for all $i < n-1$, for some $a_0, \ldots, a_{n-1}$.

A BA (or TGCA) is deterministic if $|\{q' \in Q \mid (q, a, q') \in \delta\}| \leq 1$ for all $q \in Q, a \in \Sigma$. We denote a deterministic BA and TGCA by DBA and DTGCA.

2.3. Realizability Checking

In designing a reactive system, it is effective to describe the specifications in LTL or to check realizability.[1,2] Realizability is the property such that there exists a system model that satisfies given specifications in all situations. Realizability checking can detect dangerous situations that may arise that were not expected while drawing up the specifications. However, such verification typically involves complex, intricate analyses.

Realizability can be checked using ω-automata as follows:

(1) We construct a deterministic ω-automaton $\mathcal{D}$ such that $\mathcal{D}$ accepts behaviors that satisfy the specification.
(2) We analyze $\mathcal{D}$, and check whether there exists a system such that all of the behaviors satisfy the specification.

The construction of $\mathcal{D}$ is expensive and intricate. A normal construction is as follows: (i) we construct a (non-deterministic) ω-automaton $\mathcal{N}$ such that $\mathcal{N}$ accepts behaviors that satisfy the specification f, (ii) then we determinize $\mathcal{N}$ using Safra's determinization procedure.[3] A construction with complementation is as follows: (i) we construct a (non-deterministic) ω-automaton $\overline{\mathcal{N}}$ such that $\overline{\mathcal{N}}$ accepts the behavior that satisfies $\neg f$, (ii) we obtain a deterministic ω-automaton $\overline{\mathcal{D}}$ from $\overline{\mathcal{N}}$ using Safra's determinization, (iii) we obtain a complement automaton $\mathcal{D}$ of $\overline{\mathcal{D}}$ (the complementation of deterministic automata is easy). Safra's determinization is expensive and intricate, and it is difficult to get an efficient implementation.

3. Already-known LTL Subsets for Efficient Verification

The LTL subsets LTL^{safety}, $\text{LTL}^{guarantee}$ (see Refs. 4, 5, etc.), and LTL^{det} (presented in Ref. 6) can be translated into deterministic ω-automata by using the powerset determinization.[d] The powerset determinization is less expensive and simpler than Safra's determinization. While the worst number of states of a deterministic automaton with Safra's determinization is $(12)^n n^{2n}$ ($2n^n n!$ for the improved version in Ref. 9) where n is the number of states of the non-deterministic automaton, that of the powerset determinization is 2^n. Moreover, the powerset determinization uses simple set-operations only, while Safra's determinization needs operations of tree structures. Therefore, it is easy to get an efficient implementation.

The definitions of these LTL subsets are as follows:

Definition 3.1 (Syntax of LTL^{safety} and LTL^{guarantee}). *Formulas* f *in LTL^{safety} are defined inductively as follows:*

$$f := p \mid \neg p \mid f \wedge f \mid f \vee f \mid f\mathbf{R}f.$$

Formulas f in LTL^{guarantee} are defined inductively as follows:

$$f := p \mid \neg p \mid f \wedge f \mid f \vee f \mid f\mathbf{U}f.$$

Definition 3.2 (Syntax of LTL^{det}). *Formulas f in LTL^{det} are defined inductively as follows[e]:*

$$f := p \mid \neg f \mid f \wedge f \mid f \vee g \mid g\mathbf{R}f \mid f\mathbf{U}g,$$

---

[d]The powerset determinization is used in the determinization of finite state automata on finite words.

[e]Although this definition is changed slightly from the original definition in Ref. 6, these definitions are essentially the same.

where g is a Boolean formula, which contains only the Boolean operators $\neg$, $\vee$ *and* $\wedge$.

The subsets LTL^{safety} and LTL^{guarantee} are dual. The negation formula $\neg f$ of formula f in LTL^{safety} (LTL^{guarantee}) can be transformed into a formula in LTL^{guarantee}(LTL^{safety}).

The negation formula $\neg f$ of formula f in LTL^{safety} (a formula f in LTL^{guarantee}) can be translated into a BA, which has the following structural feature (called *terminal*) [10]:

- for all $q \in F$ and $q' \in Q$, if $q \to^+ q'$ then $q' = q$.

The negation formula $\neg f$ of formula f in LTL^{det} can be translated into a BA with the following structural feature (called *very weak*) [6,7]:

- for all $q \in Q$ and $q' \in Q$, if $q \to^+ q'$ and $q' \to^+ q$ then $q' = q$.

A BA with these structural features can be determinized by using the powerset construction. Therefore, the above LTL subsets can be transformed into deterministic automata $\mathcal{D}$ efficiently (LTL^{safety} and LTL^{det} can be transformed into $\mathcal{D}$ based on the construction with complementation, and LTL^{guarantee} can be transformed into $\mathcal{D}$ based on the normal construction).

4. Towards Larger LTL Subsets for Efficient Verification

In this paper, we present new subsets LTL^{ep} and LTL^{gp} that are larger than the subsets described in the previous section (LTL^{ep} and LTL^{gp} are dual).

We anticipate that LTL^{gp} can be transformed into deterministic automata based on the powerset construction, for the following conjecture:

- A formula in LTL^{gp} can be transformed into BA, which has a weaker feature than terminal and a very weak BA.
- BA with this feature can be determinized based on the powerset construction.

LTL^{ep} can be transformed to deterministic automata based on the powerset determinization, by construction with complementation, because LTL^{ep} and LTL^{gp} are dual (The negation formula $\neg f$ of formula f in LTL^{ep} can be transformed into a formula in LTL^{gp}).

4.1. LTL^{ep} and LTL^{gp}

LTL^{ep} and LTL^{gp} are defined as follows:

Definition 4.1 (Syntax of LTL^{ep} and LTL^{gp}). *Formulas f in LTL^{ep} are defined inductively as follows:*

$$f := p \mid \neg p \mid f \wedge f \mid f \vee f \mid f\mathbf{U}g \mid f\mathbf{R}f,$$

where g is a Boolean formula. Formulas f in LTL^{gp} are defined inductively as follows:

$$f := p \mid \neg p \mid f \wedge f \mid f \vee f \mid f\mathbf{U}f \mid f\mathbf{R}g,$$

where g is a Boolean formula.

From the definition, it is obvious that LTL^{ep} is larger than LTL^{safety} and LTL^{det}, and that LTL^{gp} is larger than $LTL^{guarantee}$.

4.2. *Structural Features of Non-deterministic Automata*

We conjecture that a formula f in LTL^{gp} can be translated in a BA that has the following structural feature (called feature A):

- for all $q \in F$ and $q' \in Q$, if $q \to^+ q'$ and $q' \to^+ q$ then $q' = q$.

To support the conjecture, we introduce a procedure for constructing a BA $\mathcal{N}$ from an LTL^{gp} formula. This procedure is based on a procedure for converting (general) LTL formulas into generalized Büchi automata in Refs. 11 and 12.

Let ψ be an input LTL^{gp} formula in nnf. In the procedure, each state of BA consists of a subset of $cl(\psi)$ that represents the constraints of the state, where $cl(\psi)$ is the set of sub-formulas of ψ. The initial state is $\{\psi\}$. We decompose the formulas in a state and obtain the set of successive states, repeatedly. This decomposition is based on the following properties:

- '$f_1\mathbf{U}f_2$ holds' equals that 'f_2 holds', or 'f_1 holds and $f_1\mathbf{U}f_2$ holds at the next time'.
- '$f_1\mathbf{R}f_2$ holds' equals that 'f_2 holds', and 'f_1 holds or $f_1\mathbf{R}f_2$ holds at the next time'.

That is, we calculate a set of formulas that must hold at the next time (this set corresponds to a successive state) and a set of formulas that must hold at this point (a transition condition is defined by atomic propositions in this set).

The satisfaction of formula $f_1 \mathbf{U} f_2$ needs the eventual satisfaction of f_2. Therefore, we need to reject a run such that f_2 does not hold globally from the point occurring at $f_1 \mathbf{U} f_2$ (that is, the constraint $f_1 \mathbf{U} f_2$ remains global), by setting the acceptance component F.

Decomposition Procedure
Input: a set S of formulas

(1) $D := \{(S, \emptyset, \emptyset)\}$
(2) For all $(Proc_i, Cur_i, Next_i) \in D$ and $f_{ij} \in Proc_i$ apply one of the following, according to f_{ij}. Repeat this operation until $Proc_i = \emptyset$ for all $(Proc_i, Cur_i, Next_i) \in D$. Here, $Proc'_i := Proc_i - \{f_{ij}\}$, $Cur'_i := Cur_i \cup \{f_{ij}\}$.

   (a) if $f_{ij} = p$ or $\neg p$, replace $(Proc_i, Cur_i, Next_i)$ with $(Proc'_i, Cur'_i, Next_i)$.

   (b) if $f_{ij} = f_1 \wedge f_2$, replace $(Proc_i, Cur_i, Next_i)$ with $(Proc'_i \cup \{f_1, f_2\}, Cur'_i, Next_i)$.

   (c) if $f_{ij} = f_1 \vee f_2$, replace $(Proc_i, Cur_i, Next_i)$ with $(Proc'_i \cup \{f_1\}, Cur'_i, Next_i)$, $(Proc'_i \cup \{f_2\}, Cur'_i, Next_i)$.

   (d) if $f_{ij} = f_1 \mathbf{U} f_2$, replace $(Proc_i, Cur_i, Next_i)$ with $(Proc'_i \cup \{f_2\}, Cur'_i, Next_i)$, $(Proc'_i \cup \{f_1\}, Cur'_i, Next_i \cup \{f_{ij}\})$.

   (e) if $f_{ij} = f_1 \mathbf{R} f_2$, replace $(Proc_i, Cur_i, Next_i)$ with $(Proc'_i \cup \{f_2, f_1\}, Cur'_i, Next_i)$, $(Proc'_i \cup \{f_1\}, Cur'_i, Next_i \cup \{f_{ij}\})$.

(3) For $(Proc_i, Cur_i, Next_i) \in D$, if $p, \neg p \in Cur_i$ or $\bot \in Cur_i$, then remove $(Proc_i, Cur_i, Next_i)$ from D. If $f_1 \mathbf{U} f_2, f_2 \in Cur_i$ and $f_1 \mathbf{U} f_2 \in Next_i$, then remove $f_1 \mathbf{U} f_2$ from $Next_i$. If $f_1 \mathbf{R} f_2, f_1, f_2 \in Cur_i$ and $f_1 \mathbf{R} f_2 \in Next_i$, then remove $f_1 \mathbf{R} f_2$ from $Next_i$.
(4) Output $\{(C, N) \mid (\emptyset, C, N) \in D\}$

$Proc_i$ denotes a set of formulas to process, Cur_i denotes a set of formulas that must hold at the point, and $Next_i$ denotes a set of formulas that must hold the next time.

Example 4.1. Let ψ be $\mathbf{F}(p1 \wedge \mathbf{G}p2)$, that is $\top \mathbf{U}(p1 \wedge \bot \mathbf{R} p2)$. The result of the decomposition procedure for ψ is as follows: $\{(\{\top, \psi\}, \{\psi\}), (\{p1, p2, \mathbf{G}p2, \psi\}, \{\mathbf{G}p2\})\}$. The result of the decomposition procedure for $\mathbf{G}p2$ is as follows: $\{(\{p2, \mathbf{G}p2\}, \{\mathbf{G}p2\})\}$.

BA Construction
Input: LTL^{gp} formula ψ in nnf.
Output: BA $\mathcal{N} = (2^{Prop}, Q, q_I, \delta, F)$

22

(1) $Q := \{q_I\}$ $q_I := \{\psi\}$ $\delta := \emptyset$

(2) Let *Decomp* be the result of the decomposition procedure for a state $q \in Q$ (q is a set of formulas). Update Q and δ as follows:
$Q := Q \cup \{N \mid (C, N) \in Decomp\}$
$\delta := \delta \cup \{(q, s, N) \mid (C, N) \in Decomp, p \in C \Rightarrow p \in s, \neg p \in C \Rightarrow p \notin s\}$.
Repeat this operation until Q and δ do not change.

(3) Set F as described below.

In the construction of LTL^{gp}, due to the restriction of the syntax, any accepting runs ρ satisfy the following conditions:

- For $f \neq f_1 \mathbf{R} f_2$, $\exists i.\forall j > i.(f \notin \rho[j])$.
- For $f = f_1 \mathbf{R} f_2$, $\exists i.\forall j > i.(f \notin \rho[j])$ or $\exists i.\forall j > i.(f \in \rho[j])$.

Therefore, the acceptance component F can be defined as follows:

$$F := \{q \mid \forall f \in q.\ f = f_1 \mathbf{R} f_2\}.$$

Moreover, from this property, we derive that automata obtained by this procedure have feature A.

Example 4.2. Let ψ be $\mathbf{F}(p1 \wedge \mathbf{G}p2)$, that is $\top \mathbf{U}(p1 \wedge \bot \mathbf{R}p2)$. The result of the BA construction procedure for ψ is the BA illustrated in Fig. 1.

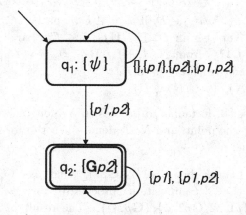

Fig. 1.   The result of the BA construction procedure in Example 4.2

Conjecture 4.1. *Let ψ be an LTL^{gp} formula. Then, we can construct* a BA $\mathcal{N}$ with feature A such that $L(\mathcal{N}) = \{\sigma \mid \sigma \models \psi\}$, by the above procedure.

4.3. Determinization

We conjecture that a BA with feature A can be determinized based on the powerset determinization procedure.

For any accepting runs ρ of a BA with feature A, $\exists i \forall j > i.\rho[j] = q_{loop}$ for some q_{loop}. We can characterize the existence of an accepting run on the powerset construction by using the acceptance condition of TGCA.

We introduce a determinization procedure based on this idea.

Determinization Procedure
Input: BA $\mathcal{N} = (\Sigma, Q, q_I, \delta, F)$ with structural feature A
Output: DTGCA $\mathcal{D} = (\Sigma, Q', q'_I, \delta', \mathcal{F}')$

(1) $Q' := \{\{q_I\}\}$ $q'_I := \{q_I\}$ $\delta' := \emptyset$.
(2) For any $q' \in Q'$ and $a \in \Sigma$, update Q' and δ' as follows:
$Q' := Q' \cup \{q'_{succ}\}$,
$\delta' := \delta' \cup \{(q', a, q'_{succ})\}$,
where $q'_{succ} = \{q_{succ} \in Q \mid q \in q', (q, a, q_{succ}) \in \delta\}$.
Repeat this operation until Q and δ do not change.
(3) $\mathcal{F}$ is defined as follows:
$\mathcal{F}' = \{T'_q | q \in F\}$
$T'_q := \{(q', a, q'_{suc}) \in \delta' \mid q \in q' \Rightarrow (q, a, q) \notin \delta\}$

Example 4.3. Let $\mathcal{N}$ be the BA illustrated in Fig. 1. The result of the determinization procedure for $\mathcal{N}$ is the DTGCA illustrated in Fig. 2, where $\mathcal{F} = \{T_{q_2}\}, T_{q_2} = \delta \setminus \{(q'_2, \{p2\}, q'_2), (q'_2, \{p1, p2\}, q'_2)\}$.

Conjecture 4.2. *Let $\mathcal{N}$ be a BA with feature A. Then, we can construct a DTGCA $\mathcal{D}$ such that $L(\mathcal{D}) = L(\mathcal{N})$, by the above procedure based on the powerset determinization.*

5. Related Works

Other LTL subsets. In this work, we focused on LTL subsets that can be translated into deterministic ω-automata using the powerset determinization. Other approaches for LTL subsets for efficient realizability checking have also been studied. Ref. 13 shows the complexity

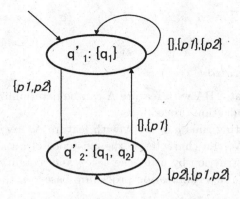

Fig. 2.   The result of the determinization procedure in Example 4.3

of constructing deterministic ω-automata and checking realizability for LTL($op_1, op_2, \ldots, op_n$), where LTL($op_1, op_2, \ldots, op_n$) is a fragment that allows only $op_1, op_2, \ldots, op_n$ operators (e.g., LTL(**F**, **X**), LTL(**G**, **F**), and so on). In Ref. 14, an LTL subset called *generalized reactivity (1)* is proposed, together with a checking procedure based on a BDD-based symbolic technique. Specifications written in the subset can be translated into deterministic automata, directly and briefly. The tools Anzu[15] and Ratsy[16] based on the procedure have been developed.

Approximation approach. The approximation approach, which is another approach to avoid Safra's determinization, has been studied. Refs. 17, 18 and 19 have proposed approximate procedures that avoid Safra's determinization. The procedures in Refs. 18 and 19 are refinements of the procedure in Ref. 17. In the procedures in Refs. 18 and 19, the acceptance condition of the ω-automaton is bounded. The condition that the number of occurrences of accepting states is *at most k*, instead of *finite* is used as an acceptance condition. Several tools that are based on these procedures have been developed, including Acacia+[20] and Unbeast[21]. In addition, a procedure that considers witnesses of size k is proposed in Refs. 18 and 22, and an improved version of this is given in Ref. 23. In these procedures, bounded realizability checking is reduced to a SAT problem or a satisfiability modulo theories (SMT) problem, and the problem is solved using an efficient SAT solver or SMT solver.

6. Conclusion and Future Work

In this paper, we discussed LTL subsets that can be translated into deterministic ω-automata by using the powerset determinization, to avoid the difficulty of realizability checking. The powerset determinization is less expensive and simpler than the general determinization (Safra's determinization) of ω-automata. We offered ideas for LTL subsets larger than already-known LTL subsets.

In the future, we will present a sophisticated procedure for constructing deterministic ω-automata for our new larger LTL subsets, and will prove the correctness of this procedure. Moreover, we will develop a tool with our LTL subsets, and demonstrate its effectiveness in experiments.

References

1. A. Pnueli and R. Rosner, On the synthesis of a reactive module, in *Proc. 16th ACM SIGPLAN-SIGACT Symposium on Principles of Programming Languages*, (ACM, 1989).
2. M. Abadi, L. Lamport and P. Wolper, Realizable and unrealizable specifications of reactive systems, in *Proc. 16th International Colloquium on Automata, Languages, and Programming*, LNCS Vol. 372 (Springer, 1989).
3. S. Safra, On the complexity of omega-automata, in *Proc. 29th Annual Symposium on Foundations of Computer Science*, (IEEE Computer Society, 1988).
4. Z. Manna and A. Pnueli, A hierarchy of temporal properties, in *Proc. 6th Annual ACM Symposium on Principles of Distributed Computing*, (ACM, 1987).
5. E. Y. Chang, Z. Manna and A. Pnueli, Characterization of temporal property classes, in *Proc. 19th International Colloquium on Automata, Languages and Programming*, LNCS Vol. 4623 (Springer, 1992).
6. M. Maidi, The common fragment of CTL and LTL, in *Proc. 41st Annual Symposium on Foundations of Computer Science*, (IEEE Computer Society, 2000).
7. R. Ehlers, ACTL ∩ LTL synthesis, in *Proc. 24th International Conference on Computer Aided Verification*, LNCS Vol. 7358 (Springer, 2012).
8. A. Pnueli, The temporal semantics of concurrent programs, *Theor. Comput. Sci.* **13**, 45 (1981).

9. N. Piterman, From nondeterministic Büchi and Streett automata to deterministic parity automata, in *Proc. 21st Annual IEEE Symposium on Logic in Computer Science*, (IEEE Computer Society, 2006).

10. I. Cerna and R. Pelanek, Relating hierarchy of temporal properties to model checking, in *Proc. 28th International Symposium on Mathematical Foundations of Computer Science*, LNCS Vol. 2747 (Springer, 2003).

11. T. Aoshima, K. Sakuma and N. Yonezaki, An efficient verification procedure supporting evolution of reactive system specifications, in *Proc. 4th International Workshop on Principles of Software Evolution*, (ACM, 2001).

12. S. Mochizuki, M. Shimakawa, S. Hagihara and N. Yonezaki, Fast translation from LTL to Büchi automata via non-transition-based automata, in *Proc. 16th International Conference on Formal Engineering Methods*, LNCS Vol. 8829 (Springer, 2014).

13. R. Alur and S. La Torre, Deterministic generators and games for LTL fragments, *ACM Trans. Comput. Logic* **5**, 1 (2004).

14. N. Piterman and A. Pnueli, Synthesis of reactive(1) designs, in *Proc. Verification, Model Checking, and Abstract Interpretation*, LNCS Vol. 3855 (Springer, 2006).

15. B. Jobstmann, S. Galler, M. Weiglhofer and R. Bloem, Anzu: A tool for property synthesis, in *Proc. 19th International Conference on Computer Aided Verification*, LNCS Vol. 4590 (Springer, 2007).

16. R. Bloem, A. Cimatti, K. Greimel, G. Hofferek, R. Könighofer, M. Roveri, V. Schuppan and R. Seeber, Ratsy – a new requirements analysis tool with synthesis, in *Proc. 22nd International Conference on Computer Aided Verification*, LNCS Vol. 6174 (Springer, 2010).

17. O. Kupferman and M. Y. Vardi, Safraless decision procedures, in *Proc. 46th Annual IEEE Symposium on Foundations of Computer Science*, (IEEE Computer Society, 2005).

18. S. Schewe and B. Finkbeiner, Bounded synthesis, in *Proc. 5th International Symposium on Automated Technology for Verification and Analysis*, LNCS Vol. 4762 (Springer, 2007).

19. E. Filiot, N. Jin and J.-F. Raskin, An antichain algorithm for LTL realizability, in *Proc. 21st International Conference on Computer Aided Verification*, LNCS Vol. 5643 (Springer, 2009).

20. A. Bohy, V. Bruyère, E. Filiot, N. Jin and J.-F. Raskin, Acacia+, a tool for LTL synthesis, in *Proc. 24th International Conference on Computer Aided Verification*, LNCS Vol. 7358 (Springer, 2012).

21. R. Ehlers, Unbeast: Symbolic bounded synthesis, in *Proc. 17th International Conference on Tools and Algorithms for the Construction and Analysis of Systems*, LNCS Vol. 6605 (Springer, 2011).
22. B. Finkbeiner and S. Schewe, SMT-based synthesis of distributed systems, in *Proc. Second Workshop on Automated Formal Methods*, (ACM, 2007).
23. M. Shimakawa, S. Hagihara and N. Yonezaki, SAT-based bounded strong satisfiability checking of reactive system specifications, in *Proc. International Conference on Information and Communication Technology (ICT-EurAsia2013)*, LNCS Vol. 7804 (Springer, 2013).

First-class Environments in Categorical Combinators

Hiroki JOKO and Shin-ya NISHIZAKI

*Department of Computer Science, Tokyo Institute of Technology,
Tokyo, 152-8552, Japan
E-mail:nisizaki@cs.titech.ac.jp*

The categorical combinatory logic CCL$\beta\eta$SP is a combinatory logic motivated by the cartesian closed category, proposed by Pierre-Louis Curien. The combinatory logic is used for modeling of the lambda calculus and gives a design of an abstract machine, the Categorical Abstract Machine (CAM). The first-class environment is a mechanism in programming languages which enables us to manipulate an environment, that is, a mapping of variables to bound values. We have studied the lambda calculus with first-class environments for several years.

In this paper, we depict that the first-class environment indwells in the categorical combinatory logic, giving the translation of the simply-typed lambda calculus with first-class environments into the categorical combinatory logic. We show the translation respects the typing and the reduction.

Keywords: Lambda Calculus; Categorical Combinator; First-class Environment.

1. Introduction

In this section, we present several notions related to this paper, such as categorical combinators, first-class environments and the environment calculus.

1.1. *Categorical Combinators*

The combinatory logic is a formal system formalizing computation and mathematical logic, which is an variation of the lambda calculus. The first system of the combinatory logic is the SKI combinator calculus[1]. The primary difference of the combinatory logic between the lambda calculus is the mechanism of variable-binding: a function of the lambda calculus takes actual parameters through formal parameters, on the other hand, the combinatory logic represents a function as combination of combinators. Generally speaking, an expression of the combinatory logic is difficult to understand in comparison with the lambda calculus. But, the combinatory logic such as the SKI-combinators, is Turing-complete similarly to the lambda calculus; the SKI combinatory logic has the same computational power as the lambda calculus.

The categorical combinatory logic is proposed by Curien 2 based on the cartesian closed category. The categorical combinators are defined as morphisms (sometimes calls arrows) of the cartesian closed category and the reduction rules are derived from the equivalence between arrows in the cartesian closed category.

Definition 1.1 (Categorical Combinatory Logic). The
categorical combinatory logic CCL^2 is the algebra of terms built from a countable set **Var** of variables by the following grammar:

$$M ::= Id \mid Fst \mid Snd \mid App \mid \Lambda(M) \mid (M \circ N) \mid \langle M, N \rangle$$

We use the following notation:

$$\langle M_1, M_2 \ldots, M_n \rangle \overset{def}{=} \langle \cdots \langle M_1, M_2 \rangle, \cdots, M_n \rangle.$$

A equational system $CCL\beta\eta SP$ is defined by the following equations.

- (Ass) $(x \circ y) \circ z = x,$
- (IdL) $Id \circ x = x,$
- (IdR) $x \circ Id = x,$
- (Fst) $Fst \circ \langle x, y \rangle = x,$
- (Snd) $Snd \circ \langle x, y \rangle = y,$
- (DPair) $\langle x, y \rangle \circ z = \langle x \circ z, y \circ z \rangle,$
- (Beta) $App \circ \langle \Lambda(x), y \rangle = x \circ \langle Id, y \rangle,$
- (Dλ) $\Lambda(x) \circ y = \Lambda(x \circ \langle y \circ Fst, Snd \rangle),$
- (AI) $\Lambda(App) = Id,$
- (FSI) $\langle Fst, Snd \rangle = Id.$

The *cartesian closed category*[3,4], CCC, is a category with products, exponential objects, and the terminal object, which models pairs and currying in functional programming languages.

The constants Id, Fst, Snd and App are arrows of the cartesian closed category.

For objects A, B, and C,

$$Id : A \rightarrow A,$$
$$Fst : A \times B \rightarrow A,$$
$$Snd : A \times B \rightarrow B,$$
$$App : (A \Rightarrow B) \times A \rightarrow B.$$

For an arrow $f : C \times A \rightarrow B$,

$$\Lambda(f) : C \rightarrow (A \Rightarrow B).$$

for an exponential For arrows $f : A \rightarrow B$ and $g : B \rightarrow C$,

$$g \circ f : A \rightarrow C.$$

For arrows $f : C \rightarrow A$ and $g : C \rightarrow B$,

$$\langle f, g \rangle : C \rightarrow A \times B.$$

for a product of A and B.

The conditions of CCC is formulated by the following equations between arrows, except the terminal object.

(Ass) $(x \circ y) \circ z = x$,
(IdL) $Id \circ x = x$,
(IdR) $x \circ Id = x$,
(Fst) $Fst \circ \langle x, y \rangle = x$,
(Snd) $Snd \circ \langle x, y \rangle = y$,
(SPair) $\langle Fst \circ x, Snd \circ x \rangle = x$.
(App) $App \circ \langle \Lambda(x) \circ Fst, Snd \rangle = x$,
(SΛ) $\Lambda(App \circ \langle x \circ Fst, Snd \rangle) = x$.

The equations Fst and Snd gives us the existence of a pair and SPair the uniquness of a pair.

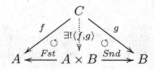

The existence means that for any arrow $f : C \rightarrow A$ and $g : C \rightarrow B$, there exists $\langle f, g \rangle : C \rightarrow A \times B$ satisfying that $Fst \circ \langle f, g \rangle = f$ and $Snd \circ \langle f, g \rangle = g$, which are Fst and Snd, respectively. The uniqueness means that if there is an arrow:

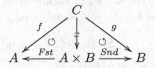

then $x = \langle f, g \rangle$ holds, that is, $\langle Fst \circ x, Snd \circ x \rangle = x$, which is SPair.

Similarly, equations App and SΛ describe existence and uniqueness, respectively.

It is known that the former equation system Ass, IdL, IdR, Fst, Snd, DPair, Beta, Dλ, AI, FSI and the latter Ass, IdL, IdR, Fst, Snd, SPair, App, SΛ are equivalent[2,5].

1.2. *Interpretation of the Lambda Calculus in the Categorical Combinators*

The lambda calculus with surjective pairing[2], λc, can be interpreted in the categorical combinatory logic CCL$\beta\eta$SP.

Definition 1.2 (Lambda Calculus with Surjective Pairing, λc).
The terms of the calculus are defined by the following grammar.

$$M ::= x \mid \lambda x.M \mid (MN) \mid (M, N) \mid fst(M) \mid snd(M)$$

The equivalence of the calculus is defined by the following equations.

(β) $(\lambda x.M)N = M[x:=N]$,
(η) $\lambda x.Mx = M$ if $x \notin FV(M)$,
(fst) $fst((M, N)) = M$,
(snd) $snd((M, N)) = N$,
(SP) $(fst(M), snd(M)) = M$.

The equivalence above-defined is called $\beta\eta SP$ and written $=_{\beta\eta SP}$ if we should distinguish from the other equivalences. If you regard the equations as the rewrite rules from their left-hand side to right-hand side, then it gives us the reduction.

The pairing mechanism with not only fst and snd but also SP, is called *surjective*.

The lambda calculus can be interpreted in the categorical combinatory logic, by the following translation.

Definition 1.3 (Translation of λ_c into CCL$\beta\eta$SP). The translation of the lambda calculus into the categorical combinatory logic is a mapping of the λc-terms and finite sequences of variables to terms of the categorical combinatory logic defined by the following equations.

$$[\![x_i]\!]_{x_0,\dots,x_n} = Snd \circ Fst^i,$$
$$[\![(\lambda x.M)]\!]_{x_0,\dots,x_n} = \Lambda([\![M]\!]_{x,x_0,\dots,x_n}),$$
$$[\![(MN)]\!]_{x_0,\dots,x_n} = App \circ \langle [\![M]\!]_{x_0,\dots,x_n}, [\![N]\!]_{x_0,\dots,x_n} \rangle,$$
$$[\![(M,N)]\!]_{x_0,\dots,x_n} = \langle [\![M]\!]_{x_0,\dots,x_n}, [\![N]\!]_{x_0,\dots,x_n} \rangle,$$
$$[\![fst(M)]\!]_{x_0,\dots,x_n} = Fst \circ [\![M]\!]_{x_0,\dots,x_n},$$
$$[\![snd(M)]\!]_{x_0,\dots,x_n} = Snd \circ [\![M]\!]_{x_0,\dots,x_n},$$

where i is the minimum number satisfying that $x = x_i$.

The interpretation of the variable x_i, $Snd \circ Fst^i$ is an arrow from $((((1 \times A_n) \times \cdots) \times A_1) \times A_0)$ to A_i:

$$Snd \circ Fst^i : ((((1 \times A_n) \times \cdots) \times A_1) \times A_0) \to A_i,$$

which is the i-th projection of the $(n+2)$-ple product. In this interpretation, the current environment is encoded as an $(n+2)$-ple product, if there are $(n+1)$ variables in the current scope.

The author who knows Lisp dialects such as Scheme, should be careful since the custom of Lisp is opposite to that of the categorical combinatory logic: a sequence is encoded as right-associative and the first component is left, in the custom of Lisp, like

$$(A_0 \times (A_1 \times (\cdots \times (A_n \times 1)))).$$

We access the nth component by function `cad`$\cdots$`dr`.

It is known the following property[2].

Proposition 1.1. If $M =_{\beta\eta SP} N$, then $[\![M]\!]_{x_0,\dots,x_n} =_{\beta\eta SP} [\![N]\!]_{x_0,\dots,x_n}$ where $\{x_0,\dots,x_n\} \subseteq FV(M) \cup FV(N)$.

1.3. *First-class Environments and Environment Calculus*

An *environment* is a mapping of variables to values, which is mentioned in the context of programming languages' semantics. For example,

```
(let ((x 1) (y 2))
  (+ x y))
```

In this expression, it is explained a sub-expression (+ x y) is evaluated under an environment in which a variable x is bound to 1 and y to 2.

In the context of programming language theory, we use the notion of environment. For the simply-typed lambda calculus, we give a set theoretic model such as

$$[\![x^\alpha]\!](\rho) = \rho(x) \ (\in [\![\alpha]\!]),$$
$$[\![(\lambda x^\sigma . M)]\!](\rho) = \lambda v \in [\![\sigma]\!]. [\![M]\!](\rho[x \mapsto v]),$$
$$[\![(MN)]\!](\rho) = [\![M]\!](\rho)\Big([\![N]\!](\rho)\Big).$$

In this semantics, a lambda term is interpreted as a function from an environment to a value of the term.

A *first-class entity* in a programming language is an object which can be passed to a function as an actual parameter and returned from a function as a result. For example, integers are first-class entities in many programming languages including programming language C. However, functions are not first-class entities in C but in functional languages such as Haskell and Scheme[6,7] and scripting languages like JavaScript. Some implementations of Scheme, such as MIT/GNU-Scheme[7], GNU Guile[8,9] provide first-class environments. In the terminology of reflective programming, we can reify a runtime environment and reflect the reified environment to the runtime. For example,

```
(define env (let ((x 1) (y 2)) (the-environment))
(eval '(+ x y) env)
```

The first expression binds the variable env to an environment in which variable x and y are bound to 1 and 2, respectively. In the second expression, the expression (+ x y) is evaluated under the environment. Strictly speaking, local-eval is used in place of eval, since an environment for local variables is reified, in GNU Guile[8,9]. In the MIT/GNU-Scheme[7], the-environment can return only the top-level environment.

In the model above-mentioned, the semantics of (the-environment) and (eval ' ⟨expression⟩ ⟨environment⟩) is defined as follows.

$$[\![(\texttt{the-environment})]\!](\rho) = \rho,$$
$$[\![(\texttt{eval } 'M \ N)]\!](\rho) = [\![M]\!]\Big([\![N]\!](\rho)\Big).$$

The first expression represents that (the-environment) returns the current environment ρ and the second that the value of N obtained by evaluation under the environment ρ should mean an environment and the expression M is evaluated under the environment value. The meaning of (the-environment) corresponds to the identity function on the semantic domain and that of (eval '···) to the function composition operator ∘.

$$[\![(\text{the-environment})]\!](\rho) = \rho = (\lambda v.v)\rho,$$

$$[\![(\text{eval '}M\ \ N)]\!](\rho) = [\![M]\!]\big([\![N]\!](\rho)\big) = \big([\![M]\!] \circ [\![N]\!]\big)(\rho).$$

We have studied the first-class environment in the framework of the lambda calculus[10,11]. In order to formalize environments, we adopt a method called *explicit environments*, proposed by P.-L. Curien *et al.*[12,13]. In this paper, we refer to this idea as *"environment-as-substitution."* In the traditional lambda calculus, a substitution of variables is defined in the meta-level, but in the lambda-sigma calculus, based on the idea of explicit substitution, it is defined in the object-level, in other words, the substitution operation is defined as a part of the reduction of the calculus. Accordingly, environments in the lambda-sigma calculus are formalized as substitutions defined in the object-level. However, the lambda-sigma calculus does not give us a first-class environment since the terms and the environments are categorized as different syntax classes. In our previous works[10,11], we mix the terms and the environment together in the same syntax class, which enables us to have first-class environments in the calculus. We call a lambda calculus with a first-class environment an *environment calculus*. In paper 10, we proposed a simply typed environment calculus and investigated fundamental properties, such as its confluence, strong normalization theorem, type inference algorithm, and principal typing theorem. In paper 11, we extended it to an ML-polymorphic type system and studied its type inference algorithm and principal typing theorem. In Paper 14, we make it possible to modify the first-class environment as a function code. In Paper 15, we extend reduction of the environment calculus. In Paper 16, we study formal system PCF with first-class environments, PCF_{env}.

2. Lambda Calculus with First-class Environments

In this section, we introduce the simply lambda calculus $\lambda_{\text{env}}^{\rightarrow}$ with first-class environments proposed in Paper 10.

Definition 2.1 (Raw Terms of λ_{env}). We assume a countable set of *variables,* **Var**. We define the *raw terms* or *pre-typed terms* of the λ_{env}-calculus by the following grammar.

$$M ::= x \ \mid\ (\lambda x.M) \ \mid\ (MN) \ \mid\ id \ \mid\ (M/x) \cdot N \ \mid\ (M \circ N)$$

where x is a variable.

Terms $(\lambda x.M)$ and (MN) are called a *lambda abstraction* and *function application* respectively, similarly to the usual lambda calculus. Intuitive meanings of the lambda abstraction and the function application are the same as the ones of the lambda calculus. Terms id, $(M/x) \cdot N$, and $(M \circ N)$ are called the *identity environment*, an *environment extension*, and an *environment composition* respectively. The identity environment id returns the current environment like `the-environment` of the Scheme programming language. The environment composition $(M \circ N)$ means a value of M which is obtained by evaluation under the environment N, which corresponds to an expression (`eval` 'M N) in Scheme.

Definition 2.2 (Reduction of λ_{env}). The *weak reduction* of λ_{env} is defined as a binary relation between terms by the following rules.

$$((L \circ M) \circ N) \to (L \circ (M \circ N)) \qquad \text{Ass}$$
$$id \circ M \to M \qquad \text{IdL}$$
$$M \circ id \to M \qquad \text{IdR}$$
$$((L/x) \cdot M) \circ N \to ((L \circ N)/x) \cdot (M \circ N) \qquad \text{DExtn}$$
$$x \circ ((M/x) \cdot N) \to M \qquad \text{VarRef}$$
$$y \circ ((M/x) \cdot N) \to y \circ N \qquad \text{VarSkip}$$
$$(M_1\ M_2) \circ N \to (M_1 \circ N)(M_2 \circ N) \qquad \text{DApp}$$
$$((\lambda x.M) \circ L)N \to M \circ ((N/x) \cdot L) \qquad \text{Beta1}$$
$$(\lambda x.M)N \to M \circ ((N/x) \cdot id) \qquad \text{Beta2}$$

$$\frac{M \to N}{(ML) \to (NL)}\ \text{AppL} \qquad \frac{M \to N}{(LM) \to (LN)}\ \text{AppR}$$

$$\frac{M \to N}{\lambda x.M \to \lambda x.N}\ \text{Lam}$$

$$\frac{M \to N}{(M \circ L) \to (N \circ L)}\ \text{CompL} \qquad \frac{M \to N}{(L \circ M) \to (L \circ N)}\ \text{CompR}$$

$$\frac{M \to N}{(M/x) \cdot L \to (N/x) \cdot L}\ \text{ExtnL} \qquad \frac{M \to N}{(L/x) \cdot M \to (L/x) \cdot N}\ \text{ExtnR}$$

Example 2.1.

$$((\lambda y.\lambda x.id)M)N$$
$$\rightarrow ((\lambda x.id) \circ ((M/y) \cdot id))N \qquad\qquad \text{Beta2}$$
$$\rightarrow id \circ ((N/x) \cdot (M/y) \cdot id) \qquad\qquad \text{Beta1}$$
$$\rightarrow ((N/x) \cdot (M/y) \cdot id) \qquad\qquad \text{IdL}$$

Next, we give a simple type system to the environment calculus.

Definition 2.3 (Types of $\lambda_{\text{env}}^{\rightarrow}$). We define a *type* of the simply-typed environment calculus $\lambda_{\text{env}}^{\rightarrow}$ by the following grammar.

$$A ::= \alpha \mid (A \rightarrow B) \mid \{x_1{:}A_1\} \cdots \{x_n{:}A_n\}$$

We call $(A \rightarrow B)$ a *function type*, and $\{x_1{:}A_1\} \cdots \{x_n{:}A_n\}$ an *environment type*. We use meta-variables $E, E', H, H', \ldots$ for environment types.

Note. In our previous work[10], we define an environment type as

$$\{x_1{:}A_1\} \cdots \{x_n{:}A_n\}\rho,$$

where ρ is a variable which can be replaced by another environment type. We attach the environment type variable ρ, because we deal with type inference algorithm and generality of typing, in Paper 10. Since we do not handle this issue in this paper, we omit the environment type variable ρ in order to make the type system simple.

Typablity is formulated as type judgement $E \vdash M : A$, which is a ternary relation among an environment type E, a raw term M, and a type A.

Definition 2.4 (Type Judgement and Typing Rules). The typing judgement $\Gamma \vdash M : A$ is defined inductively by the following *typing rules*.

$$\frac{0 \leq i \leq n}{\{x_0{:}A_0\} \cdots \{x_n{:}A_n\} \vdash x_i : A_i} \text{ Var}$$

$$\frac{E \vdash M : (A \rightarrow B) \quad E \vdash N : A}{E \vdash (MN) : B} \text{ App} \qquad \frac{\{x{:}A\}E \vdash M : B}{E \vdash (\lambda x.M) : (A \rightarrow B)} \text{ Lam}$$

$$\frac{}{E \vdash id : E} \text{ Id} \qquad \frac{E \vdash N : H \quad H \vdash M : A}{E \vdash (M \circ N) : A} \text{ Comp} \qquad \frac{E \vdash M : A \quad E \vdash N : H}{E \vdash (M/x) \cdot N : \{x{:}A\}H} \text{ Extn}$$

Example 2.2 (Typing Derivation Tree). The following is a typing derivation tree which consists of the typing rules.

$$\dfrac{\dfrac{\dfrac{}{\{y{:}\beta\}\{x{:}\alpha\} \vdash id : \{y{:}\beta\}\{x{:}\alpha\}} \text{ Id}}{\{x{:}\alpha\} \vdash \lambda y.id : \beta \to \{y{:}\beta\}\{x{:}\alpha\}} \text{ Lam}}{\vdash \lambda x.\lambda y.id : \alpha \to \beta \to \{y{:}\beta\}\{x{:}\alpha\}} \text{ Lam}$$

3. Translation of the Environment Calculus into the Categorical Combinatory Logic

In this section, we propose a translation of the lambda calculus with first-class environments into the categorical combinatory logic. The translation is an extended version of the translation of the lambda calculus, mentioned in Section 1.3.

Definition 3.1 (Type Translation of $\lambda_{\text{env}}^{\to}$ into CCL$\beta\eta$SP). We define a translation of a type into an object of the cartesian closed category, inductively as follows.

$$[\![\alpha]\!] = \alpha,$$
$$[\![(A \to B)]\!] = ([\![A]\!] \Rightarrow [\![B]\!]),$$
$$[\![\{x_1{:}A_1\} \cdots \{x_n{:}A_n\}]\!] = (((1 \times [\![A_n]\!]) \cdots) \times [\![A_1]\!])$$

Here, the terminal object **1** can be an arbitrary object since we will not use the condition of the terminal object in our translation.

Definition 3.2 (Term Translation of $\lambda_{\text{env}}^{\to}$ into CCL$\beta\eta$SP). We define a translation of a typed term into an arrow of the cartesian closed category, inductively as follows. For a variable x_i typed as

$$\dfrac{1 \le i \le n}{\{x_1{:}A_1\} \cdots \{x_n{:}A_n\} \vdash x_i : A_i} \text{ Var}$$

$$[\![x_i]\!] = Snd \circ Fst^i.$$

For a function application (MN) typed of

$$\dfrac{E \vdash M : (A \to B) \quad E \vdash N : A}{E \vdash (MN) : B} \text{ App}$$

$$[\![(MN)]\!] = App \circ \langle [\![M]\!], [\![N]\!] \rangle.$$

For a lambda abstraction $(\lambda x.M)$ typed of

$$\frac{\{x{:}A\}E \vdash M : B}{E \vdash (\lambda x.M) : (A \to B)} \text{ Lam}$$

$$[\![(\lambda x.M)]\!] = \Lambda([\![M]\!]).$$

For the identity environment id typed of

$$\frac{}{E \vdash id : E} \text{ Id}$$

$$[\![id]\!] = Id,$$

where Id is the identity arrow between $[\![E]\!]$ and itself.

For the environment composition $(M \circ N)$ typed of

$$\frac{E \vdash N : H \quad H \vdash M : A}{E \vdash (M \circ N) : A} \text{ Comp,}$$

$$[\![(M \circ N)]\!] = [\![M]\!] \circ [\![N]\!].$$

For the environment extension $(M/x) \cdot N$ typed of

$$\frac{E \vdash M : A \quad E \vdash N : H}{E \vdash (M/x) \cdot N : \{x{:}A\}H} \text{ Extn,}$$

$$[\![(M/x) \cdot N]\!] = \langle [\![N]\!], [\![M]\!] \rangle.$$

The term translation is well-defined with respect to arrow composition:

Theorem 3.1. *Let an environment type E, a term M, and a type A of $\lambda_{env}^{\to}$ be*

$$E \vdash M : A.$$

Then, $[\![M]\!]$ is an arrow from an object $[\![E]\!]$ to an object $[\![A]\!]$:

$$[\![M]\!] : [\![E]\!] \to [\![A]\!].$$

Proof. We prove this theorem by induction on the derivation tree of $E \vdash M : A$.

The cases on a variable, a lambda abstraction and a function application are the same as the proof of the similar theorem on the lambda calculus and therefore we omit them for want of space.

Case of the identity environment id type of

$$\frac{}{E \vdash id : E} \text{ Id}.$$

$[\![id]\!]$ is translated as Id such that

$$Id : [\![E]\!] \to [\![E]\!]$$

by the definition of the translation.

Case of the function composition $(M \circ N)$ type of

$$\frac{E \vdash N : H \quad H \vdash M : A}{E \vdash (M \circ N) : A} \text{ Comp.}$$

By the induction hypothesis, we have $[\![N]\!] : [\![E]\!] \to [\![H]\!]$ and $[\![M]\!] : [\![H]\!] \to [\![A]\!]$. Then we have

$$[\![M]\!] \circ [\![N]\!] : [\![E]\!] \to [\![A]\!].$$

Case of an environment extension $(M/x) \cdot N$ type of

$$\frac{E \vdash M : A \quad E \vdash N : H}{E \vdash (M/x) \cdot N : \{x{:}A\}H} \text{ Extn.}$$

By the induction hypothesis, we have $[\![M]\!] : [\![E]\!] \to [\![A]\!]$ and $[\![N]\!] : [\![E]\!] \to [\![H]\!]$. Then we obtain $\langle [\![M]\!], [\![N]\!] \rangle : [\![E]\!] \to [\![H]\!] \times [\![A]\!]$. $\square$

The following theorem shows that the translation of terms respects the reduction. The reduction of the $\lambda_{\text{env}}^{\to}$-calculus corresponds to that of CCL$\beta\eta$SP.

Theorem 3.2. *If $M \to N$, then $[\![M]\!] \overset{*}{\to} [\![N]\!]$.*

Proof. We prove this theorem by induction on $\to$. The step cases are easy. We focus on the base cases.

Cases of Ass. This case is trivial by Ass of CCL$\beta\eta$SP.

Cases of IdL and IdR. These cases are trivial by IdL and IdR of CCL$\beta\eta$SP, respectively.

Case of DExtn:

$$((L/x) \cdot M) \circ N \to ((L \circ N)/x) \cdot (M \circ N).$$

The left-hand side is

$$([\![(L/x) \cdot M) \circ N]\!] = \langle [\![M]\!], [\![L]\!] \rangle \circ [\![N]\!]$$

and the right-hand side

$$
\begin{aligned}
&[\![((L \circ N)/x) \cdot (M \circ N)]\!] \\
={}&\langle [\![(M \circ N)]\!], \ [\![(L \circ N)]\!] \rangle \\
={}&\langle [\![M]\!] \circ [\![N]\!], \ [\![L]\!] \circ [\![N]\!] \rangle.
\end{aligned}
$$

$$\langle [\![M]\!], [\![L]\!] \rangle \circ [\![N]\!] \to \langle [\![M]\!] \circ [\![N]\!], \ [\![L]\!] \circ [\![N]\!] \rangle$$

is derived from Rule DPair of CCL$\beta\eta$SP.

Case of VarRef:

$$x \circ ((M/x) \cdot N) \to M.$$

We suppose that the left-hand side is typed as

$$\frac{E \vdash (M/x) \cdot N : \{x{:}A\}H \quad \{x{:}A\}H \vdash x : A}{E \vdash x \circ ((M/x) \cdot N) : A}.$$

Then we have $[\![M]\!] : [\![E]\!] \to [\![A]\!]$, $[\![N]\!] : [\![E]\!] \to [\![H]\!]$, and

$$[\![(M/x) \cdot N]\!] : [\![E]\!] \to [\![H]\!] \times [\![A]\!].$$

Moreover,

$$
\begin{aligned}
[\![x \circ (M/x) \cdot N]\!] &= [\![x]\!] \circ \langle [\![N]\!], [\![M]\!] \rangle \\
&= Snd \circ \langle [\![N]\!], [\![M]\!] \rangle \\
&\to [\![M]\!].
\end{aligned}
$$

Case of VarSkip:

$$y \circ ((M/x) \cdot N) \to y \circ N.$$

The left-hand side is typed as

$$\frac{E \vdash (M/x) \cdot N : \{x{:}B\}H \quad \{x{:}B\}H \vdash y : A}{E \vdash y \circ ((M/x) \cdot N) : A}.$$

where we let H be $\{x_1{:}A_1\} \cdots \{x_n{:}A_n\}$ and y the variable x_i. Then we know

$$
\begin{aligned}
&[\![y \circ ((M/x) \cdot N)]\!] \\
={}& (Snd \circ Fst^{i+1}) \circ (\langle [\![N]\!], [\![M]\!] \rangle) \\
\to{}& (Snd \circ Fst^{i}) \circ [\![N]\!] \\
={}& [\![y]\!] \circ [\![N]\!] = [\![y \circ N]\!].
\end{aligned}
$$

Case of DApp:

$$(M_1 \ M_2) \circ N \to (M_1 \circ N)(M_2 \circ N).$$

We have

$$[\![(M_1 \, M_2) \circ N]\!]$$
$$= (App \circ \langle [\![M_1]\!], [\![M_2]\!] \rangle) \circ [\![N]\!]$$
$$\rightarrow App \circ (\langle [\![M_1]\!], [\![M_2]\!] \rangle \circ [\![N]\!])$$
$$\rightarrow App \circ \langle [\![M_1]\!] \circ [\![N]\!], [\![M_2]\!] \circ [\![N]\!] \rangle$$
$$= App \circ \langle [\![M_1 \circ N]\!], [\![M_2 \circ N]\!] \rangle$$
$$= [\![(M_1 \circ N)(M_2 \circ N)]\!]$$

Case of Beta1: $((\lambda x.M) \circ L)N \rightarrow M \circ ((N/x) \cdot L)$.
  We have

$$[\![((\lambda x.M) \circ L)N]\!]$$
$$= App \circ \langle \Lambda([\![M]\!]) \circ [\![L]\!], [\![N]\!] \rangle$$
$$\rightarrow App \circ \langle \Lambda([\![M]\!] \circ \langle [\![L]\!] \circ Fst, Snd \rangle), [\![N]\!] \rangle$$
$$\rightarrow ([\![M]\!] \circ \langle [\![L]\!] \circ Fst, Snd \rangle) \circ \langle Id, [\![N]\!] \rangle$$
$$\rightarrow [\![M]\!] \circ (\langle [\![L]\!] \circ Fst, Snd \rangle \circ \langle Id, [\![N]\!] \rangle)$$
$$\rightarrow [\![M]\!] \circ \langle ([\![L]\!] \circ Fst) \circ \langle Id, [\![N]\!] \rangle, Snd \circ \langle Id, [\![N]\!] \rangle \rangle$$
$$\xrightarrow{*} [\![M]\!] \circ \langle [\![L]\!], [\![N]\!] \rangle$$
$$= [\![M \circ ((N/x) \cdot L)]\!].$$

Case of Beta2: $(\lambda x.M)N \rightarrow M \circ ((N/x) \cdot id)$.
  We have

$$[\![(\lambda x.M)N]\!] = App \circ \langle \Lambda([\![M]\!]), [\![N]\!] \rangle$$
$$\rightarrow [\![M]\!] \circ \langle Id, [\![N]\!] \rangle = [\![M \circ ((N/x) \cdot id)]\!].$$

$$\square$$

4. Concluding Remarks

In this paper, we discuss the relationship of the simply-typed lambda calculus with first-class environments, $\lambda^{\rightarrow}_{\text{env}}$, to the categorical combinatory logic, CCL$\beta\eta$SP. We introduced the syntax and the operational semantics of the both systems and then defined the translation of the typed terms of the $\lambda^{\rightarrow}_{\text{env}}$-calculus into terms of CCL$\beta\eta$SP. We showed that the translation preserves typing and that the translation maps the reduction of $\lambda^{\rightarrow}_{\text{env}}$ to that of CCL$\beta\eta$SP.

The primary difference between this paper's version of the environment calculus and the previous version[10] is the data structure of the environment. An environment type in this paper is considered of an ordered sequence of variable-type pairs but the one in Paper 10 a partial mapping of variables to types. For example, in this paper, we distinguish $\{x{:}A\}\{y{:}B\}$ from $\{y{:}B\}\{x{:}A\}$. However, in Paper 10, we do not distinguish these two environment types.

It is not trivial to extend the translation to the one of the previous version[10] of the calculus, which is our future work.

References

1. J. R. Hindley and J. P. Seldin, *λ-calculus and Combinators: An Introduction* (Cambridge University Press, 2008).
2. P.-L. Curien, Categorical combinatory logic, in *Automat, Languages and Programming*, Lecture Notes in Computer Science Vol. 194 (Springer-Verlag, 1995).
3. S. M. Lane, *Categories for the Working Mathematician* (Springer, 1978).
4. A. Asperti and G. Longo, *Categories, Types, and Structures: An Introduction to Category Theory for the Working Computer Scientist* (The MIT Press, 1991).
5. P.-L. Curien, *Categorical combinators, sequential algorithms, and functional programming*, second edn. (Birkhäuser, 1993).
6. M. Sperber, R. K. Dybvig, M. Flatt and A. van Straaten (eds.), *Revised [6] Report on the Algorithmic Language Scheme* (Cambridge University Press, 2010).
7. C. Hanson, *MIT/GNU Scheme Reference Manual (Release 9.1)* MIT, 1.105 edn. (10, 2011).
8. *Guile Reference Manual 1/2* (Samurai Media Limited, 2015).
9. *Guile Reference Manual 2/2* (Samurai Media Limited, 2015).
10. S. Nishizaki, Simply typed lambda calculus with first-class environments, *Publication of Research Institute for Mathematical Sciences Kyoto University* **30**, 1055 (1995).
11. S. Nishizaki, Polymorphic environment calculus and its type inference algorithm, *Higher-Order and Symbolic Computation* **13** (2000).
12. M. Abadi, L. Cardelli, P.-L. Curien and J.-J. Lévy, Explicit substitutions, *Journal of Functional Programming* **1**, 375 (October 1991).

13. P.-L. Curien, T. Hardin and J.-J. Lévy, Confluence properties of weak and strong calculi of explicit substitutions, *J. ACM* **43**, 362 (March 1996).
14. Programmable environment calculus as theory of dynamic software evolution, in *Proceedings of International Symposium on Principles of Software Evolution: ISPSE2000*, (IEEE Computer Society Press, 2000). doi:10.1109/ISPSE.2000.913242.
15. Strong reduction for typed lambda calculus with first-class environments, in *Proceedings of the Third International Conference on Information Computing and Application, ICICA2012*, Lecture Notes in Computer Science Vol. 7473 (Springer, 2012).
16. Evaluation strategy and translation of environment calculus, in *Proceedings of the Fourth International Conference on Information Computing and Application, ICICA2013*, Communications in Computer and Information Science Vol. 391 (Springer, 2013).

An Automated Way of Characterizing Protein Sequence Entries Stored in a Database

J.D. Pacilan[†] and K.P. Alferez

Department of Computer Science, University of the Philippines Cebu,
Cebu City, Cebu 6000, Philippines
[†]E-mail: jpacilan@gmail.com
www.upcebu.edu.ph

D.M. Lao

Bioinformatics Research Interest Group, BRIG, University of the Philippines Cebu
Cebu City, Cebu 6000, Philippines
E-mail: dmlao1@up.edu.ph

The ever increasing biological data deposited in databases worldwide requires corresponding bioinformatics tools that can quickly reveal its hidden information. We describe here Protein Sequence Profiler (PsP) that was developed to characterize protein sequence entries (stored in database) which gives the user a simplified description about proteins sequences as well as the capability to generate new dataset, either subjected to redundancy check or not for prediction purposes. The system is built using PHP as the computing language and the use of arrays as data structure. The system could filter-out and retrieve from the protein sequence database entries according to the following groupings (or in combination): signal peptide, taxonomy, protein type, transmembrane type, non-membrane type, and evidence level. Consequently, the filtered protein sequence entries could be downloaded, which in effect creates a new data set, or could further be subjected to the integrated redundancy checker to remove "highly" similar protein sequences.

Keywords: Characterize protein; protein sequence profiler; PHP; array; redundancy check.

1. Introduction

In the drama of life on a molecular scale, proteins are where the action is [1]. Proteins are important elements of the human physiology. They hold cellular tissues, perform intra-cellular communication and transport, responsible for metabolic processes among others. Characterizing proteins in simplified form is vital in determining the current state of the protein, which has severe implications to better understanding of the biological processes [2].

In the 90's there was an explosive growth in the amount of biological data stored in online publicly-available databases that seemingly grow in number as each day passes. For the sheer volume of data deposited, the quality becomes compromised as it came from different sources. To provide a solution to this problem, data profiling came into the picture where a systematic analysis of the content of a data source is done.

Although, there are already a lot of existing data profilers available online, and to name a few we have UniProt (http://www.uniprot.org) and SPdb (http://www.signalpeptide.de), retrieving the protein sequence(s) of interest maybe a challenge especially for those with minimal or zero background in biology due to a lot of details presented to the user.

In this study, we proposed a protein sequence profiling system which aims to characterize protein sequence entries stored in the database by a simplified approach in retrieving and describing protein sequence entries that would result to a better understanding of the protein sequence(s) of interest. Moreover, the system provides the capability to generate new dataset from the filtered-out entries, either subjected to redundancy check or not, for prediction purposes. The Protein Sequence Profiler (PsP) is a system that characterizes protein sequences with signal and non-signal peptide annotations stored in the database through the use of data filters according to taxonomy (i.e. archaea, bacteria, eukaryote or viruses), protein type (i.e. transmembrane or non-transmembrane), membrane type (i.e. single-spanning membrane, multi-spanning membrane or beta-barrel), non-membrane type (i.e. secretory or non-secretory), and evidence level (i.e. experimental or non-experimental). The system has similarities with UniProt where it provides a comprehensive, high-quality and freely accessible resource of protein sequence and functional information albeit without the complicated accessibility features.

2. Methodology

2.1. *Data Sets*

The study was focused in making sure that the protein information obtained from filtering is correct and reliable. To do this, we created data sets that contain protein sequence entries with signal and non-signal peptide annotations obtained from the UniProt release 2016_04 (http://www.uniprot.org).

Protein sequence entries with signal and non-signal peptide annotations were examined in this study. The data sets obtained belong to the SwissProt section of the UniProtKB and were downloaded in text format. SwissProt or UniProtKB (UniProt Knowledgebase) is a subset of UniProt where entries have been manually annotated by experts and reviewed by UniProtKB curators [3]. These entries are tagged with a yellow star in their entry status and were the subject of this study.

2.2. Data Set Retrieval

2.2.1. Protein Sequences with Signal Peptide Annotation

A term 'Signal' indicated in the Sequence Annotation found in the Features (FT) section, or in Keywords (KW) section determines the presence of signal peptide thus retrieving such entry. The data set with signal peptide annotation were then grouped according to their taxonomic classification. These are indicated in the Taxonomy (OC) section of the 'Names and Taxonomy' subsection. Table 1 below shows the breakdown of the dataset based on Taxonomy.

Table 1. Summary of reviewed signal peptide proteins.

Taxonomy	Number of Entries	Percentage
Archaea	152	0.38 %
Bacteria	9,775	24.26 %
Eukaryota	28,773	71.42 %
Viruses	1,587	3.94 %
Total	40,287	100.00 %

2.2.2. Protein Sequences without Signal Peptide Annotation

A term without 'Signal' indicated in the Sequence Annotation, the Features (FT) section or in the Keywords (KW) section, retrieved a protein sequence with non-signal peptide annotations. Similar to those with signal peptide annotations, it was also grouped according to their taxonomic classification. Table 2 below shows the breakdown of reviewed protein sequence with non-signal peptide annotation based on their taxonomy.

Table 2. Summary of reviewed non-signal peptide proteins.

Taxonomy	Number of Entries	Percentage
Archaea	19,233	3.76 %
Bacteria	322,792	63.18 %
Eukaryota	153,839	30.11 %
Viruses	15,042	2.94 %
Total	510,906	100.00 %

2.3. *Reducing Number of Protein Sequence Entries in Dataset by Systematic Sampling*

The data sets used for testing was not the whole UniProt release 2016_04 (551, 193 entries) but only a sample of it. We took a sample to represent the population of the UniProt release 2016_04 for testing purposes since testing a large number of entries in the system would take some time to process. To accomplish this, systematic sampling was adapted. Here, the determination for the periodic interval (k) was fixed, and instead, the sample size was computed by the formula: sample size = population size/interval (k).

Although, we fixed the interval to pick a sample in every 10th of the protein sequence entries (i.e. $k = 10$, which is the default value), the system has a sampling tool where the user could input his desired k value.

By applying the abovementioned formula for computing the sample size, we obtained the number of entries for each data set as shown in Table 3. We did a little modification in the case of the entries with non-signal peptide annotation because of the big difference in the ratio to the entries with signal peptide annotation. In the table, the values in the Factor column was derived by getting the proportion of the number of entries with signal peptide annotation for each taxonomic group to the total protein sequence entries (with the same signal peptide annotation). Then, these values were multiplied to the corresponding original number of entries without signal peptide annotation, which still resulted to a very big gap in the number of entries. Hence, we decided just to pick the equivalent number of protein sequence entries as that with signal peptide annotation following the same sampling procedure. However, k was calculated this time by the formula k = population size/sample size.

Table 3. Number of protein sequence entries for each data set after sampling.

Taxonomy	Signal Peptide		Non-Signal Peptide			
	Original No. of Entries	No. of Entries After Sampling	Original No. of Entries	Factor	Target Entries	No. of Entries After Sampling
Archaea	152	15	19,233	0.0038	73	15
Bacteria	9,775	978	322,792	0.2426	78,309	978
Eukaryota	28,773	2,878	153,839	0.7142	109,871	2,878
Viruses	1,587	159	15,042	0.0349	525	159
Total	40,287	4,030	510,906			4,030

2.4. *Protein Sequence Entries Classification Criteria*

2.4.1. *Evidence Level*

All protein sequence entries are grouped by the presence of experimental evidences. The criteria below were adapted from the UniProt manual for protein resources (http://www.uniprot.org/manual).

2.4.1.1. Non-Experimental Evidence

Entries whose protein existence have not been strictly proven yet, have probable evidence, have unsure evidence or without protein existence are labeled as protein sequence entries with non-experimental evidence. In Protein Attributes, the Protein Existence (PT) section, is searched to determine if a protein sequence entry has non-experimental evidence. The following annotations in the PT section indicate non-experimental types of evidences [4]:

- *'Evidence at transcript level'* which indicates that the existence of a protein has not been strictly proven but that expression data (such as existence of cDNA(s), RT-PCR or Northern blots) indicate the existence of a transcript.
- *'Inferred by homology'* which indicates that the existence of a protein is probable because clear orthologs exist in closely related species.
- *'Predicted'* which indicates that an entry is without evidence at protein, transcript, or homology levels.
- *'Uncertain'* which indicates that the existence of the protein is unsure.

2.4.1.2. Experimental Evidence

Entries in which protein existence are clear and have been proven are classified under protein sequence with experimental evidence. The following Protein Attributes were looked into the PT section in order to retrieve protein sequence entries with experimental evidence [4]:

- *'Evidence at protein level'* which indicates that there is a clear experimental evidence for the existence of the protein. The criteria include partial or complete Edman sequencing, clear identification by mass spectrometry, X-ray or NMR structure, good quality protein-protein interaction or detection of the protein by antibodies as stated in the user manual of UniProt.

2.4.2. *Classification Based on Taxonomy*

All protein sequence entries were classified into the following Taxonomy (i.e. Superkingdom): Archaea, Bacteria, Eukaryota and Viruses. These are indicated in the Taxonomy (OC) section of the 'Names and Taxonomy' subsection. This contains the taxonomic hierarchical classification lineage of the source organism. Only the first listed classification in the hierarchy, i.e. the Superkingdom, was being used as the keyword.

2.4.3. *Classification Based on Subcellular Location*

A protein sequence entry can either be classified as a Transmembrane or a Non-Transmembrane protein. To classify where an entry belongs, three sections were checked in the text record:

1. Keyword (KW) section;
2. Features (FT) section; and,
3. Subcellular Location (CC) section.

Any of the three (3) sections signifies a membrane-spanning or a non-membrane-spanning region of the protein. For example, if a 'Transmembrane' keyword exists in KW section, a protein is classified as a Transmembrane protein. Otherwise, a protein is classified as a Non-transmembrane protein.

2.4.3.1. *Classifying Protein Sequences as Transmembrane Protein*

For Transmembrane proteins, each of the sections have different use as a keyword filter. In KW section, this would signify a Transmembrane entry. In FT section, the count of 'TRANSMEM' keyword signifies a Single-pass (single instance of 'TRANSMEM') or a Multi-pass membrane (multiple instance of 'TRANSMEM'). In CC section, this signifies a more detailed classification of a Single-pass membrane protein such as 'Single-pass Type I', 'Single-pass Type II', 'Single-pass Type III', and 'Single-pass Type IV'.

There are Multi-spanning entries having 'Transmembrane' keywords but do not have 'FT TRANSMEM' line which contradicts our method of classifying a transmembrane protein, i.e. all Multi-spanning membrane proteins have transmembrane regions. This situation only occurs for beta-stranded transmembrane regions, which were purposely not annotated as explained by a curator of UniProt, Elisabeth Gasteiger (personal communication, 2015) of the Swiss Institute of Bioinformatics (SIB). Furthermore, such transmembrane domains are, however, not predicted by transmembrane prediction programs (e.g. TMHMM or ESKM). As a consequence, such entries frequently have no 'FT

TRANSMEM' annotations, although they contain the 'Transmembrane' keywords in KW section. Hence, for this study, the system classified protein sequence entries 'Beta-barrel Transmembrane' protein whenever it encounters such kind of annotation.

2.4.3.2. Classifying Protein Sequences as Non-Transmembrane Protein

For non-transmembrane protein sequence entries, also called Globular proteins, there are two (2) possible classifications. One is the secretory protein and the other is non-secretory, in which no further classification was implemented by the system, but provided the location of where the protein exits or resides. This is shown in the 'Place of Excretion/Residence' column, 'Non-Transmembranes' filter under 'Display Filter Results by'.

2.5. Export of Filtered Protein Sequence Entries

Protein sequence entries can be exported either in fasta file or text file, or both. This feature allows the creation of new data set where the user could use in prediction for assessment purposes. Each exported files displays the download details:

   i.   File Name
   ii. Date (dd/mm/yyyy)
   iii. Total Entries
   iv. Filter Setting
   v.   Subjected to Redundancy Checking
   vi. Redundancy Percentage

Clicking on the 'Fasta' download button, exports a fasta formatted file while clicking on 'Text Record' download button exports a text formatted file.

2.5.1. FASTA Format

A fasta format is a text-based format for representing peptide sequences, where amino acids are represented using single-letter codes. A protein sequence entry begins with a single-line description, followed by lines of sequence data [5].

The description line consists of the 'Entry Id' and the 'Entry Name' and begins with a greater-than (">") symbol followed by "sp" then followed by the Entry Id and Entry Name which is separated by a vertical line ("|"). See example below:

```
>sp|D4GSY9|ANTRB_HALVD
MAIERRRFLQAAGVGAVLGLSGCTGNTSPP
QANNETAEGSGGSESGDGSTQELTLATTTS
TYDTGLLDALNPVFEEKFNARVKTISQGTG
AAIETARNGDADVILVHARGAEDEFLQDGY
GVNRRDVMFNDFVVVGPADDPAGISGMESA
ADAFATVADAGATFVSRGDDSGTNKKELLI
```

Fig. 1. Snapshot of sample protein sequence entry in FASTA format.

2.5.2. *Text Format*

A text format consists of the following keyword headers (aligned left vertically). The Text Record format is similar to the SwissProt/UniProtKB format, except that, we added the information on the number of Transmembrane segments using KW keyword for Transmembrane proteins.

```
ID    KEX1_TUBMM 625 AA
AC    DG5G4B1
DT    15-06-2010(Date Created)
DT    08-06-2016(Date Modified)
OC    Eukaryota
CC    -!- FUNCTION: Protease with a
carboxypeptidase B-like function
CCinvolved in the C-terminal
processing of the lysine and arginine
CCresidues from protein precursors.
Promotes cell fusion and is
CC involved in the programmed cell
death (By similarity).
CC {ECO:0000250}.
CC    -!- SUBCELLULAR LOCATION: Golgi
apparatus, trans-Golgi network
CC membrane {ECO:0000250}; Single-pass
type I membrane protein
CC {ECO:0000250}.
PE    Inferred from homology
KW    Transmembrane (1)...
```

Fig. 2. Snapshot of sample protein sequence entry in text record format.

2.6. *Protein Sequence Redundancy Check*

After protein sequence entries are filtered, the user may apply data reduction or data redundancy check procedure if the intention is to create a new (non-redundant) data set for prediction purposes. According to Sikic [6], the inclusion of similar sequences in certain analyses will introduce undesirable biases. Therefore, performing data redundancy is an important step in creating new dataset for it removes protein sequences that go beyond certain similarity thresholds to qualify as 'representative' dataset.

Biological data are vastly increasing and it needs tools to eliminate similar sequences so that when training prediction methods, it can generalize well its performance through learning diverse representation of protein sequences. And, preferably, such tool is integrated with data filtering/extraction system just like what is implemented here.

2.6.1. *The Redundancy Checking Tool*

There are different software tools available to check data redundancy, and to name a few: 'Pisces' [7], 'BlastClust' [8], 'Decrease redundancy' [9], 'cd-hit' [5], and 'SkipRedundant' [6]. The non-redundant datasets resulted from the five programs mentioned are moderately similar to each other for the same dataset fed and with the same percentage of identity threshold setting [5]. All of their outputs are more than acceptable in terms of residual similarity between the entries that were grouped from the outputs [5].

For the proposed system, we opted to integrate the 'Pisces' tool (http://dunbrack.fccc.edu/Guoli/PISCES_InputD.php) as the data redundancy removal program. The basis in choosing this software tool over the other four (4) is that, it is an open-source software and the sequence percentage identity or similarity can be set from a range of 0 to 100.

2.6.2. *Setting Limits for the Redundancy Checker*

For server back-end processing manageability purposes, however, the current version of the system sets a limit on the number of protein sequence entries to be processed in real-time by the redundancy checker. Initially, the limit is set to 300 entries, and beyond that, the system will ask for an email where it will send the output. After subjecting to redundancy checking (for real-time processing), the results can be automatically shown in the data table. This was done to avoid long waiting times for the users to get the results and still be able to perform other functionalities of the system.

2.7. *Overall Process of the PsP System*

Figure 3 illustrates the whole process in the retrieval and the display of the filtered-out protein sequence entries of the database. The process starts with the user specifying whether the protein sequence entries to be retrieved is with 'signal peptide' annotation or without after activating the data filter function. Then, from here, the user may set the following filter options, namely, according to: the organism's taxonomy, the protein type, and the evidence level of the protein sequence entries; and, may not necessarily of that same specific order also. Although, for illustrative purposes, it is presented sequentially in the process flowchart.

After execution of filtering the protein sequence entries, the user may perform these subsequent tasks, again in no particular order and for the same reason as above, either to display graph or table statistical summaries, redundancy check, download the filtered-out protein sequence entries either as text-record file or as FASTA file formats, and further filter-setting for the screen display of the database filtering output.

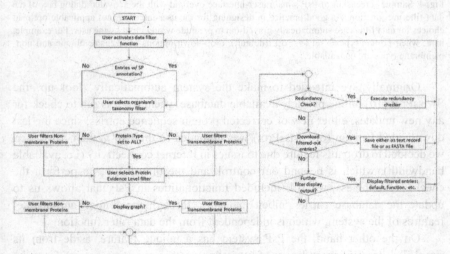

Fig. 3. PsP's overall process in filtering protein sequence entries and its associated functionalities.

3. Results and Discussion

3.1. *Main Webpage and Dialog Box for Database Filters of PsP*

The PsP system is designed to be easily accessible and navigated by the user. In fact, the protein sequence entries filtering function can be effortlessly located and activated by the use of either the menu tab or the 'data filter' icon found in the opening webpage of the system (Fig. 4).

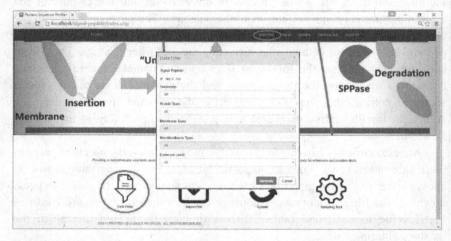

Fig. 4. Sample screenshot of PsP's main user-interface overlaid with the activated dialog box of the data filtering function. As good practice in designing for the user-interface, not applicable optional choices for data filters are automatically grayed-out to preclude wrong input by the user. For example, here, when protein type is set to 'ALL'(default), drop-down options for transmembrane and non-membrane types are unavailable.

Originally, we intended to make the system automatically "look-up" the SwissProt [10] online publicly available database whenever it is run to check for any new updates, either new or corrected protein sequence entries, since the last downloaded version (of SwissProt) was uploaded to the PsP system. However, we decided to drop this feature due to issues in Internet connectivity (i.e. available bandwidth), which is beyond our control, and the time it took to perform the check. Nevertheless, we still included functionalities in PsP that allows us to update the database entries, albeit manually, through the 'import-and-update' features of the system, which is independent from the data filter function.

On the other hand, the PsP system has a unique feature, aside from its simplified description and way of retrieving protein sequence entries from the database, by incorporating a data redundancy checker to the system, which in effect allows the user not to leave the system to perform similarity check for the filtered-out protein entries. Although, currently, we are looking at fixes to improve the system's sluggish performance when executing this feature.

3.2. Consistency Test

There are 8,060 total number of entries of protein sequences that were selected through systematic sampling from the 551,193 entries of the manually annotated and reviewed UniProt release 2016_04. Table 4 shows the summary of the breakdown of data sets for both signal and non-signal protein sequence entries.

Table 4. Summary of data sets.

Taxonomy	Signal Peptide	Non-signal Peptide	Grand Total
Archaea	15	15	30
Bacteria	978	978	1,956
Eukaryota	2,878	2,878	5,756
Viruses	159	159	318
Total	4,030	4,030	8,060

The correctness or reliability of the profiler using these data sets were tested by using the permutation formula to determine the maximum number of possible combinations in the settings for the different data filters without repetition and order. Table 5 shows the values for each data filter used in retrieving protein sequence entries. These are the values that were used for the different data filter settings (i.e. combinations).

Table 5. Settings for data filters used in testing the system.

Taxonomy	Protein Type	Membrane Type	Non-membrane Type	Evidence Level
ALL	ALL	ALL	ALL	ALL
Archaea	Transmembrane	Single-spanning	Secretory	Experimental
Bacteria	Non-transmembrane	Multi-spanning	Non-secretory	Non-experimental
Eukaryota		Beta-barrel	Beta-barrel	
Viruses				

We also eliminated the possible occurrence of either protein type (i.e. 'Transmembrane' or 'Non-transmembrane'), membrane type and non-membrane type in the list of combinations when protein type is set to 'All'. Consequently, the filter for membrane type or non-membrane type also becomes unavailable. Furthermore, if Protein type is 'Transmembrane', filter option would be unavailable for non-membrane type, and the opposite would happen for non-transmembrane choice in protein type. With this process of filter-setting reduction, we came up with 120 combinations for protein sequence entries with signal and non-signal peptide annotations making a total of 240 combinations of filter settings. To determine the accuracy of the filtering output, we compared the filtering results of the system with that of the excel file containing the information of the protein sequence entries used for testing downloaded straight from UniProtKB website. Then, the different test runs were conducted using the combinations generated. Two rounds of testing were made to ensure that the data filter truly resulted to a correct output.

By investigation, we found out that the first test run resulted to 21 errors. The errors were effected by beta-barrel membranes when set to 'Non-transmembrane' protein type filter during retrieval of protein sequence entries. The beta-barrel annotation causes an error in the code and the non-transmembrane filter due to a flaw in the database's data type setting which is 'text'. And, we fixed this bug by changing the data type to 'longtext' instead. In addition, during debugging the codes, we discovered that we mistakenly input a blank value instead of putting beta-barrel in the system's parser, which resulted to not able to read correctly beta-barrel membrane annotations. As for the non-transmembrane error, the database data type for subcellular location, which is the dependency for the non-membrane type filter, was set to 'text property' which can hold only a maximum of 65,535 bytes of data. As a consequence, an error was generated because there were some information that were not stored. Hence, the data type was changed to 'longtext' in order to accommodate more bytes of data and fix the bug.

The issues were then resolved, and another test run was conducted. This time all the combinations gave 100% similar results. Table 6 shows the summary of test results.

Table 6. Summary of test results for filter-setting combinations with errors.

Test Run	No. of Filter Setting Combinations (n = 240)		% Correct
	Correct	Incorrect	
First Round	198	42	82.5 %
Second Round	240	0	100.0 %

3.3. *Function Test*

The system also generates graphs and tables (results not shown) to visualize the distribution of data and to describe the statistical summaries, respectively, of the filtered-out protein sequence entries. The statistics displayed should correspond to the number of the total number of entries for the filtered protein sequences, which serves as means of determining accuracy and consistency in the output.

3.4. *Redundancy Check Efficiency*

Table 7 shows a snapshot of the results for the experiment done with different number of protein sequence entries subjected to redundancy check. For total number of entries 312 and 223, redundancy checking was quite fast. Thus, we decided that 300 be the number of protein sequence entries considered (at a time) as the limit/cut-off for real-time processing. The reason for slow processing time for the 714 entries (or perhaps, more) might be the number of lines the checker has to scan, and/or might be the limited memory installed in our test platform. For more than 300 protein entries, the system displays a dialog box asking the user for an email address whenever data reduction function is called.

Table 7. Summary of test made for redundancy check using different number of protein sequence entries.

Number of Entries	Time
312	52 seconds
223	34 seconds
714	9 mins, 10 seconds

4. Conclusion and Recommendation

In this study, we were able to develop successfully a Protein Sequence Profiler (PsP) system that allows the user to retrieve and characterize protein sequence entries stored in the database using simplified description and presentation of protein sequence information. Furthermore, PsP can create new data sets (from the filtered-out protein sequence entries) using the following filtering options by: 'Taxonomy', 'Protein Type', 'Membrane Type', 'Non-membrane Type' and 'Evidence Level'. The system is also capable of exporting the filtered-out protein sequence entries in 'text record' or FASTA formats. Hence, we can say that somehow the developed-system has the capability to generate new dataset for prediction purposes.

In addition, the developed-system has features to display statistical summaries by either tables or graphs based from the filtered-out protein sequence entries. On the other hand, we were able to integrate somewhat successfully a data redundancy checker in our developed system.

For future research direction, it is worthwhile to explore parallel computing techniques, i.e. GPU programming, in processing large number of protein sequence entries since the current version of the system expectedly cannot handle efficiently for large amount of entries, in which response time of the system greatly affects the following processes: viewing of the entries, import, update and redundancy checking. Moreover, we are entertaining the idea of expanding the functionality features of the system specifically providing the prospective user a sort of built-in datamining *cum* analytical tool, which hopefully enriches the protein (sequence) entries characterization process.

References

1. A. M. Lesk, *Introduction to Protein Architecture*, (OUP, Oxford, 2001).
2. V. Buntrock, MALDI-TOF MS, an Adaptable Method for Protein Characterization, Visualized in a JoVE-Chemistry Video Article (2013), https://blog.mendeley.com/tag/protein-characterization/.
3. The UniProt Consortium, UniProt: a hub for protein information, *Nucleic Acids Res.*, **43**: D204-D212 (2015).
4. S. Poux, M. Magrane, C.N. Arighi, A. Bridge, C. O'Donovan, K. Laiho, The UniProt Consortium. Expert curation in UniProtKB: a case study on dealing with conflicting and erroneous data, *Database (Oxford)*, bau016 (2014).
5. W. Li and A. Godzik, Cd-hit: a fast program for clustering and comparing large sets of protein or nucleotide sequences, *Bioinformatics*, **22**:1658-1659 (2006).
6. P. Rice, I. Longden, and A. Bleasby, EMBOSS: The European Molecular Biology Open Software Suite, *Trends in Genetics*, Vol. **16** No. 6, pp. 276-277 (2006).
7. G. Wang and R. L. Dunbrack, Jr., PISCES: a protein sequence culling server, *Bioinformatics*, **19**:1589-1591 (2003).
8. V. Alva, S.Z. Nam, J. Söding, A.N. Lupas, The MPI bioinformatics Toolkit as an integrative platform for advanced protein sequence and structure analysis, *Nucleic Acids Res.*, **44**(W1):W410-415 (2016). DOI: 10.1093/nar/gkw348.
9. P. Artimo, M. Jonnalagedda, K. Arnold, D. Baratin, G. Csardi, E. de Castro, S. Duvaud, V. Flegel, A. Fortier, E. Gasteiger, A. Grosdidier, C. Hernandez, V. Ioannidis, D. Kuznetsov, R. Liechti, S. Moretti, K. Mostaguir, N. Redaschi, G. Rossier, I. Xenarios, and H. Stockinger, ExPASy: SIB bioinformatics resource portal, *Nucleic Acids Res*, **40**(W1):W597-W603, (2012).
10. Boutet E, Lieberherr D, Tognolli M, Schneider M, Bansal P, Bridge AJ, Poux S, Bougueleret L, Xenarios I., UniProtKB/Swiss-Prot, the Manually Annotated Section of the UniProt KnowledgeBase: How to Use the Entry View, *Methods Mol. Biol.* **1374**:23-54 (2016).

CALVIS:
Educational Tool in Learning
Intel x86-32 Instruction Set Architecture

Jennica Grace Alcalde, Goodwin Chua, Ivan Marlowe Demabildo, Marielle Ashley Ong
and Roger Luis Uy

College of Computer Studies, De La Salle University,
Manila, 0922, Philippines
E-mail: {jennica_alcalde, goodwin_chua, ivan_demabildo}@dlsu.edu.ph,
{marielle_ong, roger.uy}@dlsu.edu.ph
www.dlsu.edu.ph

Computer Assembly Language Visualizer and Simulator (CALVIS) is an assembler that executes assembly code instructions from x86-32 Instruction Set Architecture. This includes basic integer and floating-point as well as Single Input/Multiple Data (SIMD) instructions such as MMX, SSE and SSE2. CALVIS provides a display of the contents of the assembly components - registers, memory and flags, allowing assembly programmers to visibly see the values that were affected during the simulation. Correspondingly, CALVIS contains visual demonstrations of the process of an instruction, which aides students in understanding assembly instructions. CALVIS is an educational tool for computer architecture and assembly language programming that eases the delivery of concepts taught from teacher to students and provides students with a supplementary learning tool for assembly.

Keywords: x86-32 Instruction Set; Assembly Language; Computer Architecture; Code Simulator; Code Visualization.

1. Introduction

Undoubtedly, programming is justified to be a significant element in undergoing further research and study. Subsequently, different programming languages are being used today for developing personal or business software. As explained by [1, 2], using a learning approach in programming without a proper basis of knowledge is difficult to completely understand as a whole.

Computer Architecture, a subject, which deals with introducing the three aspects of computer design-based concepts: instruction set architecture (ISA), organization or micro-architecture and hardware implementation. Hence, properly visualizing of these design-based concepts are important part for the students to get the integral idea. Identified by [3] that it becomes demanding to associate the theoretical aspects and practical experiments. Thus it is necessary to have a tool, an assembly programming that acts as a middle-man in manipulating hardware components resulting to a software application. Likewise, assembly programming connects the abstract computer and software concepts. According to [4], assembly programming helps an individual to comprehend the internal process of a computer and functionality of a high-level programming language in accessing direct hardware components.

Occasionally, there are instances where students cannot figure-out the abstract computer concepts. Thus, giving negative effect on the students performance to master the basics of assembly programming. Though committing errors is a factor in a person's development of programming skills, a fitting method can be used in teaching and learning assembly programming with the use of visualizations. Visualization means that showing the executed assembly code instruction with its real-time values such as registers, memory and flags. This use of visualization corresponds in a method called visual learning. [5] emphasized that visual learning takes advantage of the visual instruments to transmit knowledge to an individual. Visual instruments such as images, representations and simulations processed to a person's brain that results to a visual thinking.

On the other hand, there are available software that demonstrate the debugging of assembly programs. Mostly, these software are platform-specific and have limited support to x86 instruction set family such as [3, 6, 7]. These software lack visualizations that does not cater the core concepts for students regarding ISA. In short, CALVIS is an educational tool that provides the following elements: visualization, simulation and customization for Intel x86-32 Architecture. It aims to be a supplementary companion for students in learning assembly programming using the different elements. Moreover, this paper aims to present CALVIS as an assembler, catering the students' needs to get the hang of assembly concepts and programming.

2. Related Works

2.1. *Usability Test of CALI86*

Developed by [6], CALI86 is an x86 assembly micro-architecture simulator used to provide a visual overview of the processes undertaken by an assembly program. It was designed for student use, as it provided a detailed visualization of the micro-architecture operations for each instruction simulated. Students can trace their code better with CALI86 because the values of the registers, flags, and memory are readily displayed.

CALI86 was conceptualized with the help of three faculty members with first-hand teaching experience in assembly programming from the Computer Technology department of De La Salle University, Manila. Accordingly, three focal points were recommended to improve the delivery of assembly concepts to students; which are to display the complete Von Neumann architecture, to produce detailed visualizations for arithmetic operations, and to pattern the interface design with existing assemblers.

2.2. *Usability Test of EduMIPS64*

EduMIPS64 by [3] is an educational MIPS64 assembly simulator used to help students visualize the processes undertaken within the MIPS64 architecture. EduMIPS64 provides a visualization of the five stages of pipelining during the execution of a program. Moreover, it uses a DINEROIV cache simulator to show specific traces of files that access the memory. In addition, students are provided with a command line via DINEROIV cache simulator to configure different test instances of caches without the need to exit EduMIPS64.

Usability tests for EduMIPS64 were conducted to assess the consistency, complexity, clarity and utility of the system [8]. A sample of ninety-three students from three different courses were asked to accomplish an online survey to assess the general speed and responsiveness of EduMIPS64. Table 1 shows the result of the online survey, with EduMIPS64 being evaluated as generally good in terms of simulator performance and excellent in terms of its user interface.

Table 1. EduMIPS64 Usability Test Results [3]

Metrics	Simulator Performance	Graphical User Interface
Excellent	19%	60%
Good	60%	20%
Sufficient	18%	19%
Poor	3%	1%

2.3. *Graphical User Interface and Visualization*

Different approaches and techniques in designing educational systems are developed with the intent of fully engaging the student [9]. According to [10], the following are good user interface design practices: strive for consistency, cater to universal usability, offer informative feedback, design dialogs to yield closure, prevent errors, permit easy reversal of actions, support internal locus of control, and reduce short-term memory load. These practices embody a user-centered designed in which the system is intuitive to the needs of the user. Furthermore, [11] emphasizes the need of a continuous process in developing a better user experience.

Additional techniques that can be used to improve user experience include information grouping, information sequencing, and information distribution. Information grouping is done by highlighting the relationships of relevant information through the use of same colored groupings or graphical boundaries; improving its readability. Information sequencing is done by arranging the displayed information depending on importance, convention, usage sequence, usage frequency, and alphabetical or chronological order. This enables the user to quickly extract and process information. Information distribution pertains to the volume of information presented to the user. This should be controlled so as to not overwhelm the user with information [12]

2.4. *System Usability Scale*

The System Usability Scale (SUS) is a metric used to measure the usability of applications and websites. [13] states that the SUS is an established metric with over 1,200 publication references. It is composed of a ten item questionnaire, answered with either strongly disagree, disagree, neutral, agree, and strongly agree.

The SUS helps assess the effectiveness, efficiency, and user satisfaction of a system. It centers on the value of the user's subjective view. With SUS, users do not need to expound on their choices, and they simply need to focus on the response that most appeals to them. The robustness and reliability of the SUS helps in understanding the user's perspective on the system.

2.5. *SASM: Simple ASM*

Developed by [7], Simple ASM (SASM) is a cross-platform IDE for Netwide Assembler (NASM), Microsoft Macro Assembler (MASM), GNU Assembler

(GAS), Flat Assembler (FASM) assembly languages. SASM is capable of displaying the contents of the assembly components in tabular form. However, the entire memory block is not displayed, and only specified variables can be tracked. Its console is split into an input and output window. Moreover, SASM functions as a debugger which uses the GNU Project Debugger (GDB). SASM also allows font and color customization of the assembly code editor. Furthermore, SASM is an assembly IDE that can run executable code.

3. The CALVIS System

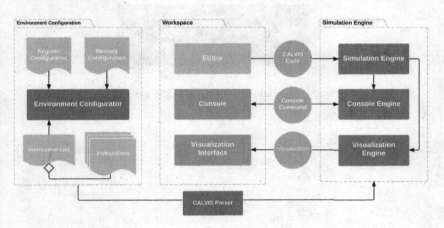

Fig. 1. Architectural diagram of the CALVIS system

Figure 1 shows the architectural diagram of the CALVIS system. CALVIS is composed of three modules namely, the environment configuration module, the workspace module, and the simulation module.

The environment configuration module is responsible for building the assembly simulation environment from three input configuration files, which are the register configuration file, the memory configuration file, and the instruction list file. These 3 files contain the input parameters in building the simulation environment, and produces the CALVIS parser. After the environment configuration module has finished building the assembly simulation environment, a CALVIS parser will be created and passed to the simulation module. This indicates that CALVIS is now ready to accept input assembly code.

Fig. 2.　User interface of the CALVIS system

Fig. 3.　Play mode visualization and simulation of the CALVIS system

The workspace module is responsible for processing the input assembly code, and passing the processed code to the simulation module. The main

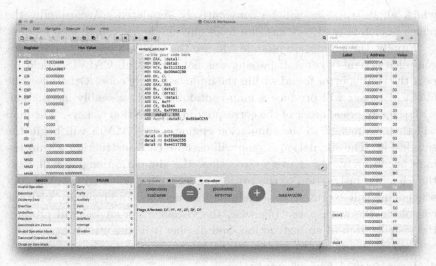

Fig. 4.   Step mode visualization and simulation of the CALVIS system

workspace of CALVIS is composed of the editor, the registers, flags, and memory interfaces, the console tab, the visualization tab, and the simulation control bar. The editor is where the assembly code can be inputted. The values of the registers, flags, and memory are displayed on the sides of the editor, allowing a complete and simultaneous tracking of the assembly components during code simulation. In addition, the relevant registers and memory segments of a simulated instruction are highlighted to help identify the assembly components affected by the instruction. The console tab acts as a dummy console to simulate console related instructions. Consequently, the visualization tab is where the visualization of an executed instruction will appear. Next, the simulation control bar is used to control the simulation of the assembly code present within the editor; with controls such as build, next step, previous step, play, and pause. Build is used to compile the input assembly code, and pass it to the simulator-visualizer module to begin the simulation.

By default, CALVIS simulates the input assembly code one instruction at a time, called step mode. The next step and previous step buttons are used to control the simulation of CALVIS by respectively stepping into, or stepping back from a line of code. This mode allows a controlled simulation to better track the contents of the different assembly components. Next, the play button is used to change the simulation mode to play mode, in which all instructions will be consecutively simulated. Accordingly, the pause button is used to transition from play mode back in to step mode.

Finally, the simulation module will use the CALVIS parser to parse the compiled assembly code. If parsing was not successful, CALVIS would report the syntax error found within the input assembly code. Otherwise, the CALVIS parser will produce a map containing each assembly instruction, with the numerical order of the corresponding instruction as keys. The map will then be passed to the simulation engine, and CALVIS will begin the simulation. The simulation engine will execute each instruction within the map accordingly. After every execution, the simulation engine will relay the executed instruction to the console and visualization engines. The console engine will execute console related instructions, and interface with the console in the workspace. Likewise, the visualization engine will produce the visualization of an instruction, and display it in the visualization tab.

4. Results and Experimentation

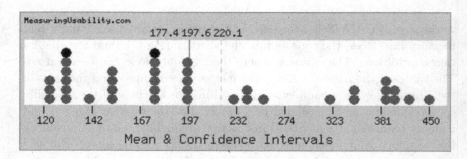

Fig. 5. Time to accomplish the tasks of all the test users

For the usability test, we used the System Usability Scale (SUS) for the questionnaire answered by the students. From a scale of 1 to 100, CALVIS scored 68.63 which is regarded to be above-average in rating. The score shown by SUS shows that the test users who are also the target users of CALVIS were satisfied with the performance and usability of the system application. However, improvements are still open for the software. In that regards, the test users were able to accomplish all tasks at hand. Figure 5 displays the average time to accomplish the tasks of both the professors and students where the red solid line represents the geometric mean and the green dashed line represents the upper and lower bounds with 95%

confidence interval. In addition, the scale of the horizontal axis represents the number of seconds the test user consumed in accomplishing the tasks. In the case that the maximum number of dots exceed a certain second, it is then represented by a black dot.

Additional parameters for the usability testing were used such as the geometric mean which computed the average time of the 53 students to accomplish the given tasks to execute using CALVIS. The result shows that the average time of the 53 students was three minutes and seventeen seconds (3:17). The time of each student is spread along within the graph as some of the students may have used a slow performing machine and others could have had problems in dealing with the user-interface of the software application. The outliers at the right most side of the graph represents the students without prior knowledge to both the ISA and programming. Since the students without prior knowledge to ISA do not have a background knowledge or information to what an IDE usually looks like, they had a hard time in using and understanding the contents of CALVIS. The researchers then observed that most of the test users who had a longer time compared to the average time in accomplishing the tasks is for the reason that they had difficulty locating the visualization pane. With that aside, some of the test users had difficulties understanding the functions of the simulation buttons such as the play, pause, execute next line and previous line buttons since it lacks a tool tip to inform the user of the specific function of each button. As a result, the lack of tool tips shows that it can cause the confusion of users in using the simulation buttons of CALVIS.

Despite what is mentioned previously, most of the test users stated that the visibility of the registers, flags and memory values are indeed helpful in tracing a given assembly program. In fact, this is what encourages the test users to use CALVIS in their future assembly projects and debugging as it displays the contents of the assembly components effectively. Moreover, most of them also remarked that the positioning of the registers, memory and flags is intuitive as it is how it is normally displayed in a computer architecture class. Furthermore, the test users said that necessary information in learning Assembly are all present, thus, there were none that the users were expecting to see that were not present in CALVIS. Although some had problems with the simulation buttons of CALVIS, most of the test users said that the position of the simulation buttons are standard as to how an IDE would like, therefore, the positioning of the panes are also intuitive. Additionally, the test users mentioned that CALVIS is comfortable to use as it close to an IDE. One of the professors also mentioned that if he teaches Computer Architecture, he would use CALVIS as it is clean, does not stray away from a normal IDE, and only provides necessary information in learning Assembly Programming. Overall, the test users said that the layout of the interface of CALVIS has good placing and balanced priority.

After conducting the test, the researchers asked the test users if the visualization is effective in guiding the students in learning a new instruction. According to most of the test users, the visualization is helpful as it provides the necessary information to understand the function of an instruction. However, they said that the layout of the visual representations need improvement. The researchers observed that the inconsistencies with the font and color used were the cause.

5. Conclusion

As discussed previously, it is a noteworthy mention that it is truly difficult for novice or aspiring assembly programmers to fully grasp the concept of computer architecture. With that in mind, CALVIS is an assembly compiler and simulator that initially accepts an assembly code written under the x86-32 assembly architecture in which the code is parsed, simulated and visualized by means of displaying the registers, flags and memory values along with the proper animations of the instruction used. The notable Instruction Set Architecture (ISA) that CALVIS supports are currently MMX, SSE, SSE2 and x87 FPU instructions. The researchers then assessed the performance and capabilities of CALVIS as an educational tool by means of using a sample size of 119 students from the De La Salle University. Analysis of the survey data were then post-processed afterwards. Upon the post-processing of the survey data of the sample, the researchers have found that the simulator was indeed useful in terms of helpfulness and responsiveness in debugging the assembly program by means of showing the registers, flag and memory values upon execution of the said program. The visualization of each instruction at hand were also met with positivity as it helped the students understand the logic of the specific instruction that was visualized. All in all, the software CALVIS is a helpful tool for both students and assembly programmers alike. The researchers recommends that further testing of CALVIS along with a larger sample size would be helpful in making improvements of the software by the researchers in the future.

References

[1] M. Saeli, Pedagogical content knowledge in programming education for secondary school, in *Proceedings of the Seventh International Workshop on Computing Education Research*, ICER '11 (ACM, New York, NY, USA, 2011).

[2] A. Sengupta, Cfc (comment-first-coding)–a simple yet effective method for teaching programming to information systems students, *Journal of Information Systems Education* **20**, 393 (2009).

[3] D. Patti, A. Spadaccini, M. Palesi, F. Fazzino and V. Catania, Supporting undergraduate computer architecture students using a visual mips64 cpu simulator, *Education, IEEE Transactions on* **55**, 406 (Aug 2012).

[4] P. A. Carter, *PC Assembly Language* (No Starch Press, 2006).

[5] J. Walny, S. Carpendale, N. Riche, G. Venolia and P. Fawcett, Visual thinking in action: Visualizations as used on whiteboards, *Visualization and Computer Graphics, IEEE Transactions on* **17**, 2508 (Dec 2011).

[6] J. Deriquito, T. Roseller, E. R. J. Diaz, J. J. H. Torreno and R. L. Uy, CALI86: computer assembly language illustrator for the intel 80x86 software architecture, unpublished thesis, (2004).

[7] D. Manushin, Sasm (simple asm) (2013).

[8] V. Catania, D. Patti, M. Palesi and A. Spadaccini, An open and platform-independent instruction-set simulator for teaching computer architecture, *World Scientific and Engineering Academy and Society (WSEAS)* **11** (2014).

[9] S. Panjwani, L. Micallef, K. Fenech and K. Toyama, Effects of integrating digital visual materials with textbook scans in the classroom, *Internation Journal of Education and Development using Information and Communication Technology (IJEDICT)* **5** (2007).

[10] R. Stopper, R. Sieber, S. Wiesmann and O. Schnabel, *Graphical User Interface - Layout and Design*, tech. rep., Cartography for Swiss Higher Education (CartouCHe) (January 2012).

[11] R. Saini, Graphical user interface design essentials and process, *International Journal of Advanced Research in Computer Science and Software Engineering* **3** (2013).

[12] B. Jansen, *The Graphical User Interface: An Introduction* (SIGCHI Bulletin, Seoul, Korea, 1998).

[13] J. Brooke, Sus: A retrospective, *Journal of Usability Studies (JUS)* **8**, 29 (February 2013).

Assembly Optimization Loop Unroll Implementation for RISC and CISC Processors and Metrics for Testing Optimization Effectiveness

Jonathan Paul Cempron[1], Jonathan Benedict Gonzales[2], Yuuki Hayakawa[3], Chudrack Salinas[4] and Roger Luis Uy[5]

Computer Technology Department, De La Salle University, Manila, Philippines
jonathan_cempron@dlsu.edu.ph[1], jonathan_benedict_gonzales@dlsu.edu.ph[2], yuuki_hayakawa@dlsu.edu.ph[3], chudrack_salinas@dlsu.edu.ph[4], roger.uy@delasalle.ph[5]

This paper presents a software implementation of program performance enhancement, specifically implementation of loop unroll. Loop unroll is an optimization where loops are converted into longer sequential code to avoid branches. Branches are to be avoided because it introduces high latency or pipeline stalls. Implementation of loop unroll is different for a Reduced Instruction Set Computer (RISC) and a Complex Instruction Set Computer (CISC). Differences in a supposed implementation of loop unroll for a RISC system and a CISC system will be presented. Our method in computing for effectiveness of optimization will be presented, as well as, the difference in computation of program performance for a RISC and a CISC system. The sample RISC system used for this paper is MIPS64 while the CISC system is x86_64.

Keywords: Assembly programming; RISC; CISC; code optimization; loop unroll.

I. INTRODUCTION

Assembly programming is a low level programming language that closely resembles the operations that a processor performs. The assembly language of the processor is dictated by its instruction set architecture thus assembly languages are different for different processors as compared to High Level Languages which are the same across different processors.

Processors generally have two classifications: CISC and RISC. The idea behind a CISC processor is that it has an abundance of instructions available to aid the programmer in development of programs. While a RISC processor reduces the number of instructions available, only having essential instructions with focus on hardware optimization on the processor such as uniform pipeline length [1-3].

Programs written specifically for processors are best optimized. One optimization method is loop unrolling. Loop unrolling is the transformation of the assembly codes from loops into longer sequential set of instructions [9]. The purpose of loop unrolling in a CISC program is to decrease the usage of branch instructions. While in a RISC program is to avoid stalls in the processor pipeline.

To evaluate the effectiveness of an optimization performed in a source code, two metrics are created and presented in this paper. One is Program Latency which will be used for evaluation for optimization effectiveness on CISC programs. The other is Instructions Performed for RISC programs.

II. CISC AND RISC

A CISC processor has an abundance of instructions in its ISA to aid the programmer in creation of programs. While it was realized that only a subset of a typical instruction from a CISC was used. Then the RISC idea was created. Only keeping the essential, commonly used, instructions. For the processor developers to focus more on hardware optimizations [3].

Common property of a CISC processor is that it has an abundance of instructions [1]. Because of the wide range of complexities that an instruction performs, each instruction is of different latency. These latencies are a result of the instruction being decoded to be used by the processor. The decoded instructions are called micro operations or micro-ops. This decoding process is a large influence in developing the CISC architecture and instruction set; a focus on simple decoding results in low latency.

A common feature on CISC processors are the availability of Single Instructions Multiple Data (SIMD) instructions which can process multiple set of data in a single instruction. An optimization that can be done is to maximize the usage of SIMD instructions, also called vectorization. A prerequisite to vectorization is loop unrolling.

A common property of a RISC processor is that it only has the essential simple instructions. Because of the limited number and simplicity of instructions, commonly a RISC processor has a hardwired implementation wherein the decoding process is reduced to have uniform latencies as the available instructions are simple enough.

A RISC processor usually has a uniform pipeline length for each instruction [1]. A pipeline is a processor feature that allows execution of multiple instructions at a time. The operation of the processor is slowed down by pipeline stalls, which is a safety mechanism employed by the processor to ensure correctness. Thus, an optimization on RISC programs can be done through loop unrolling which will ideally reduce the stalls that the program might cause.

It is to be noted that common in the implementation of CISC processors invoke the use of micro-operations, or micro-ops. Micro-operations are sub-operations that make up the larger, more complex CISC instructions. These micro-operations produce an in-between architecture of sorts which is CISC-like in the view of the programmer but RISC-like in view of the processor. This approach is used specifically to utilize the advantages of RISC architectures while providing the toolset to the programmer provided by CISC instruction sets. This type of design provides a form of abstraction which still has to be decoded before being executed by the processor therefore the effects of this abstraction is already accounted for by the overall latencies for each operation or instruction in the instruction set. The same can be said for the effects of hyperthreading; their effects can also be accounted for by the overall latency of each operation or instruction. The latency of a program instruction is usually given by the manufacturer of the processor. Because the latency value is dictated by its hardware implementation. The Intel provides an approximate latency of instructions across their different implementation of the x86_64 architecture listed in [9].

III. LOOP UNROLL

Loop unrolling in assembly language programming is the optimization wherein loops are transformed into a longer sequential set of instructions. The two general steps in loop unrolling are detection and unrolling.

Before loop unrolling is performed. The input assembly code must first be broken down into basic programming blocks. Basic programming blocks are defined as a series of program instructions that ideally would not be interrupted by a branch. There are several types of blocks as defined by [7] and are determined by how the series of code ends:

1) 1 way - ends in an unconditional branch
2) 2 way - ends in with a conditional branch
3) n way - ends in an unconditional branch on a register
4) call - ends in a call instruction
5) ret - ends in a return instruction
6) fall - if the next instruction is labelled

Figure 1 displays a sample MIPS64 code in which blocks are detected and are boxed. The determined type of block is stated at the right of the box.

In the detection portion, after the code is separated into blocks, each block is checked if it is a looping block. Looping blocks are usually type 2 blocks wherein the block is labelled and the target address of the conditional jump instruction is the same as the address or the label of the block.

```
1       .data
2       abc: .word64 0x01
3       def: .word64 0x0F
4       .code
5       ld r1, abc(r0)
6       ld r4, def(r0)
7       label1:                fall through
8       daddu r3, r3, r1
9       bne r4, r3, label1     2-way
10      label2:                fall through
11      dsubu r3, r3, r1
12      bnez r3, label2        2-way
13      syscall 0              call
```

Fig. 1. Block detected sample.

After a block is determined if it is a looping block, the next step is to determine if the number of iterations that the block will perform can be discovered statically. The purpose of this is to determine how many times the operation portion of the block will be repeated. Looping blocks whose iterations cannot be discovered statically will not be unrolled.

After the detecting if the block is unrollable which are looping blocks. It will then be unrolled. An Unrollable block typically has the four basic parts. These are: label, operations, counter, and branch. The unrollable block should be detected to contain these parts or else it will not unroll. If the detection was not able to detect, it will not unroll. The label will be kept at the top. The operations will be repeated several times. The counter is updated each time the operations are repeated. The branch is sometimes kept at the bottom or it will be removed altogether.

The number of times the operations are repeated is dependent on the loop counter which is usually located above the label. If it detects that the loop counter is initialized by an immediate, it will unroll the operations based on the said immediate. After unrolling the operations, the branch will then be removed because it already unrolled the operations that it needs to loop. Removing the branch will reduce branch stalls. This will reduce the cycles that it needs to run.

A. CISC Loop Unroll

Loop unrolling in CISC architectures, specifically in x86, acts as both an optimization in itself and an initial step or prerequisite before vectorization. As an optimization, loop unrolling reduces program latencies. Of particular interest in latency reduction is the reduction of branch instructions as these have high latencies. These instructions are usually placed at the end of loops to return to a label and perform the code segment again, given the instruction's conditions. When loop unrolling, the given code is lengthened but the number of iterations a branch is to be performed is also reduced meaning the use of branch instructions decreases. Consequently, this also reduces the total amount of latency in the block of code and therefore the entire program.

Loop unrolling is also closely associated with another optimization called vectorization. Vectorization is the use of special instructions which operate on an array of data elements (vectors) rather than the normal single data element. These special instructions are called SIMD (Single Instruction, Multiple Data) instructions. For the x86 architecture, these instructions are augmented as extensions of the original instruction set as Streaming SIMD Extensions or SSE. The use of these instructions is what is referred to as vectorization as using these instructions converts the scalar implementation of software into a vector implementation [9]. This process is not necessarily done automatically, the process of performing the transformation is called auto-vectorization. Vectorization improves code similarly as loop unrolling by reducing latencies with the additional benefit of not increasing code length as a set of instructions can be reduced to a single line of code. Latencies are also potentially even further reduced due to the use of a single native instruction in contrast to multiple instructions with their own inherent latencies.

Loop unrolling in relation to vectorization acts as a prerequisite wherein an unrolled loop can be seen as a prime candidate for vectorization. Vectorization, although an effective optimization is one that requires a strict criteria on which to adhere. From Intel's Guide to Vectorization in [9], the criteria is as follows:

1. Countable - the number of iterations of the loop must be known statically. Meaning, it can be detected within the program code.

2. Single Entry and Single Exit - the loop does not contain any conditional instructions within nor can there be alternative ways of entering the loop.

3. Straight-line Code - no alterations in the control flow must occur within the loop.

4. The innermost loop of a nest - the loop must not contain other loops.

5. No function calls.

The criteria used for vectorizable loops in [9] has also been used as the criteria for the implementation of the loop unrolling.

Figure 2 displays a sample of an unrolled loop. On the left is the original code block while on the right is the unrolled loop. The sample code is an x86_64 syntax. It should be noted that the counter is not displayed as the CX register is

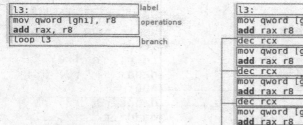

Fig. 2. Unrolled x86_64 loop sample.

used as the counter and it is already updated and used by the loop instruction in the branch portion. The loop is unrolled by four and the branch portion is kept. The number of iterations in the detected loop is divisible by four, but it is not shown in the example.

B. *RISC Loop Unroll*

The benefits of latency reduction via loop unrolling in CISC architectures also carries over to RISC architectures. However, the benefits are not as great due to the design philosophy followed by the RISC architecture pipeline and instruction set design. The RISC instruction set and pipeline are designed to achieve an average Instruction Per Cycle of one; latency is almost a non-issue. Loop unrolling however can still be performed in order to maximize the pipeline design of the RISC architecture. Because reduction of branch instructions also reduces pipeline stalls. However, the trade-off still exists where code is lengthened in exchange of reduced branches.

Figure 3 shows how the code is loop unrolled. It should contain label, operations, counter, and a conditional branch. It is shown that the counter is above the label which is 4. It will unroll the operation lines four times because the counter immediate value is 4 which is shown on the left side on the unrolled code. Then the branch will be removed because the loop is already unrolled.

IV. SAMPLE AND RESULTS

As of writing, the most viable and fundamental metric used for measuring code performance with respect to both CISC and RISC architectures uses the variable instruction count [4-5]. But as prominent as it is, it is arguably unreliable in

76

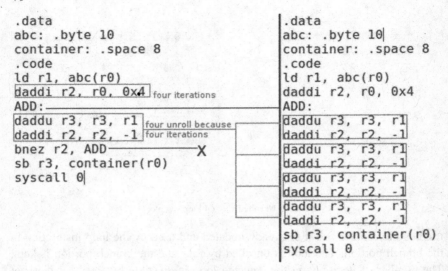

Fig. 3. MIPS loop unrolling.

determining the actual performance of a program code especially in the context of a common code optimization known as loop unrolling. This is due to its simplistic view of the program. As such, an alternative method for measuring program performance based on code blocks is proposed. The resulting metrics concluded from this proposed alternative method are instructions performed and program latency.

The difference between instruction count and instructions performed is that Instruction Count is determined through a sequential counting of instructions in an entire code. While the Instruction Performed includes considerations in the underlying runtime behavior of looping instructions, making it more accurate in determining realistic performances. Our proposed method is to replace Instruction Count with Instruction Performed in computations for comparing code performance.

The reasoning for replacing instruction count in use of program measurement stems from its use in the commonly used metrics, Cycles Per Instruction (CPI) and Execution Time (ET). As Instructions Performed would supposedly have a more accurate prediction of ET.

The equation for CPI is: $CPI = (CPU\ clock\ cycles\ for\ a\ program)\ /\ (Instruction\ Count)$. $ET = CPI*Instruction\ Count\ /\ Clock\ Rate$.

When a program is evaluated through CPI, the evaluation results in a measurement that takes into account the entire code, line-per-line. This way of measurement is considerably only accurate when the evaluated program is linear. When branches and loops are introduced however, the evaluation becomes inaccurate due to including blocks of code that would either be executed multiple times or not at all. This leads the focus of the measurement to move away from instruction count and instead toward instructions performed.

Figure 4 shows the results of the original code while Fig. 5 shows the results of the unrolled code. The original and unrolled code being referred to by Figs. 4 and 5 is shown in Fig. 3. It can be seen that the cycles are reduced to an extent because of the removed branches. The instruction count will increase because of the unrolled instructions. It can be also seen that the RAW stalls are reduced because of the removed conditional branch.

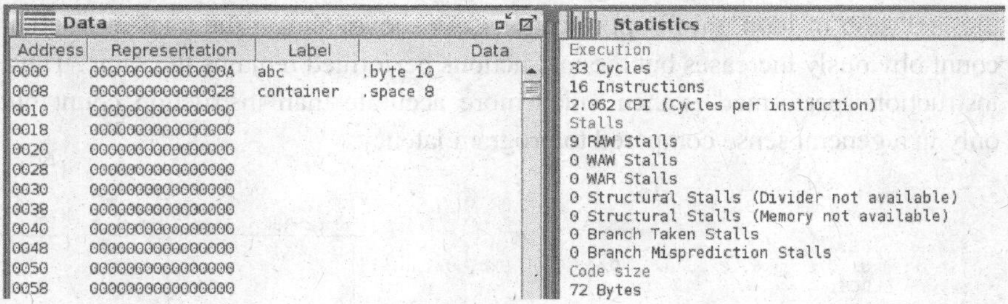

Fig. 4. MIPS loop unrolling original results.

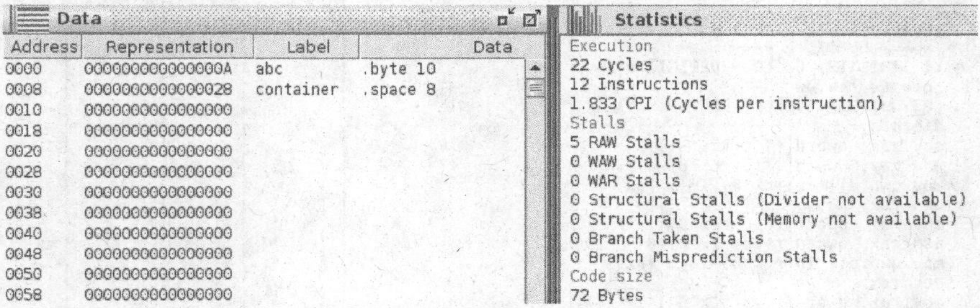

Fig. 5. MIPS loop unrolling unrolled results.

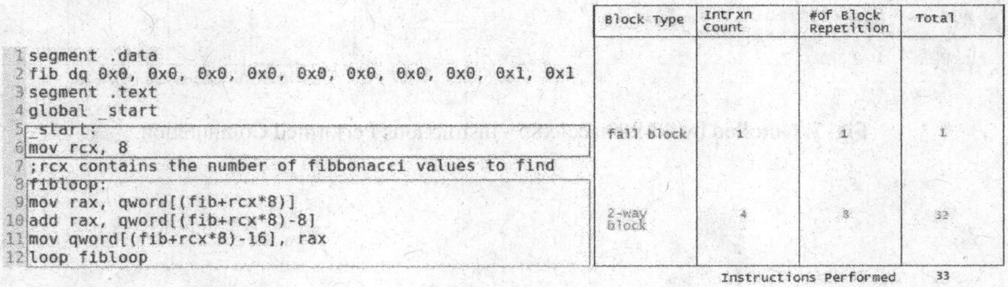

Fig. 6. Original Fibonacci x86 - Instructions Performed Computation.

78

Shown above in Fig. 6 is an x86-64 assembly algorithm (with a loop) of a sample Fibonacci computation and an illustration of how each of the created metrics are computed. As shown above, the total instruction count is computed by simply counting the number of instructions in each block and in a sequential manner, then adding the instruction count of all blocks. On the other hand, the instructions performed is computed by multiplying the number of repetitions of each block to their corresponding instruction count. After which, the products obtained for each block is then added in order to obtain the total instructions performed of the entire program.

With reference to Fig. 6, Fig. 7 and Fig. 8 are of the same case but now with the inclusion of loop unroll optimizations. As shown above, the total instruction count obviously increases but the instructions performed remains the same. Thus, instructions performed is then much more accurate than instruction count but only in a general sense compared to program latency.

	block type	instrxn count	block repetition	total
1 segment .data				
2 fib dq 0x0, 0x0, 0x0, 0x0, 0x0, 0x0, 0x0, 0x0, 0x1, 0x1				
3 ;===== BLOCK, 0 =====				
4 segment .text				
5 global _start				
6 ;===== BLOCK, 1 =====				
7 _start:				
8 mov rcx, 8	fall block	1	1	1
9 ;rcx contains, the number of fibbonacci values to find				
10 ;===== BLOCK, 2 =====				
11 ;!!!THIS IS, CX LOOP OPTIMIZED!!!				
12 ;please review				
13 ;QZYOUIPMIXTOUNROLLEDPQZOP				
14 fibloop:				
15 mov rax, qword[(fib+rcx*8)]				
16 add rax, qword[(fib+rcx*8)-8]				
17 mov qword[(fib+rcx*8)-16], rax				
18 dec rcx				
19 mov rax, qword[(fib+rcx*8)]				
20 add rax, qword[(fib+rcx*8)-8]	2-way block	16	2	32
21 mov qword[(fib+rcx*8)-16], rax				
22 dec rcx				
23 mov rax, qword[(fib+rcx*8)]				
24 add rax, qword[(fib+rcx*8)-8]				
25 mov qword[(fib+rcx*8)-16], rax				
26 dec rcx				
27 mov rax, qword[(fib+rcx*8)]				
28 add rax, qword[(fib+rcx*8)-8]				
29 mov qword[(fib+rcx*8)-16], rax				
30 loop fibloop				

instructions performed | 33

Fig. 7. Unrolled by 4 Fibonacci x86 - Instructions Performed Computation.

	block type	instrxn count	block repetition	total

```
segment .data
fib dq 0x0, 0x0, 0x0, 0x0, 0x0, 0x0, 0x0, 0x0, 0x1, 0x1
;===== BLOCK, 0 =====
segment .text
global _start
;===== BLOCK, 1 =====
 start: |
mov rcx, 8
;rcx contains, number of loops to find
;===== BLOCK, 2 =====
;!!!THIS IS, CX LOOP OPTIMIZED!!!
;please review
;QZYOUIPMIXTOUNROLLEDPQZOP
fibloop:
mov rax, qword[(fib+rcx*8)]
add rax, qword[(fib+rcx*8)-8]
mov qword[(fib+rcx*8)-16], rax
dec rcx
mov rax, qword[(fib+rcx*8)]
add rax, qword[(fib+rcx*8)-8]
mov qword[(fib+rcx*8)-16], rax
dec rcx
mov rax, qword[(fib+rcx*8)]
add rax, qword[(fib+rcx*8)-8]
mov qword[(fib+rcx*8)-16], rax
dec rcx
mov rax, qword[(fib+rcx*8)]
add rax, qword[(fib+rcx*8)-8]
mov qword[(fib+rcx*8)-16], rax
dec rcx
mov rax, qword[(fib+rcx*8)]
add rax, qword[(fib+rcx*8)-8]
mov qword[(fib+rcx*8)-16], rax
dec rcx
mov rax, qword[(fib+rcx*8)]
add rax, qword[(fib+rcx*8)-8]
mov qword[(fib+rcx*8)-16], rax
dec rcx
mov rax, qword[(fib+rcx*8)]
add rax, qword[(fib+rcx*8)-8]
mov qword[(fib+rcx*8)-16], rax
dec rcx
mov rax, qword[(fib+rcx*8)]
add rax, qword[(fib+rcx*8)-8]
mov qword[(fib+rcx*8)-16], rax
dec rcx
```

	block type	instrxn count	block repetition	total
	fall block	1	1	1
	last block	32	1	32
	instructions performed			33

Fig. 8. Unrolled Full Fibonacci x86 - Instructions Performed Computation.

Defining Program Latency as the sum of all latencies of instructions that will performed in an entire program. Program Latency is basically a weighted version of the Instructions performed where the weight of an instruction is defined by [9] for the x86_64 architecture. The significance of this metric is that when loop unroll is performed, program latency is significantly reduced. This is because upon loop unrolling, the number of repetitions of a looping block is reduced, thus the multiplication of the high-value latency of the LOOP instruction is reduced as well.

Shown in Fig. 9, Fig. 10, and Fig. 11 are illustrations of how program latency is computed on the same Fibonacci code example above. As shown above, the latency of each instruction is added for each block, then the total latency of each block is multiplied to their corresponding block repetition value. After which, the products for each block is added in order to obtain the program latency. Since there is a significant decrease in program latency for each type of loop unroll, the loop unroll is then affirmed to have optimized code performance and thus making it a viable and more practical metric for performance.

	instrxn latency	total block latency	block repetition	total
| ```
1 segment .data
2 fib dq 0x0, 0x0, 0x0, 0x0, 0x0, 0x0, 0x0, 0x0, 0x1, 0x1
3 segment .text
4 global _start
``` | | | | |
| ```
5 _start:
6 mov rcx, 8
7 ;rcx contains the number of fibbonacci values to find
``` | 1 | 1 | 1 | 1 |
| ```
8 fibloop:
9 mov rax, qword[(fib+rcx*8)]
10 add rax, qword[(fib+rcx*8)-8]
11 mov qword[(fib+rcx*8)-16], rax
12 loop fibloop
``` | 1<br>1<br>1<br>8 | 11 | 8 | 88 |
| | | | Total Latency | 89 |

Fig. 9. Original Fibonacci x86 - Program Latency Computation.

	instrxn latency	total block latency	block repetition	total
| ```
1 segment .data
2 fib dq 0x0, 0x0, 0x0, 0x0, 0x0, 0x0, 0x0, 0x0, 0x1, 0x1
3 ;===== BLOCK, 0 =====
4 segment .text
5 global _start
6 ;===== BLOCK, 1 =====
``` | | | | |
| ```
7 _start:
8 mov rcx, 8
9 ;rcx contains, the number of fibbonacci values to find
10 ;===== BLOCK, 2 =====
11 ;!!!THIS IS, CX LOOP OPTIMIZED!!!
12 ;please review
13 ;QZYQUIPMIXTOUNROLLEDPQZOP
``` | 1 | 1 | 1 | 1 |
| ```
14 fibloop:
15 mov rax, qword[(fib+rcx*8)]
16 add rax, qword[(fib+rcx*8)-8]
17 mov qword[(fib+rcx*8)-16], rax
18 dec rcx
19 mov rax, qword[(fib+rcx*8)]
20 add rax, qword[(fib+rcx*8)-8]
21 mov qword[(fib+rcx*8)-16], rax
22 dec rcx
23 mov rax, qword[(fib+rcx*8)]
24 add rax, qword[(fib+rcx*8)-8]
25 mov qword[(fib+rcx*8)-16], rax
26 dec rcx
27 mov rax, qword[(fib+rcx*8)]
28 add rax, qword[(fib+rcx*8)-8]
29 mov qword[(fib+rcx*8)-16], rax
30 loop fibloop
``` | 1<br>1<br>1<br>1<br>1<br>1<br>1<br>1<br>1<br>1<br>1<br>1<br>1<br>1<br>1<br>8 | 23 | 2 | 46 |
| | | | Total Latency | 47 |

Fig. 10. Unrolled by 4 Fibonacci x86 - Program Latency Computation.

	instrxn latency	total block latency	block repetition	total
`segment .data`				
`fib dq 0x0, 0x0, 0x0, 0x0, 0x0, 0x0, 0x0, 0x0, 0x1, 0x1`				
`;===== BLOCK, 0 =====`				
`segment .text`				
`global _start`				
`;===== BLOCK, 1 =====`				
`start:`				
`mov rcx, 8`	1	1	1	1
`;rcx contains, number of loops to find`				
`;===== BLOCK, 2 =====`				
`;!!!THIS IS, CX LOOP OPTIMIZED!!!`				
`;please review`				
`;QZYOUIPMIXTOUNROLLEDPQZOP`				
`fibloop:`				
`mov rax, qword[(fib+rcx*8)]`	1			
`add rax, qword[(fib+rcx*8)-8]`	1			
`mov qword[(fib+rcx*8)-16], rax`	1			
`dec rcx`	1			
`mov rax, qword[(fib+rcx*8)]`		1		
`add rax, qword[(fib+rcx*8)-8]`		1		
`mov qword[(fib+rcx*8)-16], rax`		1		
`dec rcx`		1		
`mov rax, qword[(fib+rcx*8)]`	1			
`add rax, qword[(fib+rcx*8)-8]`	1			
`mov qword[(fib+rcx*8)-16], rax`	1			
`dec rcx`	1			
`mov rax, qword[(fib+rcx*8)]`		1		
`add rax, qword[(fib+rcx*8)-8]`		1		
`mov qword[(fib+rcx*8)-16], rax`		1	32	1	32
`dec rcx`		1		
`mov rax, qword[(fib+rcx*8)]`	1			
`add rax, qword[(fib+rcx*8)-8]`	1			
`mov qword[(fib+rcx*8)-16], rax`	1			
`dec rcx`	1			
`mov rax, qword[(fib+rcx*8)]`		1		
`add rax, qword[(fib+rcx*8)-8]`		1		
`mov qword[(fib+rcx*8)-16], rax`		1		
`dec rcx`		1		
`mov rax, qword[(fib+rcx*8)]`	1			
`add rax, qword[(fib+rcx*8)-8]`	1			
`mov qword[(fib+rcx*8)-16], rax`	1			
`dec rcx`	1			
`mov rax, qword[(fib+rcx*8)]`		1		
`add rax, qword[(fib+rcx*8)-8]`		1		
`mov qword[(fib+rcx*8)-16], rax`		1		
`dec rcx`		1		

			total latency	33

Fig. 11. Unrolled Full Fibonacci x86 - Program Latency Computation.

Take note however that program latency is viable only in CISC architectures due to the fact that RISC architectures mostly have instructions of equal latencies.

Additionally, there exists a limitation where cases of the used loop unrolling method does not become viable and does no unrolling meaning a comparison measurement between an original program and a loop unrolled program will not necessarily be made because the original program is essentially the "optimized" program. Among these cases are: 1) when the loop is not detected as a viable unrollable loop, 2) the loop count is variable or unknown, and 3) the loop count is not a multiple of the unroll factor.

In case 2 as the loop variable is unknown, the block multiplier defaults to 1 in the computation for instructions performed and instruction latency.

For case 3, it is present in an unroll optimizer that will eventually be used for vectorization. In cases where the loop count is not a multiple of the unroll factor but is still known, the latency of the block can still be calculated and then multiplied by its loop count.

V. CONCLUSION

In conclusion, the implementation and potency of loop unrolling for a CISC and a RISC program is different. The computation of effectiveness of optimization is also different, using Program Latency for CISC while Instructions Performed for RISC due to the inherent differences in architecture and microarchitecture implemented in a CISC and RISC system.

The proposed metric for computation can be used in more accurately computing for, or predicting, program performance. However the presented new methods of computation is more tedious than the current Instruction Count. Thus the presented methods are recommended to be only used when needed. That is on comparing performance of two, supposedly related, programs.

VI. RECOMMENDATION

In the interest of providing ease of computation in using the proposed methods, recommendation is to implement a program that would take an assembly program as an input and the program will automatically compute for the program performance. The computation for program performance will be based from the proposed method.

REFERENCES

[1] George, A. D., "An Overview of RISC vs. CISC," in System Theory, 1990., Twenty-Second Southeastern Symposium, Cookeville, TN, 1990, pp. 436-468.

[2] El-Awwar, H., "CISC vs. RISC Hardware and Programming Complexity Measures of Addressing Modes," in Perspective Technologies and Methods in MEMS Design, 2006. MEMSTECH 2006. Proceedings of the 2nd International Conference, Lviv, 2006, pp. 43-48.

[3] Jamil, T. "RISC versus CISC," in Potentials, IEEE, 2002, Vol. 14, pp. 13-16.

[4] Patterson, D. and Hennessy, J. Computer Organization and Design The Hardware / Software Interface. Massachusetts, USA: Burlington, 2009.

[5] Patterson, D. and Hennessy, J. Computer Architecture A Quantitative Approach, 5th ed. Massachusetts, USA: Waltham, 2012, pp. 148-334.

[6] Kleir, R.L. and Ramamoorthy, C.V., "Optimization Strategies for Microprograms," in Computers, IEEE Transactions, 1971 Volume: C-20, Issue: 7, pp. 783-794.

[7] Shu, W. et al., "A Framework for Software Performance Simulation Using Binary to C Translation," in Circuits, Communications and Systems, 2009. PACCS '09. Pacific-Asia Conference, Chengdu, 2009, pp. 602-605.

[8] Hahn, H., Assembler Inside & Out. Osborne McGraw-Hill. 1992.

[9] Intel Corporation, (2010). A Guide to Vectorization with Intel C++ Compilers [Online]. Available:https://software.intel.com/sites/default/files/m/4/8/8/2/a/31848-CompilerAutovectorizationGuide.pdf

Deployable Mobile Communication Infrastructure for Emergency Services (DISTRESS)

J. A. Chua, J. P. Go-Soco, I. S. Morano, K. D. Pequiras and A. V. Ong

Center for Networking and Information Security, De La Salle University, Manila, 1004, Philippines
E-mail: {jordan_chua, joswin_go-soco, iris_morano,kielle_pequiras, arlyn.ong}@dlsu.edu.ph
www.dlsu.edu.ph

Mobile ad hoc networks (MANETs) are an alternative method of communication for mobile user devices without the need for a central infrastructure. They are helpful in emergency situations, especially when cellular networks or Internet connections are broken down. Current projects related to the use of MANET in emergencies address issues such as locating the disaster areas and connecting to the outside network (cellular or Internet); yet they require user intervention to establish a gateway in the network for external communications. This study developed a Bluetooth-based mobile application which allows smartphones to send messages out of the MANET through a gateway automatically selected from multiple candidates.

Keywords: MANET, ad hoc networks, reactive routing, emergency communications.

1. Introduction

Smartphones are used for services, such as Internet browsing, file sharing, photo capturing, media playing, and many other features for everyday use, but the most essential capability of smartphones is being able to send and receive calls and text messages for communication through the cellular infrastructure. In times of disasters or calamities, wherein public communication infrastructures can be damaged, smartphones will be useless in terms of end-to-end communication [1].

However, an alternative way that can be used in communicating with other smartphones is through the use of mobile ad hoc networks (MANETs). These networks are composed of mobile nodes connected by wireless links that communicate directly to each other via radio waves [2] without the need for a common infrastructure. In an emergency situation such as disasters, a mobile ad hoc connection can possibly allow victims to communicate with first aid responders in rescue operations. A basic MANET implementation however, limits nodes to communication only with fellow nodes within the MANET.

Examples of such are the Serval Project [3]. This can be a major disadvantage in an emergency situation when a user may need to communicate with someone who is outside the mobile ad hoc network.

In order to address such limitations, a gateway to the cellular network may be implemented to enable nodes inside the MANET to connect to the external network or the Internet. Ideally, a gateway must be stable so that nodes inside the network can have an established and reliable service connection. Factors to consider when implementing a gateway in the network, such as gateway routing protocols, gateway discovery, and gateway selection [4]. Currently, there are studies that implement MANET gateways for external communications. An example of this is the SPAN Project [5], [6] and [7]. SPAN uses a pre-configured gateway node chosen by the user of an area send data outside of the MANET. In the event that the gateway node needs to be replaced, it will require human intervention.

In an emergency scenario, the use of a pre-configured gateway node is a potential issue. Human intervention to establish the gateway of the network may not always be feasible in emergency situations. Furthermore, in the event that the gateway is rendered non-functional due to damage or resource exhaustion, user intervention will again be required to restore external communication.

This paper discusses the implementation of AODV (Ad Hoc Distance Vector) routing protocol within a MANET (mobile ad hoc network) and the implementation of a gateway election algorithm that would allow the MANET to automatically establish a connection to a cellular connection, if available, for messaging to the outside network.

2. DISTRESS System

DISTRESS is a mobile application that allows smartphone users to form a MANET to communicate with each other inside the mobile ad hoc network and also allow the sending of SMS to users outside of the MANET. Users in the MANET that have installed the application will have the capability to communicate with each other in an ad hoc manner using Bluetooth connectivity between MANET devices.

If a node within the MANET has an existing connection to the cellular network, then it can serve as a MANET gateway to enable two-way messaging with other cellular network users. MANET devices that need to communicate externally may send messages to the gateway device, which will then forward the message to the destination on behalf of the sending node. If an external node wishes to message a node within the MANET, then it can send the message via SMS to the MANET gateway which will then forward it to the destination within the ad hoc network. Note that external nodes do not need to have the application installed to do this. Figure 1 illustrates the topology formed by nodes using the application.

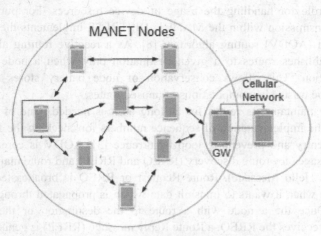

Fig. 1. Mobile device topology using the DISTRESS application

2.1. *Node Identification and Messaging Procedure*

The application provides a user interface from where users may compose messages for transmission. For the convenience of the user, the address book of the user device is imported into the application to allow selection of the destination among existing user contacts. This would be later mapped to the Bluetooth ID of the recipient during delivery. As the application is intended for use in emergency situations, immediate retrieval of contact details is prioritized; and use privacy is not considered.

If a message is to be sent to a node outside the MANET, the gateway node converts the received message to SMS format and uses the specified phone number of the destination as the recipient for sending through the cellular network connection.

In the case of an external node attempting to communicate with a node within the MANET, it is required that the external node is able to contact the MANET gateway via cellular network. The external node must send an SMS directly to the gateway, with the content following a prescribed format specifying the phone number of the intended recipient within the MANET and the message. When received, the gateway handles the message parsing, conversion of SMS to MANET message and forwarding to recipient.

2.2. *Message Routing Implementation*

Given that the users are projected to be in critical situations wherein their resources such as battery levels are limited, the routing protocol plays a significant role for handling the usage of device resources. For purposes of message transmission within the MANET, DISTRESS implements the Ad Hoc On Demand (AODV) routing algorithm [8]. As a reactive routing algorithm, AODV establishes routes to a given destination only when a node initiates communication. This allows conservation of node battery stores that can potentially be wasted by computations of unused routes.

AODV maintains its routes for as long as it is needed. One of its main features is the implementation of sequence numbers for checking the freshness of a route entry and preventing loop occurrence [3]. AODV is composed of control messages for route discovery (RREQ and RREP) and route maintenance (RERR and Hello Message). Route Request or RREQ is broadcasted by the source node when it wants to transmit data which is propagated throughout the MANET. Once the a node with a route to the destination or the desired destination receives the RREQ, a Route Reply message (RREP) is generated and sent back as unicast back to the requesting node, establishing a path through intermediate hops between source and destination.

For the purpose of sending messages, the initiating DISTRESS application begins by checking its routing table if the intended recipient is among previously known destinations. If it is not, the device starts the broadcasting process to attempt locating the destination within the MANET and establishing a route to it.

Should the route request process fail, the application assumes that the destination is outside the MANET and proceeds to locate a MANET gateway. In this step, there are 3 possible scenarios: If a gateway is not yet selected within the network, the network will proceed to the gateway election process. If a gateway is present, but is not known to the requesting node due to having missed the preceding election, then the requesting node receives gateway information from its neighbors. If the sending node already has prior knowledge of the gateway due to having previously sent an externally-bound message, then it proceeds to using AODV processes for path establishment to the gateway.

2.3. *Automatic Gateway Selection*

The selection of a gateway within the MANET is accomplished using functions that monitor gateway availability, collect candidate gateway information and most importantly, select the most suitable gateway for the MANET.

A device with a functioning connection to the cellular network is considered a candidate gateway of the MANET. It must monitor its suitability for the gateway role by maintaining a gateway priority (GP) metric computed based on external link reliability and battery level, which are given equal weight as shown in Eq. (1):

$$GP = BP\ (0.5) + ELR\ (0.5) \tag{1}$$

BP or Battery percentage is the amount of remaining energy left of a node. The minimum battery percentage required for a node to be a candidate gateway is 1%. ELR or External link reliability determines the connection stability of a candidate gateway to the external network computed using Eq. (2):

$$ELR = (TC\ sec/60\ sec)\ (0.5) + (ASL\ x\ 0.5) \tag{2}$$

ELR is tracked by getting the total time in seconds that the device remains connected to the cellular network in the span of 1 minute. ASL is average signal level (ASL) obtained by getting the signal level of a candidate gateway per second within 1 minute. The reason for choosing these factors for calculation is to rank candidate gateways based on their potential reliability. A higher residual energy and general stability of cellular connection makes a device more reliable as a gateway. In this equation, both factors are also treated with equal bearing on the overall reliability metric.

A node that requires message transmission to a destination outside the MANET initiates the process by sending out a broadcast for a gateway election or re-election. Once nodes are informed of the gateway election, possible candidate nodes will generate a self-availability broadcast (SABR) packet that contains its own computed GP metrics. The SABR packet is sent to its neighbors, propagated throughout the MANET, and acknowledged using an ACK message upon successful receipt.

Should there be multiple candidate gateways discovered within the election period, the one with the highest GP becomes the network gateway. If however, there are no candidate gateways available after the broadcasting of the election packet, the MANET will continue to function without a gateway. This event is called as failure of election. A timeout of 10 minutes will be set after the failure of election during which a new election cannot be initiated. This is to avoid successive election requests, wasting network resources even if no candidate gateway exists in the network.

88

3. Testing and Verification

In order to evaluate the performance of the application, a test set up of 6 MANET nodes as illustrated in Fig. 2 was used.

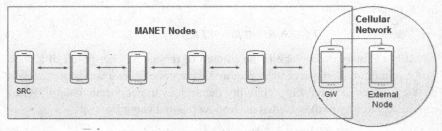

Fig. 2. Test topology setup for MANET with external connection

The topology is a cascaded connection of mobile phones, with one of the phones having an external cellular connection at the MANET edge. Phones used in these tests are listed in Table 1.

Table 1. Platforms Used for Testing

Device	CPU	RAM	OS
Message Source	1.0 GHz	512 MB	Android 4.1.2
Hop1	Quad-core 1.2 GHz	1.5 GB	Android 5.0.2
Hop 2	Quad-core 1.2 GHz	1 GB	Android 4.1.2
Hop 3	Quad-core 2.3 GHz	3 GB	Android 6.0.1
Hop 4	Quad-core 1.2 GHz	1.5 GB	Android 5.1.1
Gateway	Dual-core 1.2 GHz	1 GB	Android 4.1.2

Performance is evaluated in terms of latency of data transmissions and of gateway establishment within the MANET.

3.1. *Packet Transmission Latency (Internal)*

The objective of this test is to determine the delay for messages bound for destination ns that are within the MANET ranging from one to five hops. The delay is computed by subtracting the time wherein the message was received by the selected Receiver and the time Sender sent the message.

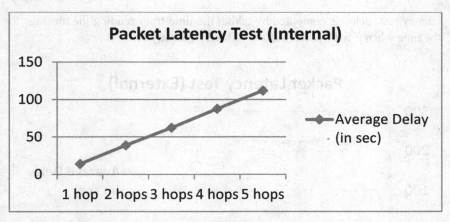

Fig. 3. Average delay of message transmission within the MANET versus number of hops to destination

As shown in Fig. 3, latency increases as more hops need to be traversed between source and destination. An average of 25 seconds of additional latency is encountered per hop due to the need to establish a Bluetooth connection as a route is created from source to destination. This amount of delay, however, is encountered only for the first message sent from source to destination.

Table 2. Transmission latency of successive messages in a 5-hop topology

Trial	MSG 1 secs	MSG 2 secs	MSG 3 secs	MSG 4 secs	MSG 5 secs
1	111.706	0.823	0.361	0.364	1.624
2	110.098	0.322	0.305	0.278	0.305
3	114.167	1.742	0.208	0.415	0.402
Average	112.133	1.032	0.257	0.347	0.354

In Table 2, as successive messages are sent between the same source and destination, latency drops after the initial message as the same route is utilized. There is therefore no need to reestablish the connections between devices for message delivery.

3.2. Packet Transmission Latency (External)

The objective of this test is to determine the delay for messages bound for destination that are bound for destinations outside the MANET. Tests are performed for topologies ranging from one to five hops. Similar to the internal latency test, delay is computed by taking the time from sending the message to the time when it was received at the MANET gateway.

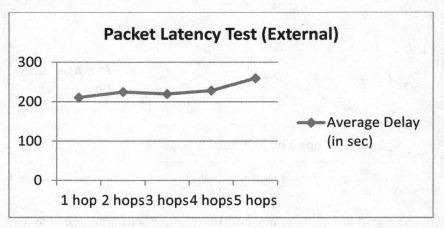

Fig. 4. Average delay of externally-bound message transmission versus number of hops to destination

Similar to the previous test on latency for intra-MANET transmission, Fig. 4 shows that latency increases as the number of hops from source to gateway is increased. Compared in intra-MANET transmission, sending of messages to external destinations takes significantly more time due to the need to first attempt to locate a node within the MANET using route discovery, then elect a gateway due to failure to locate the destination within the MANET, then finally establish a route to the gateway and transmit the message to the gateway.

3.3. Gateway Election Time

The objective of this test is to determine the duration it takes for the nodes in the MANET to elect a gateway in the case that a message from within the MANET needs to be sent outside of the MANET via SMS. The measurement of time starts when the election for a gateway is initiated until the time when the whole network identifies the elected gateway.

Based on the results in Table 3, all gateway elections were concluded in approximately one minute and thirty seconds. The time taken involves the initiation of the election process, the propagation of self-availability broadcasts (SABR), and the selection of the gateway based on highest gateway priority at every node among the received SABRs.

Table 3. Time for gateway election in MANET

Trial	1 Hop (secs)	2 Hops (secs)	3 Hops (secs)	4 Hops (secs)	5 Hops (secs)
1	90.511	91.196	141.436	85.95	91.036
2	90.894	91.196	90.773	91.724	92.905
3	103.965	101.088	91.263	90.871	93.200
Average	97.430	96.142	91.018	91.298	93.053

There is little difference in terms of election time among nodes regardless of number of network hops. In these tests, Bluetooth connections have already been established prior to election due to the nodes having attempted to locate the destination within the MANET first. With this, election occurs with existing connections among nodes; and the delay accounts for only the duration of the election process and the propagation of election control messages within the MANET.

3.4. Gateway Failover Time

The objective of this test is to determine the time it takes for a node in the MANET to switch from its current gateway to another candidate gateway. The current gateway of the node/s in the MANET will be monitored using its signal level and battery percentage. For this setup, the network will consist of two nodes as candidate gateways, both of which have viable connections to the cellular network; and an internal MANET node which will depend on the gateways for external communications.

The test is performed using two scenarios. The first assumes that the internal node maintains connectivity with the present gateway, but with the gateway losing connectivity to the cellular network. In the second scenario, the internal node loses connectivity to the current gateway. This simulates a scenario wherein a gateway may drop off the network due to movement or energy depletion. Table 4 shows the results of these tests.

Table 4. Gateway failover time in MANET

Scenario	Trial 1 (secs)	Trial 2 (secs)	Trial 3 (secs)	Average (secs)
1	135.336	135.753	136.104	135.731
2	245.496	250.647	224.713	240.285

For the first scenario, failover time will start when the gateway node loses its connectivity signal or registers the "No Signal" notification. This forces a reelection to occur in the MANET with the gateway initiating the election process. In the second scenario, the gateway becomes disconnected from the MANET altogether. This takes significantly more time compared to the first scenario because the internal node needs to first attempt message transmission to an external recipient. Path establishment to the original gateway will need to be performed, after which it will be discovered that it is no longer reachable. This process takes approximately two minutes before the election of the new gateway will be initiated.

4. Conclusion

Based on the tests conducted, it is shown that routing within a MANET, coupled with the capability to automatically establish external connectivity through a gateway device is possible. In the case of the DISTRESS application, a gateway is selected from candidates within the MANET using battery levels and stability of cellular connectivity as a basis, and an election process for selection.

Results of evaluation show that in general, the routing of messages within the MANET and to external destinations is possible; however there is significant latency. This is primarily due to the connection time required by Bluetooth technology on mobile phones and the use of reactive techniques wherein path establishment and gateway election is performed only on an as-needed basis in the interest of reducing battery consumption in the MANET.

Future work may study the use of proactive techniques and methods to determine beforehand whether destinations are within or outside the MANET in order to decrease the delays encountered in message delivery. Furthermore, additional investigation to determine the effect of varying the weights assigned to gateway desirability metrics such as residual energy, link stability and signal levels may also be performed.

References

1. D. Flanagan, *Smartphone Packet Relay Networks*, Final Paper, Rochester Institute of Technology (2012).
2. D. Tyagi, and Aarti, Study of MANET: characteristics, challenges, application and security attacks, in *International Journal of Advanced Research in Computer Science and Software Engineering*, (vol. 3, no. 5, pp. 252-257, 2013).
3. A. Bettison, *Serval Mesh*. (2011) http://developer. servalproject.org
4. I. Ahmed and R, Saeed, Review of gateway selection schemes for MANET to internet connectivity, in *International Journal of Computer Science and Telecommunications*, (vol. 5, no. 11, pp. 17-23, 2014).

5. J. Thomas, J. Roble and N. Modly, Off grid communications with android meshing the mobile world in *Homeland Security (HST), 2012 IEEE Conference on Technologies*, (2012).

6. S. Tuecke and F. Huberts, *OLSRd.* (2012) https://github.com /ProjectSPAN/android-manet-olsrd/blob/master/Olsrd/README-Olsr-Extensions

7. M. Ramesh, A. Jacob, and R. Aryadevi. Participatory sensing for emergency communication via MANET, in *2012 International Conference on Data Science & Engineering (ICDSE)*, (2012).

8. P. Maurya, G. Sharma, V. Sahu, A. Roberts, and M. Srivastava. An overview of AODV routing protocol. in *International Journal of Modern Engineering Research (IJMER)*, (vol. 2, no. 3, 728-732. 2012).

Filmification: Visual Programming Environment - Demonstrated Using Jacobi Relaxation Method as an Example

Benjo Dennis C. Uriarte and Robert R. Roxas

Department of Computer Science, University of the Philippines Cebu,
Gorordo Ave., Lahug, Cebu City, 6000, Philippines
E-mail: bcuriarte@up.edu.ph and robert.roxas@up.edu.ph
http://upcebu.edu.ph/

This paper presents a visual programming environment designed to manipulate Cyber-Films. To demonstrate the concept of a Cyber-Film, the algorithm for the Jacobi Relaxation Method is rendered in Cyber-Film format. The potential users of Cyber-Film can just view any Cyber-Film either in *"Tile View"* or *"Full Screen View"* mode if they want to learn the film's possible use for a certain kind of application. Since Cyber-Film is just a representation of a certain algorithm, a corresponding template code for a given Cyber-Film was prepared in advance. In programming, the user will just be combining Cyber-Films and will just need to supply the needed parameters like the actual sizes and some needed formula, and the system will generate the corresponding source code for the combined Cyber-Films.

Keywords: Cyber-film; filmification; visualization; visual programming tool.

1. Introduction

The representation gap is the difference between the representations the human brain uses when thinking about a problem and the representations that a computer accepts [1]. Generally, a programmer approaches a complicated task by drawing tables, matrices, or graphs. From there, he develops a solution. Implementing the solution means transforming the logic from the matrices or graphs by typing lines of text and instructions to the computer.

In order to solve the gap, a programming environment can either move the system closer to the user or move the user closer to the system [2]. Currently, the latter is the more common approach. If a programmer wants to learn algorithms, he has to read manuals and online documentations [2]. The hyperlinks for topics and concepts point to other hyperlinks, which creates a seemingly unending cycle.

Visualization is a field of study with the primary objective of minimizing the representation gap by moving the system closer to the user. This means ultimately freeing the programmers from the hassle and from the tedious work of learning from lines of text.

One visualization approach is Cyber-Filmification. It is structured based on a traditional movie format composed of films, scenes, and frames [2-5]. A frame is the smallest part of a Cyber-Film. It represents a single step in the algorithm [2-5]. A scene is composed of frames, which are doing a related task. Depending on the complexity of program, it can be made with one or more Cyber-Films.

Our goal is to create a visual programming environment where programs will be in Cyber-Film format. This paper illustrates the Cyber-Film concept using the Jacobi Relaxation Method as an example. The algorithm will be presented in a manner that is easy to understand and use. The user will only need to supply the needed parameters to have a functional program, and the system will generate the corresponding code, because each Cyber-Film has a corresponding template code.

2. Review of Related Works

Cyber-Filmification is one of the many visualization techniques, which aimed to facilitate program comprehension [2]. There are many visualization techniques existing in our days because many aspired to provide a visual programming environment that would make the programmers' lives easy. But there is still a need to develop one that can help in visualizing complex algorithmic activities.

Active Knowledge Studio (AKS) is a visual programming system wherein users can choose, watch, and execute computational algorithms in Cyber-Film format [3-5]. An entire library of Cyber-Films is available for the users to choose from. When a user chooses a film from the library, the film can be watched either in animation view or in tile view. If the users find a particular film to potentially match their needs, they can customize the film by assigning operations, which are provided by the system. Then the system will automatically generate the source code of the customized film by referring to its Code Template library.

In AKS, the algorithmic activities are visualized using some types of node flashing such as half-flash and contour-flash [3-5]. A half-flash is used to indicate that the master is making a decision. A contour-flash is used when the master is checking whether the slaves are free or not. The system uses colors to portray the different algorithmic activities. If there are many nodes communicating with each other in a single frame, colors are used to indicate which pairs of nodes are communicating with each other. Although the use of various colors and types of flashing can be useful, this introduces an extra layer of complexity to the user, that is, trying to understand the semantics of those types of flashing and the semantics of the different colors.

So in AKS, the researchers represent node states with flash types. The categories of flashing include full-flash, half-flash, contour-flash, or no flash at all. If a node is in full-flash, it means that it is under execution. When a node is in half-flash, it is ready to make a decision after waiting for subsequent frames to finish executing. If the node is being accessed or referenced, it has a contour-flash. Finally, when a node is not undergoing any process, it contains no flashing. But all of the nodes are represented as round-shaped, including the Node Observer, at all times. It needs more time to look where the Node Observer is rather than immediately differentiating it from the rest of the Space Structure.

Although AKS has gone so far, there is still a need for an improved visual programming environment in Cyber-Film format. The extra level of complexity that multiple flash-types introduce must be addressed if the system must provide an environment that will make it easier for users to comprehend program or algorithm. Their use of nodes, which were represented using the same shapes, made it difficult to distinguish the different types of algorithmic activities.

This paper presents the modified flowchart symbols to represent the different types of algorithmic activities. This to address the problems associated with the use of the different types of flashing and colors. To illustrate the idea and show the difference, the Jacobi Relaxation Method algorithm is used as an example film that the users can use when making a program.

3. Overview of Cyber-Film Format

Cyber-Film is based on the traditional film concept, wherein a film is composed scenes and frames[2,6]. A frame is the smallest part of a Cyber-Film. It represents a single step in the algorithm[3,4]. A scene is composed of frames, which are doing a particular task. And depending on the complexity of the program, a computer program can be made with at least one Cyber-Film. We will just employ the commonly used word "*film*" to refer to a Cyber-Film in the succeeding discussions.

In film programming approach, novice users will watch first some films and try to understand their behavior. If the watched films fit their algorithmic needs, the users can simply save them as part of their programs. Seasoned users may not watch some films. They can directly saved them as a part of their programs. The users can choose other films and combine them with other films as needed to meet their computational requirements.

3.1. *System Architecture*

Figure 1 illustrates the system architecture. The Films library contains the built-in algorithms in film format and the template codes. The users can open some films using the Graphical User Interface provided, but they can only view a single film at a time. It can be animated or it can be viewed as frames arranged in tile format. If the user would decide to use such a film, the Code Generation process would be executed. During this process, the template code corresponding to the chosen film would be fetched and automatically modified based on the parameters that the user would supply. Finally, a file with the "*.flm*" filename extension will be generated.

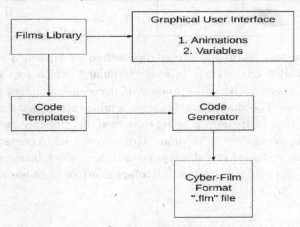

Fig. 1.   The System Architecture.

3.2. *Types of Nodes*

We use four (4) types of nodes to represent algorithmic activities, three (3) of which signify the common operations in a computer program. The three common operations include process, decision, and input/output (I/O) operations. Table 1 shows the different types of nodes that can be seen in a frame. As can be seen in Table 1, the two common operations, that is, the process and the input/output operations, are represented by modified flowchart symbols. The decision operation is represented by a diamond shape, which is the same as the flowchart symbol for decision operation. Under the column "**Referenced or Accessed**," all of these have a "Yes," because they represent some useful activities.

Table 1.   Type of nodes that can be seen in a frame.

Shape	Node Type	Referenced or Accessed
◯	Regular	No
●	Regular	Yes
■	Process	Yes
◆	Decision	Yes
▰	Input/Output	Yes

There are two additional nodes represented as circles, a shaded one and an unshaded one. Their type is "Regular," which means they are not involved in any activity like processing, decision-making, or performing I/O operations. The shaded one portrays a node that is being accessed by other nodes, that is, its data is being examined and possibly used for some computation. So under the column "**Referenced or Accessed**," it has a "Yes." The unshaded one signifies no activity, or not being accessed by other nodes. So under the column "**Referenced or Accessed**," it has a "No."

3.3. *Types of Views*

As mentioned in Section 3, the users may view some films to find the ones appropriate for their needs. The system provides two types of views that can be displayed in the Graphical User Interface in order to view some films. Figure 2 shows a sample screen shot for the first type of view, that is, the "*Tile View*." In this type of view, all the frames of the film are presented in a series of tiles. When all frames cannot fit inside the viewable screen, the users can scroll down to see the remaining frames.

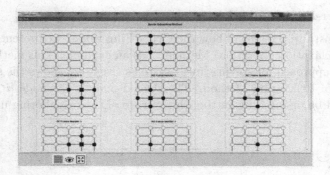

Fig. 2.   The "*Tile View.*"

Figure 3 shows the sample screen shot for the second and last type of view, the "*Full Screen View.*" In this view, the film could be played in animated form. A group of playback options will automatically appear on screen and disappear back when the type of view is changed.

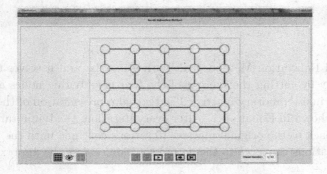

Fig. 3.   The "*Full Screen View.*"

3.4. *The Template Code*

When the users decide to take the film as part of their program, they will save it and will have to supply the needed parameters and supply the formula, if necessary. After doing so, the corresponding code in assembly language will be generated. When the users compile them, the generated assembly codes will be assembled to produce the object codes and then linked to generate the executable code.

4. Cyber-Film Example

To demonstrate the idea of how the Cyber-Film works, we present here the Jacobi Relaxation (Iteration) Method[7,8] as an example. This method is an iterative approach for solving linear systems. Figure 4 shows the stencil of the Jacobi Relaxation Method. The shaded node is the node $[i, j]$ whose value will be updated by getting the average of the neighboring nodes.

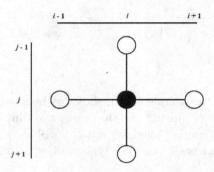

Fig. 4.   The stencil for Jacobi Iteration Method.

Jacobi Relaxation Method deals with a matrix, and it solves the inner nodes only by getting the average of the four neighboring nodes and saves the result in a temporary matrix. The textual representation of the computation is shown in Equation 1. After every iteration, the temporary matrix is saved back to the original matrix. Iterations continue until the resulting approximations converge to the actual solution, unless the approximations diverge.

$$B[i][j] = (A[i+1][j] + A[i-1][j] + A[i][j+1] + A[i][j-1])/4; \quad (1)$$

In Table 2, the flow of the Jacobi Relaxation Method is shown. It illustrated the correct traversal of the inner nodes of the matrix. This is shown in the last column under the "**Output**" heading. The first row shows the starting frame, which was composed of all the newly initialized regular nodes. Rows 2 to 10 show the whole iteration. Row 2 shows the activity of frame 2. The processing or computation is done at index $[1][1]$ (see row 2), under the "**Process Node Index**" heading. The neighboring nodes' data are accessed, that is, the indices $[0][1]$, $[1][2]$, $[2][1]$, and $[1][0]$ as shown under the "**Referenced Nodes Indices**" heading.

Table 2. One iteration of Jacobi Relaxation Method.

Frame Number	Process Node Index	Referenced Nodes Indices	Output
1	N/A	N/A	
2	[1][1]	[0][1], [1][2], [2][1], [1][0]	
3	[1][2]	[0][2], [1][3], [2][2], [1][1]	
4	[1][3]	[0][3], [1][4], [2][2], [1][2]	
5	[2][1]	[1][1], [2][2], [3][1], [2][0]	
6	[2][2]	[1][2], [2][3], [3][2], [2][1]	
7	[2][3]	[1][3], [2][4], [3][3], [2][2]	
8	[3][1]	[2][1], [3][2], [4][1], [3][0]	
9	[3][2]	[2][2], [3][3], [4][2], [3][1]	
10	[3][3]	[2][3], [3][4], [4][3], [3][2]	
11	N/A	N/A	

Figure 5 shows the magnified image of Frame 2. The square node shows that some computation is done because it is a "Process node" (see Table 1). The black circles show the nodes that are being accessed, and whose data are used in computing the average of these four nodes. As shown in Table 2, the computation goes from left to right and from top to bottom but does not include any of the boundary nodes.

As mentioned in subsection 3.4, any film has a corresponding template code. This frees the user from typing the long equation like the one shown in Equation 1, which is normally prone to error if encoded manually.

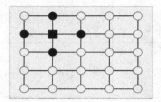

Fig. 5.   The magnified view of Frame 2.

5. Results and Discussion

To test the back end of the system, tests were ran and the results are shown in Tables 3–6. Table 3 shows the output of running the algorithm for just one iteration. As can be seen in Table 3, the values for the four inner nodes have changed, that is, the bold numbers in the "**Output**" column as compared to the italicized numbers from the "**Data**" column.

Table 3.   One iteration of Jacobi Method for a 4×4 Matrix.

Data				Iterations	Output			
3	9	8	3	1	3	9	8	3
7	*5*	*9*	7		7	**6**	**7**	7
8	*1*	*8*	9		8	**6**	**7**	9
1	6	9	5		1	6	9	5

It should be noted that Jacobi Relaxation Method is often used in numerical computation of floating-point numbers, particularly in solving systems of linear equations. In this paper, we used integers and integer division. This is for illustration purposes only and to make the numbers fit within the table, especially for the 5×6 matrices. The output of any program can easily be formatted into floating-point numbers up to a certain precision.

The same test data of a 4×4 matrix was used in Tables 3 and 4. The difference between the two test cases was that in Table 3, only a single iteration was done, while in Table 4, two iterations were done. In Table 4, the result of the first iteration is shown as the numbers in bold face found under the "**Output 1**" heading, and the result of the second iteration is shown as the numbers in bold face under the "**Output 2**" heading. The result of the first iteration in Table 4 matched with the result of the single iteration in Table 3. As can be observed in Table 4, there is just a minimal change of the data after the second iteration. In actual applications, the iterations have to be repeated until there will be no more changes.

Table 4.   Two iterations of Jacobi Relaxation Method for a 4×4 Matrix.

Data				Iterations	Output 1				Output 2			
3	9	8	3	2	3	9	8	3	3	9	8	3
7	5	9	7		7	**6**	**7**	7	7	**7**	**7**	7
8	1	8	9		8	**6**	**7**	9	8	**6**	**7**	9
1	6	9	5		1	6	9	5	1	6	9	5

Tables 5 and 6 also shared the same data. The matrix used was 5×6 to indicate that the algorithm would still work even if the rows and columns of the matrix were not the same. Table 5 shows the output of running the algorithm for just one iteration. As can be seen in Table 5, the values for the twelve inner nodes have changed, that is, the bold numbers in the "**Output**" column as compared to the italicized numbers from the "**Data**" column.

Table 5.   One iteration of Jacobi Relaxation Method for a 5×6 Matrix.

Data						Iterations	Output					
1	3	7	9	1	6	1	1	3	7	9	1	6
7	0	1	9	8	3		7	**3**	**4**	**5**	**5**	3
1	1	3	4	7	1		1	**3**	**2**	**5**	**5**	1
8	9	3	2	7	4		8	**5**	**5**	**4**	**5**	4
1	8	9	3	7	4		1	8	9	3	7	4

Once again, the result of the first iteration in Table 5 correctly matched with the result of the first iteration in Table 6. Finally, the second iteration in Table 6 showed the correct result also.

Table 6.   Two iterations of Jacobi Relaxation Method for a 5 × 6 Matrix.

Data						Iterations	Output (Iteration 1)						Output (Iteration 2)					
1	3	7	9	1	6	2	1	3	7	9	1	6	1	3	7	9	1	6
7	0	1	9	8	3		7	3	4	5	5	3	7	4	4	5	3	3
1	1	3	4	7	1		1	3	2	5	5	1	1	2	4	4	4	1
8	9	3	2	7	4		8	5	5	4	5	4	8	6	5	4	5	4
1	8	9	3	7	4		1	8	9	3	7	4	1	8	9	3	7	4

Thus the template code that was generated and was made into an executable code worked fine when ran both for the 4 × 4 matrix and the 5 × 6 matrix inputs. It produced accurate results. The same executable code can tackle big matrices as well because the template code is parameterized and can adapt to bigger sizes.

6. Conclusion and Future Work

A visual programming environment in Cyber-Film format using Jacobi Relaxation Method as an example has been presented. Its template code, after converting it into an executable code worked fine for matrices of differing sizes. The system also was able to correctly show the frame animations of the algorithm rendered in Cyber-Film format.

In order for the system to be very functional, the development of more films for other algorithms is necessary.

References

1. D. C. Smith, A. Cypher and L. Tesler, Novice programming comes of age, *Communications of the ACM* **43**, 75 (Mar. 2000).
2. R. R. Roxas and N. N. Mirenkov, "Cyber-Film": A visual approach that facilitates program comprehension, *International Journal of Software Engineering and Knowledge Engineering* **15**, 941 (Dec. 2005).
3. R. Yoshioka and N. Mirenkov, Visual computing within environment of self-explanatory components, *Soft Computing* **7**, 20 (2002).
4. R. Yoshioka, N. Mirenkov, Y. Tsuchida and Y. Watanobe, Visual notation of film language system, in *Proceedings of the 8th International Conference on Distributed Multimedia Systems*, (Knowledge Systems Institute, Sept. 2002).
5. N. Mirenkov, A. Vazhenin, R. Yoshioka, T. Ebihara, T. Hirotomi and T. Mirenkova, Self-explanatory components: A new programming

paradigm, *International Journal of Software Engineering and Knowledge Engineering* **11**, 5 (Feb. 2001).

6. R. R. Roxas and N. N. Mirenkov, A visual environment for that specifying global reduction operations, *International Journal of High Performance Computuing and Networking* **1**, 100 (2004).

7. F. T. Leighton, *Introduction to Parallel Algorithms and Architectures: Array - Trees - Hypercubes* (Morgan Kaufmann Publishers, Inc., San Mateo, CA, 1992).

8. J. Dongarra, I. Foster, G. Fox, W. Gropp, K. Kennedy, L. Torczon and A. White (eds.), *Sourcebook of Parallel Computing* (Morgan Kaufmann Publishers, San Francisco, CA, 2003).

Direction Tracking of a Single Moving Camera through Periodic Image Stitching

J. Ilao and F. K. Flores

Computer Technology, De La Salle University,
Manila, NCR, Philippines
joel.ilao@delasalle.ph and fritz.flores@dlsu.edu.ph
www.dlsu.edu.ph

Object Recognition and Tracking has been one of the top research interests in the field of Computer Vision. Methodologies such as Background Reduction, Color Thresholds, Filters, Contours and others have been used to detect these objects as well as determine their movement based on chronological data and events. However these methodologies are usually limited to and are typically used only on fixed-point cameras. Having a moving camera would present multiple difficulties in terms of background reduction and object tracking as well as determining if the object being tracked is actually moving or only due to the movement of the camera that the object seems to be moving. This research investigates a method to allow tracking of the direction of the camera, which may be used for object recognition and tracking, using a single moving camera.

Keywords: Mosaicking; BRISK; Harris Corner; SURF; SIFT; RANSAC; Affine Transform.

1. Introduction

Object Recognition and Tracking are one of the first few projects that most Computer Vision researchers perform. Steps involving this would revolve around Background Reduction, Filtering, Blurs, Contours, Threshold, and others. However it is important to take note that there are multiple methodologies that may be used to carry out this research. Also, in order to designate that an object is moving, there has to be a type of periodic data.

Periodic data in the form of consecutive images, which is usually from a fixed point camera, provides the characteristics of an object if it is moving or not. With a fixed point camera, since the background is static, Background Reduction through averaging or selection of a base image to reduce with the current image would be applicable in detecting new or moving objects in the image through algorithms such as thresholds or differencing. Filters, Blurs, Thresholds, and Contour Detections allows segmentation of the objects from the background as well as labeling them. Carrying out these procedures for multiple consecutive images, which contain moving objects, would give the direction of the moving object. However the limitation to this approach is that the images used during the Background Reduction phase is usually static and fixed, ensuring better detection of foreign objects.

Understanding that the said Object Recognition and Tracking processes is usually used for fixed-point cameras, the said steps may not be applicable when implementing on images from moving cameras. Also the use of a fixed-point camera may not always be available for other applications.

Those said, allowing Object Recognition and Tracking from a Moving Camera its next step for these applications and is thus the focus of the study. There are a few things to take note of however; first would be that camera direction tracking is described in the study as the directional difference in the movement of the camera's center of focus from one point to another; second would be that the direction of the movement of the camera may be different from the direction that the object is moving into. This would mean that non-moving objects would be seen moving at an exact reversal motion from that of the movement of the camera.

There are many possible applications to this, ranging from Multi Player Tracking and Labeling from a Moving Camera for sports games such as Football to Vehicle Detection and Motion Tracking from a Panning Security Camera.

2. Algorithm

There are multiple algorithms, which may be used for the different phases of the study. However the study revolves around the algorithms, which are implemented in Java OpenCV. This is because the application used in study was implemented using Java and OpenCV, allowing cross platform use as well as due to OpenCV being one of the widely used libraries for Computer Vision.

The algorithms used in the study for detecting key features from images are the following; BRISK or Binary Robust Invariant Scalable Keypoints, Harris Corner, and SIFT Scale Invariant Feature Transform. After which, the ones used to determine or extract the descriptions of the said key points and features in the images are BRISK, SURF or Speed Up Robust Features, and SIFT.

RANSAC, or RANdom Sample Consensus is used to trim down the good features as well as try to obtain the Homography Matrix given the periodic pair of images for image stitching. Affine Transform is then used to transform each pair of images in order to create a stitched image of two time differential images. This is used in order to determine the movement of the image from its previous value and the current value.

108

Motion Tracking may also be applied after detecting the foreign objects based on the direction of the movement of the object with respect to the direction of the movement of the camera.

It may be observed that the study described multiple algorithms used for feature extraction and descriptor extraction. The reason for this is to be able to determine which combination or set of algorithms used in testing would result into a more reliable output.

3. Process

The entire process of tracking moving objects from a moving camera requires two (2) steps, however the research focuses on the first step which is direction tracking of the camera because the result of this may be applied to Object Detection and Tracking separately in order to determine the movement of the foreign objects from the background. This would allow determining if the foreign object is moving or not with respect to the direction of the camera.

The algorithm implemented in the study is as follows. The initial data and requirements would be a continuous video from a single camera of an environment while slightly moving the camera in a slow and dynamic but continuous motion. For the test case used in the study, a motion of random continuous directions are used while panning the camera from left to right.

| Image at time x | Image at time x + 1 | Image at time x + 2 |

| Image at time x + 3 | Image at time x + 4 | Image at time x +5 |

Fig. 1. Sample Video Frame Captures

3.1. *Video Image Frame Segmentation*

The first step is to segment the video into periodic images with respect to a certain number of frames. The number of frames depicts the differences in the transition of one frame to another in a periodic manner as well as the speed and motion of the camera. For the test cases used in the study there are three (3) implementations; every 5th, 3rd, and every frames are used. However it is best to take note of that through observation, using more frames would yield in a more continuous and seamless output due to the decrease in the size and distance between each transition but at the cost of additional processing time and power.

3.2. *Feature Detection, Descriptor Extraction, and Matching*

The next step after segmentation, feature detection and descriptor extraction would be used in order to identify the significant features of an image and be able to match them with another set of features on another image. For the study, a pair of consecutive images are used in order to determine their transition from one image at time x to the next image at time x + 1 with respect to the frames.

In feature detection, BRISK, Harris Corner, and SIFT were each used to detect the features for each implementation. Then BRISK, SURF, and SIFT were used to get the feature descriptors for every feature detection algorithm used, testing for about twenty seven (27) times.

It must be taken note of that there are many algorithms which may be used to take the features as well as provide the descriptors, each one having its one set of trade-offs. However these are the only ones, which are used in the study. A more in-depth discussion of the results would be discussed in the latter part.

Fig. 2. Feature and Descriptor Mapping Representation

Once the features are mapped, each image is checked with its succeeding image and is mapped with each other in order to get the good points. In the study a threshold of ±3 was used in order to determine if a point is good or not.

After which, the RANSAC algorithm is used in order to relate the periodic pair of images from one after the other based on the given good points and in an iterative basis. This is used in order to remove or decrease the outliers of a given set as well as to determine the Homography Matrix to match or stitch the images. The RANSAC algorithm assumes that the given points are mostly a set of inliers, then random sampling would be done in an iterative manner in order to determine the most-likely matched points of the sequential images. For the

110

study, images are mapped by pairs at a time, the current image and the next, for each iteration. This would mean that for the first iteration x and x + 1 is used, then x + 1 and x + 2 and so on.

3.3. *Periodic Image Stitching using Affine Transform*

| Image at time x | Image at time x + 1 | Image at time x + 2 |
| Image at time x + 3 | Image at time x + 4 | Image at time x + 5 |

Fig. 3. Chronological Image Stitching with Centerpoint Connection

Once the Homography Matrices has been obtained with the said periodic pair of images, the current and next image, and vice versa, Affine Transform would be used to transform both images creating a stitched image. The process of the study uses a period image stitching in a way that each image is stitched with its previous as well as its next image. This is done in order to take into account the difference of the location and direction of the current image as well as the images, which are consecutive to it, in order to determine the direction and motion of the camera during capture.

3.4. *Iterative Reverse Image Frame Centerpoint Connection*

After stitching the images together, the algorithm used in the study is to map the center points of each of the images to connect them, creating a line that connects both images at the stitched image. This is the technique that the study uses in order to determine the transition of the periodic movement of the camera as well as its direction from each iteration.

While obtaining the center points for each image, the algorithm saves those points and appends the previous point as well as the current point that of a list for every iteration. This would mean that at iteration n, there would also be n − 1 pairs of points, creating n − 1 lines, which we could backtrack from. This approach is used by the study in order to create a trace and determine the motion of the camera from the continuous movement of the periodic images from one line after the other.

| Image at time x | Image at time x + 1 | Image at time x + 2 |
| Image at time x + 3 | Image at time x + 4 | Image at time x + 5 |

Fig. 4. Chronological Images with Centerpoint Path Connections

The study uses a method which is defined here as the Iterative Reverse Image Frame Centerpoint Connection method, which simply states that for a video with an image count of n, there would be n − 1 sequential relationship center points, due to the first image not having a previous point, thus the center would be the first point for the first image.

Then it also means that for every iteration from time 1 to n, the points would be mapped from the current time x decrementing to time 1, having the first point as the location of the previous transition and the second point as the location of the new centerpoint. For every iteration, the transition point would be placed as the current trace centerpoint, and is then iteratively added with the negative difference of the second point. The succeeding previous points from it would also be mapped in reverse from the current transition point as the new center point, creating a reverse trace of the path.

An example of which is a camera panning from left to right; this would mean that the X-axis is incrementing. If we would want to show this, we should start the last and most recent point, backtracking each point, creating a line from the decrementing X-axis value, or inverse of the previous point, to create the periodic motion done from the camera movement.

After completing this step the trace and direction of the camera would be available to be used in relation to the object detection and tracking to determine if the foreign object is indeed moving or only appeared to move due to the movement of the camera.

3.5. *Object Detection and Mapping*

For the object detection and mapping, it could be understood that the movement of the camera may be different from the movement of the image. Because both the camera and object may be moving at the same time, observing that if the object seems to be moving at the exact indirectly proportional rate as the camera means that the object is not moving, but if the detected object is staying at the same relative point as the camera moves, then it would mean that the object is moving, but at the same direction as the camera, else the object is moving at a different pace and direction as the camera.

4. Performance Testing

The Single Camera Directional Movement Tracking is done by first obtaining a camera feed, then features would be extracted as well as their descriptions. Those points would then be used as points for stitching images to determine the direction of the movement of the camera as described in the study. The tests would be implemented using different frame intervals, different Feature Extraction algorithms each, as well as different Descriptor Extraction for each.

The video frame interval that would be used for the first set of tests would be one (1) frame on every five (5) frames obtaining the 5th frame; for the second set of tests, one (1) frame for every (3) frames, obtaining the 3rd frame; for the third and final set of test, every frame would be included in the tests.

During each set of tests, the feature extraction algorithms of BRISK, Harris Corner, and SIFT would be used. As well as for each feature extraction algorithm used, the following descriptor extraction algorithms; BRISK, SURF, and SIFT would also be used for each. This is in order to determine the effectiveness of each feature extraction algorithm as well as description extraction algorithm with respect to each video frame interval.

However it must be noted that the following implementation parameters as well as the use of a different video data may also yield different results. The computer used for processing is an Intel Core i-5 2.4Ghz with 4 CPUs and a 4GB RAM. The program implemented also saves a 2400 by 1500 pixel image of the camera movement trace for every frame processed which is used for observation and tracing of the step by step process done by the algorithm.

4.1. *Results with a Frame Interval of Every 5th Frame*

For the first test, an interval of every 5th frame is used. This would mean that the rate or distance of the points per transition is at the largest with respect to the tests. The following figure shows the trace with respect to the extraction algorithm used where rows are for features and the columns for their descriptions. The indicated time is the time required to complete the process.

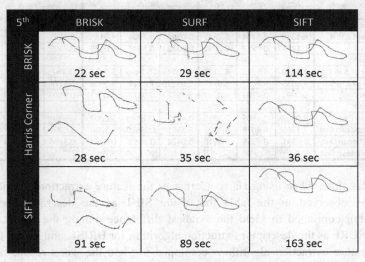

Fig. 5. Trace Results of the First Test Using a Frame Interval of Every 5ᵗʰ Frame

It may be observed from the figure above that the combination of Harris Corner and BRISK, Harris Corner, and SURF, as well as SIFT and BRISK yielded an incorrect trace due to the discontinuation of the points and segments. However among the said combinations, the combination of Harris Corner and SURF yielded the worst result from the test.

The good results are obtained when BRISK was used for feature extraction, as well as when SIFT was used as the descriptor extraction. It may also be observed that the combination of using both BRISK yielded the fastest but a slightly more jagged result as opposed of those when SIFT was used as a descriptor extractor, which took the longest.

For this test when using BRISK as the feature extraction algorithm, it may be observed in the table that using BRISK and SIFT yielded the smallest difference among the other description extraction algorithm. Also, using SURF as the descriptor extraction algorithm is the least ideal when using BRISK as a feature extraction algorithm.

Table 1. Feature Extraction Using Every 5ᵗʰ Frame

Feat Ext Algo	BRISK			HARRIS CORNER			SIFT		
Desc Ext Algo	BRISK	SURF	SIFT	BRISK	SURF	SIFT	BRISK	SURF	SIFT
Average of Δ in X	7.9419	6.7735	6.9615	6.5539	16.5068	5.8191	13.8746	3.8489	5.9324
Median of Δ in X	6.1388	5.5484	5.7845	5.0946	9.7904	4.9165	5.5859	1.9199	4.9373
Min Δ in X	0.1834	0.0827	0.0062	0.0048	0.3499	0.0229	0.2408	0.0330	0.0263
Max Δ in X	32.5211	39.9158	23.0576	34.4074	87.6986	19.5158	203.3498	132.5153	19.6058
Average of Δ in Y	7.5330	6.5718	6.1170	6.4618	15.2496	5.7427	13.7675	5.4106	5.6827
Median of Δ in Y	5.9335	4.8657	5.0247	5.0819	7.8614	5.0956	5.5178	2.1117	4.8103
Min Δ in Y	0.0091	0.0303	0.0021	0.0672	0.0377	0.0041	0.0189	0.0455	0.0111
Max Δ in Y	33.8167	66.3375	32.7068	34.4578	97.2944	29.4304	249.7762	301.5066	29.8813
Euclidean Dist	8.9907	8.1805	7.0955	8.4925	21.8445	5.8804	22.7814	7.0308	6.1190
Med Euclidean Dist	7.2769	6.4078	6.1398	5.3561	11.3510	4.3888	8.6202	2.4360	4.6915
Min Euclidean Dist	0.0251	0.0369	0.0510	0.0478	0.2653	0.0154	0.3194	0.0253	0.1386
Max Euclidean Dist	43.8139	80.9795	42.8070	57.2672	120.9729	36.4641	418.1266	431.1476	37.0791

This time, when using Harris Corner as the feature extraction algorithm, it may be observed in the table that using SIFT as the descriptor extractor algorithm continued to yield the smallest difference among the others. Also, using SURF as the descriptor extraction algorithm for BRISK and Harris Corner as a feature extraction algorithms continued to yield the worst result, causing plenty of incorrectly stitched images.

The use of SIFT as feature extraction resulted in two extreme results for the test. It may be observed that in the figure above, using SIFT and BRISK yielded the worst result for the entire test. As well as using SIFT and SURF yielded the smallest change and best overall result for the entire test. However the speed of this is about four (4) times that of when BRISK and BRISK was used.

4.2. Results with a Frame Interval of Every 3ʳᵈ Frame

For the second test, an interval of every 3ʳᵈ frame is used. The rate or distance of the points per transition should be smaller as well as the transitions should also be closer for each periodic pair. The following figure shows the trace with respect the same parameters are the ones mentioned in the first test but in this case only the frame interval used is different.

It may be observed from Fig. 6 that only those where SIFT was used as the descriptor extraction algorithm yielded the good results. Also once again, the combination of Harris Corner and SURF still yielded the worst result from this test with comparison to the first.

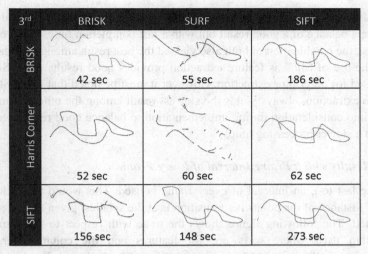

Fig. 6. Trace Results of the Second Test Using a Frame Interval of Every 3rd Frame

Table 2. Feature Extraction Using Every 3rd Frame

Feat Ext Algo	BRISK			HARRIS CORNER			SIFT		
Desc Ext Algo	BRISK	SURF	SIFT	BRISK	SURF	SIFT	BRISK	SURF	SIFT
Average of Δ in X	5.0003	5.2258	3.5962	3.3004	8.4812	2.8295	4.2697	2.6594	2.6987
Median of Δ in X	3.2423	3.1165	2.8513	2.4842	4.0510	2.2777	2.2688	1.9186	2.0909
Min Δ in X	0.0145	0.0627	0.0418	0.0113	0.0712	0.0208	0.1157	0.0330	0.0333
Max Δ in X	30.4228	73.8001	17.4230	23.9034	56.9848	11.1189	39.8385	10.1299	10.3652
Average of Δ in Y	3.9152	3.8085	3.1457	3.1652	7.9991	2.6845	4.0180	2.5749	2.6076
Median of Δ in Y	2.7600	2.7105	2.7210	2.5758	3.2560	2.2073	2.8444	2.1092	2.1483
Min Δ in Y	0.0072	0.0981	0.0048	0.0179	0.0290	0.0077	0.0451	0.0455	0.0565
Max Δ in Y	24.1478	43.0776	12.2806	12.5031	79.8004	10.4474	51.7241	11.1004	11.2465
Euclidean Dist	6.4961	6.5370	4.0897	4.2984	12.6862	3.2218	6.5003	2.9755	3.1034
Med Euclidean Dist	4.1143	3.5101	3.0862	3.1056	5.2914	2.5072	4.1293	2.3882	2.5079
Min Euclidean Dist	0.0046	0.0118	0.0235	0.0097	0.0086	0.0271	0.0193	0.0253	0.0053
Max Euclidean Dist	49.1550	115.9720	15.9893	27.4960	112.2292	13.6611	53.8898	16.3688	15.2277

When using BRISK as the feature extraction algorithm, it may be observed in the table that using SIFT yielded the smallest difference among the other description extraction algorithm. Also, using SURF as the descriptor extraction algorithm is still the least ideal when using BRISK for feature extraction.

Harris Corner Feature Extraction using every 3rd. When Harris Corner is used as the feature extraction algorithm, it is still observed in the table that using SIFT as the descriptor extractor continued to yield the smallest difference among the others. Still, using SURF as the descriptor extraction algorithm for both BRISK and Harris Corner as a feature extraction algorithms continued to yield the worst result among the others.

116

Also, similar with the previous test, using Harris Corner and SIFT allowed to have a balance of a good result but with a fast completion time. In the case of this test, the combination of both also yielded the best result among the others.

The use of SIFT as feature extraction provides good results when SIFT is also used for descriptor extraction. However it must be noted that using SIFT as feature extraction, always yields the slowest result among the others. It may be taken into consideration during implementation to balance good results with the cost of a slower processing time.

4.3. *Results with a Frame Interval of Every Frame*

For the last test, an interval of every frame is used. This would mean that the rate or distance of the points per transition is at the smallest given the video data collected. The following figure shows the trace with respect to the extraction algorithm used where rows are for features and the columns for their descriptions, still similar with the previous tests. The indicated time is the time required to complete the process given the said specifications.

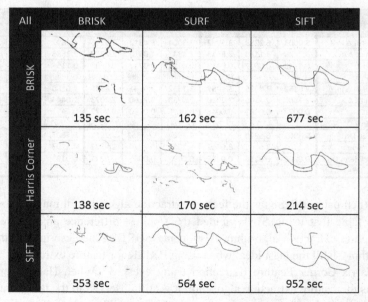

Fig. 7. Trace Results of the Third Test Using a Frame Interval of Every Frame

It may be observed from the figure above that using a combination of BRISK and SIFT as well as Harris Corner and SIFT yielded good results, but that of the latter was more than three (3) times faster. Also the combination of

Harris Corner and SURF continued to yield the worst result in all of the three tests done by the study.

Table 3. Feature Extraction Using Every Frame

Feat Ext Algo	BRISK			HARRIS CORNER			SIFT		
Desc Ext Algo	BRISK	SURF	SIFT	BRISK	SURF	SIFT	BRISK	SURF	SIFT
Average of Δ in X	4.5418	2.7083	1.5769	1.6801	4.7590	1.0800	2.0254	0.7658	0.8499
Median of Δ in X	1.7011	1.0295	0.9812	1.0577	1.0556	0.7821	0.9272	0.5371	0.4980
Min Δ in X	0.0001	0.0055	0.0003	0.0000	0.0000	0.0000	0.0008	0.0002	0.0031
Max Δ in X	75.2630	81.1489	12.9603	23.7716	91.2298	19.9315	51.4946	9.2370	17.0594
Average of Δ in Y	2.8598	1.7567	1.2739	1.4087	3.3808	0.9042	1.7693	0.6942	0.7857
Median of Δ in Y	1.1432	0.8726	0.9023	0.8636	0.8913	0.6753	0.9146	0.5007	0.4992
Min Δ in Y	0.0100	0.0043	0.0017	0.0000	0.0000	0.0000	0.0266	0.0025	0.0019
Max Δ in Y	53.4483	34.5630	16.1805	30.5328	56.7732	16.2680	40.9708	6.8454	33.3141
Euclidean Dist	5.9789	3.6235	1.9763	2.1674	7.3499	1.4118	3.0216	0.9816	1.2068
Med Euclidean Dist	2.1097	1.3434	1.2524	1.1482	1.3552	0.8618	1.4002	0.7080	0.6627
Min Euclidean Dist	0.0029	0.0021	0.0018	0.0000	0.0000	0.0000	0.0149	0.0027	0.0009
Max Euclidean Dist	93.2306	101.9300	19.2392	46.1559	113.3154	25.4643	91.2396	10.2043	49.6774

When using BRISK as the feature extraction, it may be observed that using SIFT continued to yield the smallest difference among the other description extraction when BRISK is used for feature extraction. However using BRISK as the descriptor extractor, became the least ideal when using BRISK as a feature extraction, as opposed to the previous tests where using SURF yielded the worst.

When Harris Corner is used as for feature extraction. It is still observed that using SIFT as the descriptor extractor algorithm continued to yield the smallest difference. Similar with all the other tests, using SURF as its descriptor extraction algorithm continued to yield the worst result.

Similar with the previous tests, using Harris Corner and SIFT continued to present good results with a fast completion time. However it did not yield the best result in this test, but is a close contender with the best one being the combination of using both BRISK and SIFT for the test.

The use of SIFT as feature extraction for this test did not provide any good results, but are better as opposed to the others. Again, it must be noted that using SIFT as feature extraction, always yields the slowest result among all the others based on all tests. Also the combination of using both SIFT and SIFT continued to result in the slowest time.

5. Conclusion

The study was able to detect camera directional movement through the use of a sequential image stitching and center point gathering method. In order to be able to continuously detect the path, a periodic and sequential data must be obtained from the center points of the stitched images and tracked back in reverse in order

118

to obtain the path which may be used for object detection and tracking for moving cameras.

The algorithms used by the study for the periodic image pair stitching used to determine the camera direction also determined that using SIFT as descriptor extractor yielded the best overall result among other tests while also having the slowest processing time. The combination of Harris Corner and SURF yielded the worst results in all tests. Lastly the combination of using Harris Corner and SIFT resulted in a balance of both good tracking as well as fast completion time.

Future research for this study may include extensive object detection and tracking algorithm to determine the most suitable algorithm for object tracking using a moving camera as well as other actual applications such as multiplayer tracking for moving cameras.

References

1. Azad, P., Asfour, T., & Dillmann, R. (2009, October). Combining Harris interest points and the SIFT descriptor for fast scale-invariant object recognition. In *Intelligent Robots and Systems, 2009. IROS 2009. IEEE/RSJ International Conference on* (pp. 4275-4280). IEEE.
2. Bay, H., Ess, A., Tuytelaars, T., & Van Gool, L. (2008). Speeded-up robust features (SURF). Computer vision and image understanding, 110(3), 346-359.
3. Bay, H., Tuytelaars, T., & Van Gool, L. (2006). Surf: Speeded up robust features. In Computer vision–ECCV 2006 (pp. 404-417). Springer Berlin Heidelberg.
4. Brown, L. G. (1992). A survey of image registration techniques. *ACM computing surveys (CSUR)*, *24*(4), 325-376.
5. Derpanis, K. G. (2004). The harris corner detector. York University.
6. Harris, C., & Stephens, M. (1988, August). A combined corner and edge detector. In *Alvey vision conference* (Vol. 15, p. 50).
7. Leutenegger, S., Chli, M., & Siegwart, R. Y. (2011, November). BRISK: Binary robust invariant scalable keypoints. In Computer Vision (ICCV), 2011 IEEE International Conference on (pp. 2548-2555). IEEE.
8. Lowe, D. G. (1999). Object recognition from local scale-invariant features. In *Computer vision, 1999. The proceedings of the seventh IEEE international conference on* (Vol. 2, pp. 1150-1157). Ieee.
9. Raguram, R., Frahm, J. M., & Pollefeys, M. (2008). A comparative analysis of RANSAC techniques leading to adaptive real-time random sample consensus. Computer Vision–ECCV 2008, 500-513.

10. Rublee, E., Rabaud, V., Konolige, K., & Bradski, G. (2011, November). ORB: an efficient alternative to SIFT or SURF. In Computer Vision (ICCV), 2011 IEEE International Conference on (pp. 2564-2571). IEEE.
11. Xing, J., Ai, H., Liu, L., & Lao, S. (2011). Multiple player tracking in sports video: A dual-mode two-way bayesian inference approach with progressive observation modeling. *Image Processing, IEEE Transactions on, 20*(6), 1652-1667.
12. Yilmaz, A., Javed, O., & Shah, M. (2006). Object tracking: A survey. *Acm computing surveys (CSUR), 38*(4), 13.

Score Transition of Card Game Strategy
as Personal Progress Situation
in an Applied C Programming Exercise with a Contest Style

Naoki Hanakawa, Fumiya Gemba and Hiroyuki Tominaga

Kagawa University
2217-20 Takamatsu, Kagawa 761-0396, JAPAN
†E-mail: s16g464@stu.kagawa-u.ac.jp

We have proposed an exercise of applied C programming language about card game strategy with a contest style in information engineering college. We prepare a Poker game regulation in each year and developed a contest management server WinT in order to maintain a league. A participant considers some ideas of tactics and implements a strategy code to get a high point by making a good Poker hand. He submits a code to WinT and receive the execution result and ranking order. He modifies his code repeatedly by the feedback during a contest period. He acquires the final score by the best strategy. In this paper, we propose some tracing methods as visualization for personal progress situation by code modification. STG is score transition graph as time series. We discuss a preliminary analysis in 2014 with our methods. We found out typical cases and grasped tendency. Our methods are useful for monitoring of student behavior in a programming exercise.

Keywords: score transition graph, card game strategy, personal progress situation, applied C programming, contest style exercise.

1. Introduction

In information engineering college, a basic programming exercise of C language is a required subject for beginners. After it, some applied exercises are also important subjects. Recently, in order to promote concern and motivation of learners, puzzle and game is often adopted as theme of programming problems in the exercises. Especially, a programming competition of game strategy is very attractive and useful for the educational purpose. Some contest events are held in universities as educational practices.

In our university, we have carried out applied programming exercises about game strategy with a contest style since 2010. We have two theme of game strategy programming. One is a card game for C programming. We adopt Poker card game. Another is a board game for Java programming (Yamada 2012 and Yamada 2013). We adopt an original Gogo board game like Japanese traditional Renju and Reversi called Othello in Japan.

In our research, we will establish a framework of game strategy programming with a contest style. It must treat effective methods of exercises, a local environment of learners, system functions of a contest server and adequate evaluation of results. In this paper, we discuss some visualization methods of code modification. They are one of useful analyzation approach for personal progress situation. Especially, we focus on external revision of output result and internal improvement of code quality as refactoring. The analysis suggests educational effectivity and efficiency of our proposed exercises. We introduce a preliminary analysis and the application to an educational practice in our exercise.

2. Our applied C programming exercise with card game strategy

We have proposed an applied exercise of C programming with card game strategy. We adopt a simple draw type Poker as a typical hand making game (Table 1). We indicate hand points and regulation in each year about card exchange and takes in a deck (Figure 1). We prepare execution environment and available library functions of Poker game.

Table 1. Points and probability of Poker hands in our exercises

Grade	Poker hand	Probability	Point
0	No pair (High Card)	0.501177	0
1	One Pair	0.422569	1
2	Two Pair	0.047539	2
3	Trips (Three of a kind)	0.021128	8
4	Straight	0.003925	32
5	Flush	0.001965	24
6	Full House	0.001441	16
7	Quads (Four of a kind)	0.000240	64
8	Straight flush	0.000014	128
9	Royal straight flush	0.000002	256

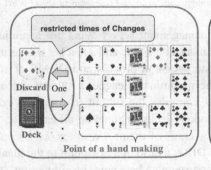 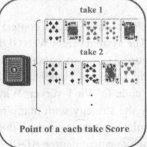

Figure 1. The rule of Poker as a draw type in a simple hand making game in our exercises

A student considers some ideas of effective strategy of exchanging a discard in hand situation like a production rule (Figure 2). He implements a strategy code from the algorithm design using the given libraries. He also revises it with trail-and-errors according to the result by many random decks. It is concerned with simple AI like production rules and heuristic evaluation in knowledge information processing.

LHS	RHS
if (**Completion of Straight or over**)	then { **Close** }
if (**Open-end Straight draw**)	then { **The isolated card** }
if (**Flush draw**)	then { **The card with different suit** }
if (**Inside Straight draw**)	then { **The isolated card** }
if (**Completion of Two Pair**)	then { **The unpaired card** }
if (**Completion of Trips**)	then { **The unpaired card** }

Figure 2. An example of production rules for Poker game strategy

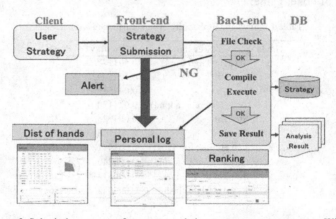

Figure 3. Submission process of a strategy code in contest management server WinT

We have developed a contest management server WinT for a preliminary league. The system offers Web GUI in a student side and a teacher side as a front-end (Figure 3). It also contains some back-end process and DBMS of strategy codes and scores of students. In the preliminary league, a student uploads his strategy code to WinT server. WinT compiles the submitted code and executes Poker by the strategy with many random decks. It sums up all execution points and calculates a result score as the average of them. A result score is converted into an achievement degree ADIP. ADIP is a ratio of a raw point to the ideal point IP as score normalization. IP is the approximate best point by simulation. It is the average point from many results for each random deck. Each point is calculated by a GA(genetic algorithm) method. A discard sequence is regarded as a gene.

WinT exhibits a ranking table of all students' scores in a classroom. It also tells each student some trend analysis of execution results. These information is used by students as a feedback for revision. During the preliminary league, a student tries to submit his codes repeatedly. After a period of the preliminary league, each strategy code with the best ADIP of every students is chosen as the best code in the final league. We decide the final score of each student by ADIP and his ranking order in the programming exercise.

3. Exercise process and score

A Student manages strategy programming in the exercise according to the 4 steps (Figure 4). One of the merit of our subject and approach is easiness of a clue of implementation in an initial stage. An expected value by a given random hand set with no exchange is 0.9 point at one take. It is calculated with probability of each Poker hand. The point is an initial result of no strategy. The easiest strategy is to exchange cards repeatedly until making any Poker hands. It shows 3.0 points in the average, though choosing a discard with random. If you implement some simple production rules with pattern matching in a hand set, the average point is increasing immediately. Therefore, in an initial stage, a little code modification with some efforts causes much increasing of score. Comparison among own programs and results stimulates motivation of even beginners.

1	Dialog execution by user input To understand rules and point system
2	Execution with sample strategies To consider ideas
3	Debugging by user-prepared decks with necessary specification
4	Test by a lot of random decks for various situation

Figure 4. Submission process of a strategy code in contest management server WinT

On the other hand, your score may stay in the same value and doesn't increase so easily. It falls in, as it were, the impasse state. In order to escape the state, a strategy must require introduction to a new idea or consideration of using algorithm. It may need minute adjustment of parameters through trial-and-errors. At that time, comparison with other students as rivals make a student promote motivation for revision. If you adopt effective evaluation values for discards in hand card set, the strategy program gets more than 10 point by one take.

Moreover, by realizing adequate forecast evaluation or efficient simulation, the strategy will acquire a very high score over 14 point. However, as the processing time is much increasing, the execution may be aborted by the system. You need some pruning technique in intellectual searching methods. You also need heuristic adjustment of parameters about searching condition with trial-and-errors. We don't think all students to achieve these level. We expect only students in the upper group to feel a sense of accomplishment.

4. The rule regulation with weighted rate

Table 2 shows operation guidelines of our proposed exercises in 2010–2014. Number of participants as proper participants is about 40 in every year. All participants include some guest s in senior students, who are auditors but act roles as the strong rival. The exercise in 2010 is a trial practice only for the final contest without a preliminary contest. The middle contests were held in 2010–2012 as the same style of the final contest. From 2011, contest management server WinT has worked. Periods in the preliminary contests are about 4 weeks until the final contest. During the preliminary contest, the results are always exhibiting in WinT. However, the contest period in 2012 was only one week because some system trouble happened. From 2013, we enhanced several functions in WinT, while we abolished the middle contest. The contest period in 2013 included one week of the winter vacation.

The first data line in Table 2 is the rule regulation in each year. It includes a change number and a take number. A good strategy in the previous year is not always good in the next year because of different regulation. In 2010–2012, there are few strategies to change tactics for a number of the deck, which act the same behavior in any takes. From 2013, weighted rate for each take is introduced (Table 3). It must require consideration about changing tactics or parameter adjustment by a number of rest cards in the deck. Moreover, at the last take, cards of deck may be lack and game is over in truncation. A number of the rest card in a deck is most important condition. You must not waste many discards at takes in a low rate. You may give up a high Poker hand and change to aim at pair instead of flush and straight exactly. We set 7 changes and 5 takes in 2014. For a weighted rate list in 2013, a rate of the last take is too high. In some of strategies, takes in the initial stage are regarded as "abandoned game". We also change some rates for the balance.

Table 2. Rule regulation in 2010–2014

	2010	2011	2012	2013	2014
Rule regulation (Cg - Tk)	5-5	7-4	8-4	6-6	7-5
Max of needed cards	50	48	52	(66)	(60)
Weighted rate	N	N	N	Y	Y
Period in an exercise (Weeks)	3	3	3	5	4
Period in Pre contest (Weeks)	-	3	1	5	4
Middle contest	Y	Y	Y	N	N
Preliminary contest	N	Y	Y	Y	Y

Table 3. Weighted rate list in 2011–2014

		1	2	3	4	5	6	7	8	Sum
2010	5-5	1.0	1.0	1.0	1.0	1.0				5.0
2011	7-4	1.0	1.0	1.0	1.0	1.0	1.0	1.0		7.0
2012	8-4	1.0	1.0	1.0	1.0	1.0	1.0	1.0	1.0	8.0
2013	6-6	1.0	1.0	**1.5**	**1.5**	**2.0**	**2.0**			9.0
2014	7-5	1.0	1.0	**1.5**	**1.5**	1.0				6.0

5. The results of the submission during the contest period

Table 4 shows results of submission from 2011 to 2014. The average of submission number per proper participants is increasing. In 2013, 37 proper participants participated a contest. A number of submission is 773. The average is 20.9 and the maximum is 84. In 2014, 36 proper participants participated a contest in 4 weeks. A number of submission is 1453. The average is 38, and the max is 187. It is remarkable increasing than 2013. The upper group has a large number of submissions. The middle group and the lower group has a little number. However, some of those who has a few submissions got high points. We regard enhanced functions about personal score transition in time series of submission as effective revision from users' opinions. Moreover, some guest participants submitted in many times and takes top level scores. They seemed strong rivals for proper participants to stimulate their competitive volition.

Figure 5 shows ogive curves of submission number in each year. The horizontal axis stands for number of days elapsed from a start of contest period. In every year, at the first lesson of the exercise, all students must upload their strategy codes as user tests. However, after it, a plateau appears in a while. Inclining of graph from 2 weeks before a deadline in 2014 and the one from 1 weeks before a deadline in 2013 seem almost the same. Submissions tend to concentrate just before a deadline every year. In 2014, some of students has many submissions more than 100. Though another problems in classroom restrain student activity for a while, the number of submission increased constantly from the 3rd week. The preliminary and middle contest promotes to submit strategy codes continuously during about three weeks until the final contest.

Table 4. Results of submission number in 2011–2014

	2011	2012	2013	2014
Proper participants	35	43	37	36
Guest participants	-	5	4	3
Total of submission of proper participants	136	446	773	1453
Average of personal submission	3.89	10.4	20.9	40.4
Personal submission per week	0.8	(3.5)	5.2	10.1
Maximum of personal submission	20	61	84	187

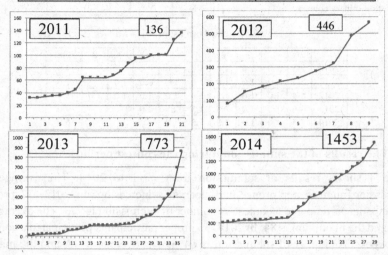

Figure 5. Graph of ogive curves of submission number in 2011–2014

6. Score transition graph STG for personal progress situation

A programming exercise with a contest style has two aspects in educational effect. One is to stimulate competitive volition by exhibition of ranking table as synchronic influence. Another is to realize own transition by comparison with used products of old versions as diachronic influence. Especially, the upper group seems to implement with a cycle of the stage of enhancing functions and the stage of refactoring. Therefore, during a period in the preliminary contest, it is important to trace transition of modification of submission code. In this study, we propose an analysis method and discuss the result in preliminary analysis.

In this study, we propose STG, which is a tracing method of code submission. STG stands for Score Transition Graph. It is a time series diagram of strategy codes for each submission as a visualization. The vertical axis Y stands for ADIP as a result score. The horizontal axis X stands for relative time from beginning to ending of a contest. All strategy codes of a target student are plotted as each dot in the X-Y plane. Each plotted dot is connected with a line in time order. A shape of a time series zigzag line in STG suggests a behavior of the target student. It shows density of submission and increasing rate of result score.

We mention related works. Jiau tried showing transition graph using some game scores in strategy programming of strategy game to enhance students' motivation (Jiau 2009). The graph is used as feedback for students' side, does not support for teachers' side. Kogure proposed a monitoring system of students' solving situation during programming lecture in classroom (Kogure 2015). It has the same point as our study in monitoring to obtain students' situation. However, it monitors their situations using answer type of programming problem. The point is different from our approach which makes try to submit repeatedly.

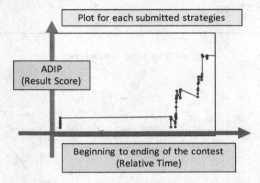

Figure 6. Instances of STG in 4 group by score grade

7. The results of STG in 2014

We discuss an educational practice in 2014. A period of the contest is about 4 weeks. As the game regulation in 2014, a change number Cg is 7, and a take number Tk is 5. If a card in the deck is lacked, the game aborts. As the weighted rate, a weight of the third and the fourth take is 1.5, and others are 1.0. The limit of execution time is 30 seconds. The number of participants is 36. The number of submission is 1453. The average is 40.4.

Figure 7 shows STG for all proper participants in 2014. 36 participants are divided in 4 groups (a) - (d) by ADIP of each best strategy. The first group (a) includes 8 members in 43–52% of ADIP. They accomplished satisfactory progress without a large of decreasing point. A half of members showed positive activity until the middle of the period. The rest did not submit continuously from the beginning. After reaching at 30% of ADIP, a little brank of submission interval appeared. The second group (b) includes 7 members in 38–43% of ADIP. There were few quick starters. The third group (c) includes 9 members in 35–38% of ADIP. There were three types in starting time, such as 0%, 50% and 75%. These

128

times were depended on exercise days in a classroom. The fourth group (d) includes 12 members in 19–35% of ADIP. In this group, many of them started from the middle of the contest period. Some fluctuations of points appeared because of groping of tactics and parameter with trial-and-errors.

As the reflection of the result, a half of players show good progress situation. However, there were some slow starters. When they start the first stage even lately, they changed an active mode with a little progress for a while. Many students tended to work this problem on and off according to exercise day in a classroom. At the last week, almost students worked very hard. The contest period may be too long, as students think of time to spare until the deadline. It must be 3 weeks for keeping concentration.

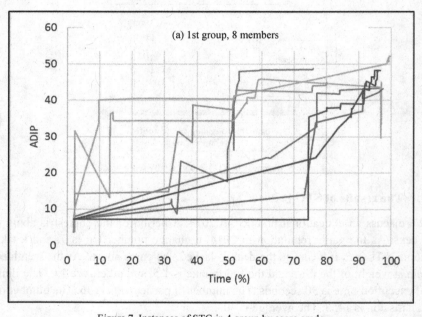

Figure 7. Instances of STG in 4 group by score grade

Figure 7 (continued)

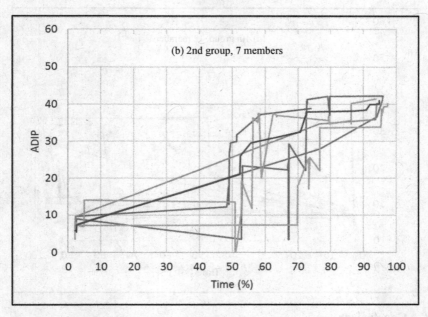

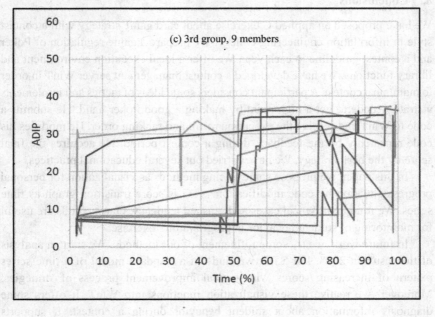

130

Figure 7 (continued)

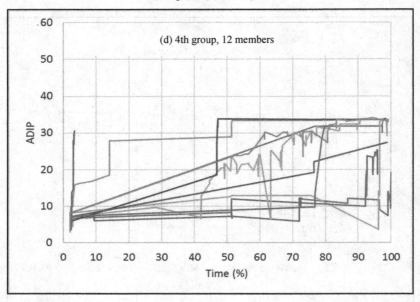

(d) 4th group, 12 members

8. Conclusions

We have proposed an applied C exercise about card game strategy with a contest style in information engineering college. We prepare a game regulation of Poker and a contest guideline in each year. We offer a local execution environment and library functions. We have developed a contest management server WinT in order to maintain a contest. A participant considers some ideas of tactics and implements a strategy code to get a high point by making a good Poker hand. He submits a code to WinT and receive the execution result and ranking order. He modifies his code repeatedly by the feedback during a contest period. He acquires the final score by the best strategy. We have carried out several educational practices.

In this paper, we propose some tracing methods as visualization for personal progress situation by code modification. STG is score transition graph as time series. We found out typical cases and grasped tendency. Our methods are useful for monitoring of student behavior in programming exercise.

In future work, we try some refinement of our methods. We start an analysis of the result in 2015. For STG, we find out a standard model of a time series pattern of increasing scores with typical improvement process of strategies. Moreover, we realize these visualization functions into WinT. It offers some diagnosis information about student behavior during a contest. It supports teacher's personal instruction for each student. It also helps students to improve their coding style and raise code quality.

References

1. K. Yamada, H. Tominaga, Ranking Analysis of Battle Result of Board-Game Strategy in Java Programming Exercise, Proceedings of WCTP 2013, pp. 173-184 (2013).
2. K. Yamada, H. Tominaga, Support System WinG and Applied Programming Exercise with Board-Game Strategy, Proceedings of ITHET 2012, PS9, pp. 1-6 (2012).
3. T. Nishimura, S. Kawasaki, H. Tominaga, Monitoring System of Student Situation in Introductory C Programming Exercise with a Contest Style, Proceedings of ITHET 2011, No. 40, pp. 1-6 (2011).
4. H. C. Jiau, J. C. Chen, K. F. Ssu, Enhancing Self-Motivation in Learning Programming Using Game-Based Simulation and Metrics, IEEE Transactions on Education, Vol. 52, No. 4, pp. 555-562 (2009).
5. S. Kogure, R. Nakamura, K. Makino, K. Yamashita, T. Konishi, Y. Itoh, Monitoring system for the effective instruction based on the semi-automatic evaluation of programs during programming classroom lectures, Research and Practice in Technology Enhanced Learning, Vol. 10, No. 1, pp. 1-12 (2016).

A User Acceptance Test on ConnectUP:
An Academic Social Networking Application
Developed Using University Ontology

Ricardo Pablo de Leon, Michelle Nazario, Ma. Rowena Solamo, Rommel Feria
Department of Computer Science
College of Engineering
University of the Philippines, Diliman
{rjdeleon|mbnazario|rcsolamo|rpferia}@up.edu.ph

ConnectUP is the proposed academic social networking application for the University of the Philippines (UP) System. It may be used by UP student and employees as an avenue for communication with regards to their research fields and topics of interest for their works. ConnectUP is developed using semantic web technologies. The data essential for the creation of the relationships among the ontology's entities are collected from members of the UP system. These data are incorporated into the university ontology. It is modelled by the Resource Description Framework (RDF), then given semantics with the use of Web Ontology Language (OWL). SPARQL Protocol and RDF Query Language (SPARQL) is used in querying the academic data that has been put against the ontology. The application has been subjected to a user acceptance test, which has rendered generally positive feedback, thus allowing the researchers to deem that ConnectUP is ready for operational use.

Keywords: Academic Data, University Ontology, Usability Testing.

1. Introduction

At present, using social network services has become part of the everyday lives of almost everyone. These services and applications serve as means of connecting two or more individuals. The use of information across different social networks is essential to the present day data-handling. With today's number of social networking applications, the availability of a platform capable of linking these various services together is an emerging problem.

The scope of this research is limited to the university domain, particularly that of the University of the Philippines (UP). The UP system - which comprises of different campuses around the Philippines, allows its students and employees to each have a unique UP Mail account with the domain *up.edu.ph*. Only these members of the UP system, with their individual UP Mail accounts have access to the information within the social networking application. Since it is a closed social networking application, the security of the data disclosed by the users is an important factor the researchers considered, thereby justifying the use of UP Mail accounts. This is to maximize the data available for the use of the application's users in looking for possible collaborators.

The web application that the researchers developed in this study serves as an aid for the university's students and employees into engaging in possible collaboration with fellow researchers or artists, in the case of creative works. As such, the researchers aimed to design and develop a social networking web application that has the following features accessible to its users:

- Sign up or log in using their UP Mail account and log out of the application
- Create a user profile
- Edit the information on their profile
- Add a publication or creative work
- Edit their publications or creative works
- Delete their publications or creative works
- Search all individual entities within the social network
- Search people by a keyword on their publication or creative work
- See a visualization of the users returned by the search results and download the CSV file used in the visualization (for both search features)
- View profile pages, including theirs and other users'
- View the individual page of a publication or creative work

Additionally, an admin account has been created by the developers. The features that have been provided for the administrator's account are not accessible to regular users, and are:

- Add a user account and create profile
- Edit the profile of a user
- Delete a single user
- Delete multiple users
- Suspend or activate a user
- Add a publication or creative work
- Edit a publication or creative work
- Delete a single publication or creative work
- Delete multiple publications or creative works

The different aforementioned features are the bases used by the researchers, or developers, to carry out the testing of the social networking application, which serves as the highlight of this paper.

2. Related Research and Literature

While this paper focuses on the use of ontology in an academic and university-based social networking application that the researchers developed, that is ConnectUP, and having it undergo user acceptance testing, there are several key concepts besides ontology and user-based software testing that are essential to this research. In this section, other concepts such as social networks, ontology-based software projects, and technologies essential to this study are explored and detailed by reviewing published studies and literary work that have great bearing to the concepts covered within this study.

A. Related Literature on Ontologies and Their Significance

According to Jung et al., ontology is widely used in fields such as philosophy, linguistics, and computer science. In the field of computer science, ontologies are recognized as machine-understandable conceptual representations of various domains of knowledge. At present, researchers have started to look at ontologies as key components in providing the current web with meaning in the hope that the Semantic Web will be realized in the near future.[5]

Ontologies can be considered as both content theories and vocabularies. As content theories, ontologies are a means of describing objects, properties of objects, and relations between them that exist in a certain domain or body of knowledge. On the other hand, ontology is the study of the nature of existence. It has been said that ontologies "carve the world at its joints". They serve as representation vocabularies that are tailored to a certain domain of knowledge.

Ontologies are significant in many fields. They play important roles in various fields such as knowledge-based systems, information systems, and natural language understanding. For all these fields and many others, ontological analysis helps give a better understanding of the structure of their knowledge systems. A certain domain's ontology functions as the core of any knowledge representation systems for that domain. One cannot simply form a vocabulary for representing the knowledge within a certain domain without the ontology for that domain. Therefore, it is critical that an effective ontological analysis be performed in that domain in order to come up with an effective knowledge representation system. Also, ontologies facilitate the process of knowledge-sharing. Shared ontologies are helpful in building knowledge bases that are to be specifically made to describe specific situations.[3]

B. Related Literature on Ontologies and Social Networks

According to Wennerberg, ontologies can be used to aid the modeling of social networks for several reasons. Firstly, ontologies give conceptual structure to a certain domain. Social networks serve a similar purpose but with focus on social entities, relationships, affinities. In this way, ontologies related to social entities and relationships can be constructed and implemented. Also, since ontologies do not permit the modeling of inconsistent information, designing social networks after ontologies is a big step in ensuring that all information within the social network are valid. Lastly, ontologies are able to obtain information with its inference mechanism. This mechanism can be applied to social networks built on ontologies to obtain new concepts and relationships from existing social entities within the network.[13]

A proposal from Liu, Shan, and Zhang identifies the characteristics of their semantic-based social network, which would prove useful for researchers and developers attempting to build social networks of the same nature:

- The entities or nodes of the network are now considered as instances of ontology concepts and now contain information represented in the network's ontology.
- The relationships or edges can now be described by various attributes contained in the ontology.
- Multiple relationships between any two entities are now possible, due to the heterogeneous nature of relationships.
- The social network now possesses some degree of intelligence and may now serve as an organization's knowledge base. Analyzing the network using inference-based methods is now possible since it had built on ontology.
- It is now easier to integrate various networks, as they always exist

in the form of OWL (Web Ontology Language) or RDF (Resource Description Framework).

As a conclusion, they recognized that a semantic-based social network where entities and relationships have actual meanings and computer-understandable have certain potentials. With its abundance of information, it can be set as a platform to come up with network analysis methods that may change the way we look at fields such as data mining today.[4]

C. Related Literature on Ontology-based University Domain Projects

Zeng, Zhu, and Ding, on the other hand, aimed to study the construction of an ontology of university courses. Their study was driven by their idea that the solution to the lack of ontology-based content in the semantic web must begin with universities having their own domain ontology constructed.

They defined the requirements for developing the ontology for university courses. Zeng et al. pointed out that the ontology must be able to capture the concepts, theories, and relationships of a certain course. A curriculum may involve several bodies or fields of knowledge. These fields, along with their relationships to each other need to be represented as well. Lastly, the university course ontology must provide a collection of basic resources for the Semantic Web, so as to contribute to the realization of the semantic web on the field of education.[14]

Another attempt in developing an ontology-based application operating within the university domain has been made by Malviya and his colleagues. They aimed to explain the terms of university by means of an ontology created using the Protege OWL tool. They identified several components that need to be considered when building the university ontology, specifically using the said tool. The components include classes and class hierarchy, object or class properties, data properties of the ontology, relationships and their properties, axioms of ontology (axioms for classes, attributes, and instances), the instance of the ontology, and the reasoning of the ontology.[8]

Lastly, a social network system based on an ontology has been developed by Kim, Han, and Song in the Korea Institute of Oriental Medicine (KIOM). They aimed to develop the network so as to allow researchers to find collaborators and share their research results with other researchers to further the advance the studies in the fields of Korean medicine.

The researchers started out by collecting data from sources such as personal profiles of researchers, scholarships, academic activities, research work, and personal connections. After analyzing the data, a social network ontology was constructed using OWL and FOAF (Friend of a friend). The social network was designed to be a closed network for use within the KIOM, making it possible for researchers to share private research content and personal information that they cannot publish on the Internet. There was, however, a consideration for external personnel in the ontology which allowed institute personnel of the KIOM to somehow connect with them, given that they are connected to each other as detailed in the FOAF.[6]

Resource Description Framework

In Miller's introduction on the Resource Description Framework or RDF, he states that the RDF is an infrastructure that allows for encoding and use of metadata. It is one of the applications of XML that provides non-ambiguous methods of expressing semantics by enforcing structural constraints.[11]

Furthermore, Candan, Liu, and Suvarna point out that RDF, being able to describe metadata, is necessary for the next-generation Web applications. It is expected that through the development of more applications that utilize RDF, areas such as knowledge discovery and data mining will advance. At present, the technologies involved in the development of RDF and the Semantic Web are the XML, the semantics of data as expressed using RDF, and ontologies or namespaces.[9]

Web Ontology Language

Pan and Uschold defines the Web Ontology Language or OWL as a collection of knowledge representation languages used for designing ontologies. It is an extension of the RDF schema and like its base grammar, it utilizes the same RDF syntax. OWL can also serve as a means to accompany the schema with semantics, allowing for more details on the classes and properties to be specified. It has the added abilities to represent more data regarding certain characteristics of properties and describe classes through the grouping of instances that meet those certain characteristics.[10]

SPARQL Protocol and RDF Query Language

Segaran et al. defines SPARQL, or SPARQL Protocol and RDF Query Language, as a semantic query language used in databases. It is capable of obtaining and manipulating data stored using the RDF format.[12]

SPARQL can also be seen as a reaction to the challenge of integrated access to various distributed RDF data sources. Quilitz and Leser mention that the current standard entails hard and lengthy query formulations and the current implementations cause network traffic overhead. As a solution to these issues, they present an engine called DARQ for use in federated SPARQL queries. It is capable of querying multiple and distributed SPARQL sources and allowing the query federation be transparent to the user.

Their tests show that DARQ works successfully in several cases though it still needs further improvements. Hence, the current SPARQL standards and implementations still hold and more research is necessary to improve these standards.[11]

E. Related Literature on User Acceptance Testing

Since the paper is a discussion of the user acceptance test on ConnectUP, it is important for researchers to align the testing processes for the application with already-established knowledge and guidelines in user acceptance testing.

Leung and Wong posit that user acceptance testing or UAT is the last stage in testing an application in software development. Once the test results show that the application being tested meet the acceptance criteria, it can already be published and released for operational use.[7]

On the other hand, for user experience (UX) expert Gerry Gaffney and his Melbourne-based user experience and usability company Information & Design, several categories are considered when testing the general usability of any web application. Categories are navigation, functionality, control, language, feedback, consistency, error prevention and correction, and visual clarity.[2]

ConnectUP is a web application, and therefore, put by the researchers as the subject application for user acceptance testing. The succeeding sections of this paper discuss how the user acceptance testing was carried out, and how the researchers patterned the test after their predefined list of features as well as Gaffney's general website usability checklist.

3. Methodology

The academic social networking application, that is ConnectUP, had been developed with the various aforementioned tools and applications. In its core is an existing benchmark university ontology from Lehigh University in Pennsylvania[1] (which was modified to suit the UP system and enhance the application's search features). Figure 1 shows the system architecture used to build ConnectUP.

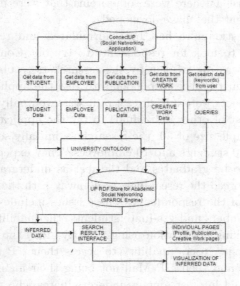

Fig. 1.   The system architecture of ConnectUP

With tools that allowed them to build an RDF store and retrieve data from it, the researchers deemed that the critical phase to follow was user acceptance testing. They needed to see how people from within the UP system would view and describe their usage of the application.

The user acceptance test for ConnectUP was done by means of a survey. First and foremost, the researchers formulated the set of questions which the respondents were to answer after using the social networking application, ConnectUP, and using it as they wished. The survey had its questions classified into two parts, namely, the functional goals and usability goals.

The functional goals that have been put in the questionnaire were based from the list of use cases or features that the researchers have come up with prior to pursuing the study. Each item under the functional goals category represented one of those aforementioned features. On the other hand, for the usability goals, the researchers opted to base the questions or items from the website usability checklist provided by Information & Design, a Melbourne-based user experience and usability company. The checklist included categories of three to six items which aimed to evaluate the overall experience of the user when using the subject website, or in this study's case, the ConnectUP application. The researchers, however, did not exactly follow the checklist as there were some items that were not applicable to the application that they have developed.

After the questionnaire had been formulated and reviewed, the researchers needed to look for respondents to try out ConnectUP. Convenience sampling was undertaken by the researchers to obtain the sample which would in turn be the respondents to test the application. A number of 30 respondents were initially set, but was eventually increased to 35 due to the interest of other individuals to try the application. Originally following the sample size of 30, the researchers initially set the sample to be composed of 20 students and 10 employees. They expected at least five of the students to be graduates and the rest as undergraduates. Several issues, however, forced the researchers to do away with the original plan on the composition of the respondents. These issues include the busy schedule of faculty members and graduate students, the inability to connect to the social networking application using a proxy-aided Internet connection within the university, users' inability to access their UP mail due to forgotten passwords and their UP Mail not being their main email account, as well as increased interest among undergraduates who want to test the application.

As a result, the researchers arrived at a final sample of 35 respondents composed of seven (7) employees who are faculty members, one (1) graduate student, and 27 undergraduate students. 34 of these respondents came from UP Diliman and one (1) came from UP Manila. Also, it is worth noting that 20 of the respondents were from the field of Computer Science and two (2) each from Economics, Music, and Home Economics. The remainder of the respondents each belong to varying fields, namely, Arts and Culture, English and Comparative Literature, Broadcast Communication, Speech Communication, History, Mathematics, Library Science, Psychology, and Visual Communication. These respondents were asked to answer the questionnaire that the researchers formulated and compiled. The questionnaire was published via a Google Form. This allowed the researchers to easily process the results of the survey, as the user acceptance tests went on. Additionally, an adjustment to the application's source code was also done to allow users to use their typical Google Mail accounts, thereby temporarily lifting the UP Mail account restriction, at least for the testing phase only. The researchers then put back the restriction after the testing phase had ended, and the temporary lifting of the restriction has, in no way, affected the initial requirement set by the researchers that users can only log in using their UP Mail accounts so as to ensure that only members of the UP system are able to be part of the social network.

After the user acceptance testing was carried out, the researches analyzed the results and inferred how ConnectUP fared in the user acceptance testing using the responses of those who have tried it out.

4. User Acceptance Test Results and Analysis

The respondents' responses for the user acceptance test were gathered by means of Google Forms and these results and their analyses are discussed in the following sections. The survey's questions are discussed in detail and the researchers attempt to explain and justify why the respondents' overall rating for that category was so. Note that in the context of this user acceptance testing, by majority, we mean more than 50% or half of the respondents.

A. Functional Goals

The first part of the questionnaire, as discussed in the methodology section of this paper, is composed of the functional goals that the researchers, or developers, have set at an earlier phase of the study, prior to development. These functional goals have then been rated by the respondents. They were asked to answer 'Comply' if they were able to complete the subject functional goal, 'Not Comply' if they were not able to do so, and 'Other' if they encountered a different experience and issue. Figure 2 summarizes the testers' responses on the different functional goals.

As part of the analysis of the results for the survey, the researchers look at each of the different features that were tested and the functional goal(s) attached to each feature.

- Sign up, log in, and log out

  It is worth noting once more that for user sign up or log in, the restriction that users were only allowed to access this functionality using their UP Mail account was lifted to allow more interested respondents who have had problems with their UP Mail account to use their typical Google Mail account. As seen in Fig. 2 (Q1 and Q22), 100% or all 35 respondents had successfully signed up

142

Question Number	Question	Comply		Not Comply		Other	
Q1	The user can sign up or log in	35	(100%)	0	(0%)	0	(0%)
Q2	The user can create his/her profile and add personal information (name, campus, college, department, phone, biography, awards and honors)	35	(100%)	0	(0%)	0	(0%)
Q3	The user can edit the information in his/her profile	35	(100%)	0	(0%)	0	(0%)
Q4	The user can add his/her publications or creative works and enter information about it (abstract/description, date published, full text/file URL)	34	(97.14%)	0	(0%)	1	(2.86%)
Q5	The user can list another user as a co-author or co-contributor to his/her work	34	(97.14%)	0	(0%)	1	(2.86%)
Q6	The user can list a non-existent user as a co-author or co-contributor to his/her work	33	(94.29%)	1	(2.86%)	1	(2.86%)
Q7	The user can edit the information in his/her publication or creative work	35	(100%)	0	(0%)	0	(0%)
Q8	The user can remove a co-author or co-contributor that is listed on his/her publication or creative work	35	(100%)	0	(0%)	0	(0%)
Q9	The user can view the publications or creative works in a profile page, along with the user's information	33	(94.29%)	0	(0%)	2	(5.71%)
Q10	The user can delete a publication or creative work from his/her 'edit profile' page	32	(88.57%)	3	(8.57%)	1	(2.86%)
Q11	The user can input a keyword and search all individuals (students, employees, publications, creative works) using that keyword.	34	(97.14%)	0	(0%)	1	(2.86%)
Q12	The user can input a keyword and search for students only	35	(100%)	0	(0%)	0	(0%)
Q13	The user can input a keyword and search for employees only	35	(100%)	0	(0%)	0	(0%)
Q14	The user can input a keyword and search for publications only	35	(100%)	0	(0%)	0	(0%)
Q15	The user can input a keyword and search for creative works only	35	(100%)	0	(0%)	0	(0%)
Q16	The user can input a keyword and search everything using any combination of the filters for students, employees, publications, and creative works	34	(97.14%)	0	(0%)	1	(2.86%)
Q17	The user can input a keyword and search students and employees based on the content of their publications or creative works	34	(97.14%)	1	(2.86%)	0	(0%)
Q18	After searching everything, the user can see a visualization of the students and employees found within the search results, and download a CSV file based on the data used in the visualization	33	(94.29%)	1	(2.86%)	1	(2.86%)
Q19	After searching for users based on the keywords found in their publications or creative works, the user can see a visualization of the students and employees found within the search results, and download a CSV file based on the data used in the visualization	32	(91.43%)	1	(2.86%)	2	(5.71%)
Q20	The user can view any user's profile, including his/hers and others'	34	(97.14%)	0	(0%)	1	(2.86%)
Q21	The user can view his/her publications or creative works in their individual pages, as well as other users' publications or creative works	35	(100%)	0	(0%)	0	(0%)
Q22	The user can log out of the application	35	(100%)	0	(0%)	0	(0%)
	Mean percentage of respondents	**97.53%**		**0.91%**		**1.56%**	

Fig. 2. A summary of the responses for the functional goals

and/or logged in, and logged out, using their Google Mail account, and have had no problems while doing so.

- Create a user profile

Upon logging in for the first time, the user is directed to the 'Create Profile' page. Users are then asked to fill out the necessary information, and are allowed to add their biographies and/or list of awards and honors. In Fig. 2 (Q2), it is clear that 100% or all 35 respondents were able to create their profiles successfully and had reported no errors while they were filling out the information and afterwards. Note that by 'successfully', this means that the respondents were, after filling out the information (at least those that have been marked required) are directed to the 'Edit Profile' page. This signifies that the profile creation was a success.

- Edit the information on their profile

The respondents were then asked to edit the information on their profile page. They were allowed to change information such as phone number, biography, and their awards and honors. Figure 2 (Q3) shows that 100% or all 35 respondents agreed that ConnectUP complies with the feature that allows users to edit the information on their profile. This means that respondents were able to edit their information without encountering any error with regards to this specific feature.

- Add a publication or creative work

The respondents were asked to add their own publications or creative works, as well as their co-authors or co-contributors. As presented in Fig. 2 (Q4) For this feature, 97.14% or 34 respondents have said that the application allows them to add their own publications or creative works (see Fig. 5). While 34 of the respondents agreed that the specific feature works, one respondent had a comment as a response.

The respondent said that while ConnectUP complies with the feature of letting a user add his/her work, there could have been an instruction on how to add multiple tags on the 'Add Publication' page. Also, it was pointed out that after adding (or editing) a publication, the application should redirect the user to the previous page, such as the profile page or 'Edit Profile' page of that user. While the first issue had already been addressed by the researchers/developers, they opted to not adhere to the second suggestion of the respondent. Instead, they added an alert message which would allow the user to choose to go back to his/her 'Edit Profile' page or view the page of the publication or creative work. The researchers believed that this would be more intuitive.

For the specific feature of adding a publication or creative work, 97.14% or 34 respondents were able to add another user within the social network as a co-author or co-contributor (see Fig. 2, Q5). 94.29% or 33 respondents were able to list in their work a non-user as a co-author or co-contributor as well (see Fig. 2, Q6). There were also 33 respondents who said that they were able to view in their profile page the publication or creative work they have added (see Fig. 2, Q9).

For other users who had other comments or said that the application did not comply, the researchers have identified issues or points surrounding their responses. One respondent, for feature of adding another user as a co-author, have said that the co-authors or collaborators of interest did not have accounts yet. The researchers addressed this by using the administrator account to create user accounts for the respondent's collaborators. The feature was later verified as working by the respondent.

On the other hand, for the feature of adding the name of a non-user as a co-author or contributor, one respondent answered 'Other', since there was no non-user to add as a collaborator to his publication. The other responded who answered 'Not Comply' reportedly had issues in adding a non-user. This was clarified to the respondent a couple of days after and was identified to have been caused by an unstable Internet connection (the changes the respondent made were not sent to the server).

Lastly, two (2) respondents have other responses when it came to viewing in their profile page the creative work or publication that they have added. One claimed that the his name should have been first in the list of authors, but the researchers deemed that it would be more intuitive to have the list of authors arrange alphabetically. The other claimed that he wasn't able to view his profile initially, and the researchers have verified this issue to be caused by an unstable Internet connection. This was resolved after a couple of days and was confirmed working by the respondent, though the survey response was never edited.

- Edit their publications or creative works

After adding a publication or creative work, the respondents were asked to edit their work and try deleting some collaborators in their work (and re-add them afterwards). As seen in Fig. 2 (both Q7 and Q8), it is clear that no respondent encountered any issue while editing the information in their work that they previously added or deleting a co-author or co-contributor in their work. 100% or all 35 respondents agreed that ConnectUP complies with the specified features.

- Delete their publications or creative works

The respondents were told as well to try deleting their publications or creative works from their 'Edit Profile' page. In some cases, respondents were asked to add a dummy or sample work that need not be re-added after deletion. Based on the results summarized in Fig. 2 (Q10), for this feature, 88.57% or 31 respondents have tried using the feature without any issue and had no other comment for the feature. Three (3) testers responded with 'Not Comply' and one (1) reportedly did not try the feature. Upon inquiry with respondents, one cause of such responses is that the respondent was too busy and deleting a work that he/she had already spent time on adding would take some more of his/her time. As a result, the researchers were not able to verify anymore with these respondents that the feature was completely working and deemed that the 88.57% of respondents, along with extensive testing done for the feature after the survey were enough to make sure that the feature was completely working.

- Search all individual entities within the social network

To try this feature out, the researchers instructed the respondents to test the 'Search Everything' feature in ConnectUP repeatedly, with each time using a different filter under the 'Advanced Search' page. The responses for this feature are divided into different items, in accordance with the usage of search filters. Filters that are incorporated into this feature are those that allow students only, employees only, publications only, and creative works only. A search using all or any combination of these features are possible as well. As summarized in Fig. 2 (Q11), with all filters on (meaning that the search results will include students, employees, publications, and creative works), 97.14% of the respondents or 34 of them were able to get their desired search results without having any error. One (1) respondent, however, encountered an error wherein the tool used to visualize the results could not process the data returned by the search. As a result, the respondent answered the item with a comment, instead of a 'Comply'. The researchers made sure that this issue was fixed, and was presented to the respondent after the error had been addressed.

For all other items pertaining to the 'Search everything' functionality except for when users were instructed to test out different combinations of the filters, all 35 or 100% of the respondents agreed that the feature is working properly and its filters, when used individually, allow them to get their desired results (see Fig. 2, Q12-Q15).

For Fig. 2 (Q6), it is clear to see that 97.14% or 34 respondents had no issues when searching everything using different filter combinations. There was, however, an issue raised by a respondent for the specific item when they were asked to try the 'Search everything' feature using any combination of filters. The respondent answered with 'Incomplete data to test'. The response was such due to the lack of, at the time of testing, another employee with a publication or creative work. The researchers ensured that after adding an employee with such work, the respondent was able to completely test out this specific sub-feature of the 'Search everything' functionality.

• Search people by a keyword on their publication or creative work

This feature allows a user to input a keyword or phrase, search the existing publications or creative works, and returns the list of authors or contributors of the works that contain the search term or phrase. The testers were asked to input a search term or phrase and examine the results returned by the research. 97.14% or 34 respondents have said that they have used this search feature without any error or issue, while one (1) respondent said that ConnectUP was not able to comply with this feature, as seen in Fig. 2 (Q17). Once more, the researchers verified the issue that the respondent encountered, and it was, once more, caused by a problem with the visualization data not being processed, thereby returning an error. This issue has since been addressed by the researchers/developers and has been extensively tested to ensure that the error has been fixed.

- See a visualization of the users returned by the search results and download the CSV file used in the visualization (for both search features)

Back to the search results pages from the two aforementioned search features, the researchers were asked to see the visualization at the lower portion of the page, as well as download a CSV file of the visualized data. Based on the summarized data in Fig. 2 (Q18), after using the 'Search Everything' feature, 97.14% or 34 respondents were able to see the visualized search results and download a visualization of the data from the results.

On the other hand, looking at Fig. 2 (Q19), after using the 'Search By Keyword' feature, 94.29% or 33 respondents were able to see the visualization and obtain a CSV file of the data in the search results.

The issues raised for this feature by the respondents who answered 'Not Comply' or 'Other' include empty search results and incomplete data. For empty search results, there is obviously nothing to visualize and more so, a CSV file to download. The 'incomplete data' comment was, as said by the respondent, due to the fact that she wanted more than publications or creative works to connect the individuals within the social network. Addressing this will force the researchers to go beyond their predefined scope, and this was made clear to the respondent after the survey.

148

- View profile pages, including theirs and other users'

From the search results pages, the respondents were asked to click on the names of the students and employees that were returned by the search. As seen in Fig. 2 (Q20), for viewing profile pages, only one (1) tester reported an issue where viewing a profile redirected to the 'Create Profile' page. This issue was caused by a faulty link and has since been fixed by the researchers/developers. The 34 other respondents (97.14%) encountered no issue with this feature at all.

- View the individual page of a publication or creative work

From the search results pages, the respondents were asked to click on the titles of the publications or creative works that were returned by the search. It is clear that in Fig. 2 (Q21), all respondents were able to view the publications and creative works returned by the search results in their individual pages without any errors or issues.

In this part of the survey, the respondents all agreed that ConnectUP complies with the following features, or items (all 35 respondents marked 'Comply'):

- The user can sign up, log in, or log out.
- The user can create his/her profile and add personal information (name, campus, college, department, phone, biography, awards and honors).
- The user can edit the information in his/her profile.
- The user can edit the information in his/her publication or creative work.
- The user can remove a co-author or co-contributor that is listed on his/her publication or creative work.
- The user can input a keyword and search for students only.
- The user can input a keyword and search for employees only.
- The user can input a keyword and search for publications only.
- The user can input a keyword and search for creative works only.
- The user can view his/her publications or creative works in their individual pages, as well as other users' publications or creative works.

On the other hand, the respondents found the following items as points for improvements as they encountered an issue with these features:

- After searching for users based on the keywords found in their publications or creative works, the user can see a visualization of the students and employees found within the search results, and download a CSV file based on the data used in the visualization.
- The user can delete a publication or creative work from his/her 'edit profile' page.

The issues that have been raised with the features listed above have since been taken note of and addressed by the researchers.

As a summary for the first part of the survey questionnaire, with the researchers treating each item to be of equal weight as the others, a mean percentage of **97.53%** of the total respondents or around **34 respondents** would say that ConnectUP complied with each of the features listed by the researchers. Rounded off to a count of 34 respondents, the researchers are confident that the application was able to comply with the features and specifications that they have formulated early on in the study.

B. Usability Goals

The second and last part of the survey dealt with having the respondents evaluate ConnectUP using more general questions based on the website usability checklist obtained from Information Design, a Melbourne-based user experience and usability company. ConnectUP is evaluated using the usability categories of navigation, functionality, control, language, feedback, consistency, error prevention and correction, and visual clarity.

- Navigation

  Figure 3 summarizes the responses of the respondents to each of the items in the checklist under the Navigation category. The answers of the respondents dwell between 'always' and 'sometimes', as shown on the mean percentages of 87.86% or around 31 respondents and 12.14% or about 4 respondent, respectively.

  Respondents' comments on Navigation include commendation on the navigability of the site and possible adjustments for the navigation bar buttons as well as the navigation bar search field. The researchers have chosen to stick to the original navigational bar layout as they believe it is intuitive after being patterned after

Navigation goal	Always	Sometimes	Never	Not applicable
There is a clear indication of my current location or page in the web application.	31 (88.57%)	4 (11.43%)	0 (0%)	0 (0%)
There is a clearly-identified link to the Home page.	32 (91.43%)	3 (8.57%)	0 (0%)	0 (0%)
Site structure is simple, with no unnecessary levels.	32 (91.43%)	3 (8.57%)	0 (0%)	0 (0%)
An easy-to-use Search function is available.	28 (80.00%)	7 (20.00%)	0 (0%)	0 (0%)
Mean percentage of respondents	**87.86%**	**12.14%**	0%	0%

Fig. 3. Responses for Navigation category

Facebook's navigation bar layout. One respondent raised an issue with the search field whose options, when changed, return the user to the top of the page. The researchers attempted to fix this after identifying it was a JQuery issue, but the issue, though being very minor, remained.

- Functionality

Figure 4 lists the count of responses for each of the checklist items listed under the Functionality category. While majority of the responses dwell between 'always' and 'sometimes' based on the mean percentages, for the last item regarding 'unnecessary plug-ins', one respondent answered 'never' and another 'not applicable'.

Functionality goal	Always	Sometimes	Never	Not applicable
All functionality is clearly labelled.	29 (82.26%)	6 (17.14%)	0 (0%)	0 (0%)
All necessary functionality is available without leaving the site.	31 (88.57%)	4 (11.43%)	0 (0%)	0 (0%)
No unnecessary plug-ins are used.	29 (82.26%)	4 (11.43%)	1 (2.86%)	1 (2.86%)
Mean percentage of respondents	**84.76%**	**13.33%**	**0.95%**	**0.95%**

Fig. 4. Responses for Functionality category

Respondents also commented that the indicator on the search bar that tells the type of search that the user is currently using be made clearer, and that a PDF/file upload module could be added for publications or creative works. Another comment was on the visualization, wherein a respondent suggested that users be also related not only by publications or creative works themselves, but by topics, too. Further suggestions such as listing frequently used keywords were made as well.

Control goal	Always	Some-times	Never	Not appli-cable
The user can cancel all operations.	29 (65.71%)	11 (31.43%)	0 (0%)	1 (2.86%)
There is a clear exit point on every page.	32 (91.43%)	3 (8.57%)	0 (0%)	0 (0%)
The site supports the user's workflow.	29 (82.26%)	6 (17.14%)	0 (0%)	0 (0%)
All appropriate browsers are supported.	29 (82.86%)	4 (11.43%)	0 (0%)	2 (5.71%)
Mean percentage of respondents	80.71%	17.14%	0%	2.14%

Fig. 5. Responses for Control category

- Control

Figure 5 summarizes the responses for the items under the Control category. Still, based on the mean percentages of responses, majority of the responses are 'always' and 'sometimes' and while no one answered 'never', some answered 'not applicable' for some of the items. Comments from respondents with regards to the Control category tend to focus on the question "All appropriate browsers are supported." The researchers infer that this is probably due the subject item being a more developer-oriented question, and that the item, which was taken directly from the usability checklist, may have been addressed.

- Language

Overall, in Fig. 6, responses tend to focus on 'always' for both of the items under the Language category. This can be seen in the 97.14% mean percentage for the 'always' response type. Only one

Language goal	Always	Some-times	Never	Not appli-cable
The language used is simple.	35	0 (0%)	0	0 (0%)
Jargon is avoided.	33 (94.23%)	1 (2.86%)	0 (0%)	1 (2.86%)
Mean percentage of respondents	**97.14%**	**1.43%**	**0%**	**1.43%**

Fig. 6.   Responses for Language category

respondent said that ConnectUP sometimes meets the language goals, and only one said that is not applicable. A respondent suggested that for Language, the employee user type be more clarified. Upon inquiry with the respondent, it was clear to the researchers that the respondent did not get to see the 'employee type' field in the results information pane in the search results page.

- Feedback

Basing from Fig. 7, the testers' respondents for the Feedback category tend to be less focused on the 'always' and 'sometimes' responses as compared to the results for the other categories. The lower mean percentage for 'always' and higher mean percentages for the other response types for this category, as compared to the mean percentages of respondents of previous usability categories,

Feedback goal	Always	Some-times	Never	Not appli-cable
It is always clear what is happening on the site.	28 (80%)	7 (20%)	0 (0%)	0 (0%)
Users can receive email feedback if necessary.	19 (54.26%)	6 (17.14%)	1 (2.86%)	8 (25.71%)
All feedback is prompt.	29 (65.71%)	4 (11.43%)	2 (5.71%)	6 (17.14%)
Users are informed if a plug-in or browser version is required.	19 (54.26%)	6 (17.14%)	2 (5.71%)	8 (22.86%)
Users can give feedback via email or a feedback form.	25 (71.43%)	5 (14.29%)	1 (2.86%)	4 (11.43%)
If necessary, online help is available.	26 (74.29%)	4 (11.43%)	1 (2.86%)	4 (11.43%)
Mean percentage of respondents	**66.67%**	**15.24%**	**3.33%**	**14.76%**

Fig. 7.   Responses for Feedback category

support the fact that the researchers focused more on other aspects of the usability of a web application, and as a result, some respondents commented that some feedback features listed in the checklist were not tested properly.

Despite this, the mean percentage tells that on average, 66.67% of the respondents, or around 23 of them would say that ConnectUP met the Feedback goals. This is still the highest mean percentage of respondents for this usability category as compared to those from the other response types.

Consistency goal	Always	Some-times	Never	Not appli-cable
Only one word or term is used to describe any item.	27 (77.14%)	8 (22.86%)	0 (0%)	0 (0%)
Links match titles of the pages to which they refer.	32 (91.43%)	3 (8.57%)	0 (0%)	0 (0%)
Standard colours are used for links and visited links.	33 (94.23%)	1 (2.86%)	0 (0%)	1 (2.86%)
Terminology is consistent with general web usage.	33 (94.23%)	2 (5.71%)	0 (0%)	0 (0%)
Mean percentage of respondents	**89.29%**	**10%**	**0%**	**0.71%**

Fig. 8.   Responses for Consistency category

- Consistency

Figure 8 presents the summary of the responses of the testers for items under Consistency. As with previous categories, answers tend to cluster around 'always' and 'sometimes', based on the mean percentages of 89.29% (around 31 respondents) and 10% (around 4 respondents), respectively. No respondent said that the application never complies with the consistency goals, and a mean of 0.71% indicates that almost no one says that the goals are not applicable to ConnectUP.

- Error Prevention and Correction

Figure 9 summarizes the respondents' answers for the checklist items listed under the Error Prevention and Correction category. Similar to the responses in the Feedback category, the answers tend

Error Prevention and Correction goal	Always	Some-times	Never	Not appli-cable
Errors do not occur unnecessarily.	26 (74.29%)	7 (20%)	0 (0%)	2 (5.71%)
Error messages are in plain language.	29 (65.71%)	3 (8.57%)	2 (5.71%)	7 (20%)
Error messages describe what action is necessary.	29 (65.71%)	3 (8.57%)	2 (5.71%)	7 (20%)
Error messages provide a clear exit point.	22 (62.86%)	5 (14.29%)	1 (2.86%)	7 (20%)
Error messages provide contact details for assistance.	29 (65.71%)	5 (14.29%)	1 (2.86%)	6 (17.14%)
Mean percentage of respondents	**66.86%**	**13.14%**	**3.43%**	**16.57%**

Fig. 9. Responses for Error Prevention and Correction category

to be less focused on the 'always' and 'sometimes' category, upon closer examination of the mean percentages. The 'always' response type, albeit having the highest mean percentage of respondents, tells that only 68.86% of the respondents or around 24 of them agree that ConnectUP has met the Error Prevention and Correction goals. The remaining respondents are spread throughout the other response types, similar to the ones in the Feedback category. This reflects more opinionated responses, as well as the fact that Error Prevention and Correction had also not given as much weight as the researchers did in categories such as Navigation, Control, and Functionality. Also similar to the Feedback category, respondents commented that some items in the checklist were not tested properly and this was due to the researchers not being able to focus on this aspect prior and during the development of ConnectUP.

- Visual Clarity

Lastly, Fig. 10 presents summarized responses for the checklist items under Visual Clarity. Like most previous categories, responses tend to focus on the 'always' and 'sometimes' responses, as reflected by the differences in the mean percentages of respondents of the different response types.

Additionally, a respondent commented that the visualization's zooming feature be made more controllable, and this issue has since been addressed by the researchers.

Visual Clarity goal	Always	Sometimes	Never	Not applicable
The layout is clear.	32 (91.43%)	3 (8.57%)	0 (0%)	0 (0%)
There is sufficient space/'white space'.	32 (91.43%)	3 (8.57%)	0 (0%)	0 (0%)
Unnecessary animation is avoided.	33 (94.23%)	2 (5.71%)	0 (0%)	0 (0%)
All images have ALT text assigned.	25 (71.43%)	3 (8.57%)	2 (5.71%)	5 (14.29%)
Mean percentage of respondents	**87.14%**	**7.86%**	**1.43%**	**3.57%**

Fig. 10.   Responses for Visual Clarity category

Category	Always	Sometimes	Never	Not applicable
Navigation	87.86%	12.14%	0%	0%
Functionality	84.76%	13.33%	0.95%	0.95%
Control	80.71%	17.14%	0%	2.14%
Language	97.14%	1.43%	0%	1.43%
Feedback	66.67%	15.24%	3.33%	14.76%
Consistency	89.29%	10%	0%	0.71%
Error Prevention and Correction	66.86%	13.14%	3.43%	16.57%
Visual Clarity	87.14%	7.86%	1.43%	3.57%

Fig. 11.   A tabulation of the mean percentages of respondents for the usability categories

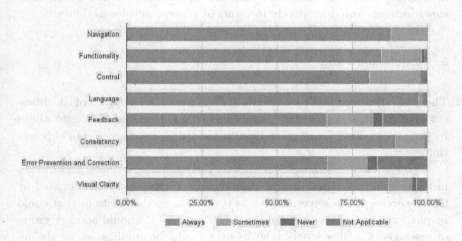

Fig. 12.   A visualized summary of the mean percentages of respondents for the usability categories

For all the categories in this second part of the survey, it is worth noting that the mean of responses for 'always' significantly outweigh the means of other response types. It is also important to note that all items in the checklist are expressed in positive statements, and that a response of 'always' will, at all times, indicate the most positive response for every item in the checklist, and 'never' the most negative. The means percentages of each response type for every category are summarized in Fig. 11 and visualized in Fig. 12.

Looking at Fig. 12, it is easy to see that categories such as Feedback and Error Prevention and Correction tend to have their responses more spread throughout the different response types. This reflects the fact that the development processes undertaken by the researchers did not focus on such categories. The researchers prioritized the use of ontology and how it fits into the picture of building an academic social network. The researchers had little consideration for the two categories, thus resulting to lesser features in the application that adhere to those categories. As a result, the respondents tended to have more opinionated responses for the categories of Feedback and Error Prevention and Correction. The mean percentages of respondents for other categories follow a different trend, showing that majority of the responses come from the 'always' response type. This is shown clearly in Fig. 11, and is an indication that the application, especially in those categories, are rated positively in terms of general website usability.

5. Conclusions and Recommendations

The generalizations made by the researchers from their analysis of the different undertakings in this study, as well as recommendations brought about by potential points for improvement in the study are discussed in this section.

The user acceptance test has allowed the researchers/developers to take in tester feedback based on the questionnaire formulated and compiled by the researchers themselves, as well as comments and suggestions that could be put forth to improve the application, ConnectUP, should another group of researchers or developers take interest in the beginnings set by the researchers of this study.

The testers' responses for the user acceptance test have generally been positive. In the first part of the survey questionnaire, the mean percentage of respondents who said that ConnectUP complied with each of the researchers' predefined features resulted to **97.53%** of the total number of respondents. This is equivalent to around 34 respondents who, in average, agree to the compliance of the application to the features listed in their questionnaire.

On the other hand, for the second part of the user acceptance survey, the researchers were able to find out that for all usability categories, majority of the respondents (with mean percentages ranging from 66.67% to 97.14%) say that ConnectUP always meets the various goals under each usability category. Of the usability categories, the one that had the least percentage of respondents saying that the application always complied with the goals under that category was Feedback category, followed by Error Prevention and Correction. This is a reflection of the path that the researchers took when developing ConnectUP wherein the usability goals concerning feedback and error handling were given less attention as compared to other aspects of the application. In spite of this trend, the responses for the usability part of the survey have been generally positive, as stated earlier.

Despite having several issues and errors encountered and raised by respondents in the midst and after the user acceptance test, the figures show that in general, the user feedback on the application is positive - that ConnectUP complies with the features and items in the checklist formulated and compiled by the researchers themselves. Both the functional and usability goals that the researchers have set, appear to have been met by ConnectUP, as a result of the analysis of the survey responses. The figures show that in retrospect, the application is ready for operational use, given that testers have generally 'accepted' it.

The issues that have been encountered during and after the testing have been noted carefully by the researchers/developers. While most of the issues and errors have been resolved, some suggestions for improvement still hold and the researchers list them as recommendations for any researcher or developer who takes interest in continuing and improving ConnectUP, or a system similar to it.

One respondent suggested that the data visualization be improved. Aside from publications and creative works connecting the different users, the respondent suggested that research fields or keywords be utilized as well to form connections between the users. Addressing the respondent's concern will open more possible areas of research for applications such as ConnectUP and will require the researchers to go beyond the predefined scope of the study. Nonetheless, it still is an important suggestion and the researchers see it as a major point for improving such an application.

Future researchers on this study, or a similar one, may try allotting more time to getting a sample of more than 35 respondents and making sure that it is representative of the population of the UP system as much as possible. As such, it is further suggested that more time be allotted to prepare for the user acceptance test to make way for additional use cases that future researchers may identify, thereby allowing them to refine and polish their checklist of items for the user acceptance test before taking in any responses from users.

With these points, the researchers see that the potentials of this study can be magnified and this will result in nothing but the improvement of the application that the researchers have developed in this study.

References

1. Lehigh University Benchmark Ontology. http://swat.cse.lehigh.edu/onto/univ-bench.owl. (Accessed on 06/10/2016).
2. Usability evaluation checklist for web sites. http://infodesign.com.au/wp-content/uploads/WebCheck.pdf.
3. B. Chandrasekaran, J. R. Josephson, and V. R. Benjamins. What are ontologies, and why do we need them? *IEEE Intelligent Systems*, 14(1):20–26, Jan. 1999.
4. L. Chen, S. Wei, and Z. Qingpu. Semantic description of social network based on ontology. In *E-Business and E-Government (ICEE), 2010 International Conference on*, pages 1936–1939, May 2010.
5. J. J. Jung, K. S. Choi, and S. H. Park. Discovering mobile social networks by semantic technologies. *Handbook of Social Network Technologies and Applications*, pages 223–239, 2010.
6. S.-K. Kim, J.-M. Han, and M.-Y. Song. A social network system based on an Ontology in the Korea Institute of Oriental Medicine. *Lecture Notes in Computer Science Recent Trends and Developments in Social Software*, pages 46–51, 2010.
7. H. K. N. Leung and P. W. L. Wong. A study of user acceptance tests. *Software Quality Journal*, 6(2):137–149, Oct. 1997.
8. N. Malviya, N. Mishra, and S. Sahu. Developing university ontology using Protege OWL tool: Process and reasoning. *International Journal of Scientific & Engineering Research*, 2(9), September 2011.
9. E. Miller. An introduction to the resource description framework.
10. J. Z. Pan and M. Uschold. A semantic web primer for object-oriented software developers.

11. B. Quilitz and U. Leser. Querying distributed rdf data sources with sparql. In *Proceedings of the 5th European Semantic Web Conference on The Semantic Web: Research and Applications*, ESWC'08, pages 524–538, Berlin, Heidelberg, 2008. Springer-Verlag.

12. T. Segaran, C. Evans, and J. Taylor. *Programming the Semantic Web*. O'Reilly, 2009.

13. P. O. Wennerberg. Ontology based knowledge discovery in social networks.

14. L. Zeng, T. Zhu, and X. Ding. Study on construction of university course ontology: Content, method and process. In *Computational Intelligence and Software Engineering, 2009. CiSE 2009. International Conference on*, pages 1–4, Dec 2009.

160

A Rule-Based Classification of ECG Rhythms Using Moving First Derivative of the Signal

Sandra Mae W. Famador[†], Anthony Eliezer C. Arellano, Charise A. Pelayo

Biomedical Imaging and Artificial Intelligence Lab, Department of Computer Science, University of the Philippines Cebu, Cebu City, 6000 Philippines
[†]E-mail: swfamador@up.edu.ph

The rhythm of a scanned ECG paper can be interpreted by extracting the first derivative of the signal. This paper discusses a first derivative method to classify five different rhythms, namely: Normal Sinus Rhythm, Sinus Bradycardia, 1st Degree AV Block, Atrial Flutter and the Asystole. The PQRST Wave complex is mapped and the different intervals are identified. Unlike other methods where learning is needed and quite a number of data are required, the method described here used rule-based method. It is capable of interpreting data with minimal samples. Based on the studied data, the method was able to produce a 95% accuracy for samples with grids that do not perfectly lie in time axis.

Keywords: Rule-based; electrocardiograph (ECG); PQRST waves, forward chaining; arrhythmia; first derivative; digital image processing.

1. Introduction

Latest equipment developed for cardiac monitoring include algorithms that are capable of interpreting signals that define condition of the heart. In abnormal cases, these equipment are capable of accurately identifying the disease. However, these are very expensive and only those that can afford can avail of the services. Unlike ordinary electrocardiograph (ECG), these equipment use special digital signal processors designed for its specific purpose embedded with advanced digital signal processing algorithms. In areas where only very few can afford these services, it is wise to develop algorithms that are also capable of interpreting these diseases but will only require inputs taken from ordinary ECG machines to lower down the cost of service.

This paper describes a way to interpret ECG rhythms, arrhythmias, from a scanned ECG paper. Digital image processing of the scanned signal is used instead of digital signal processing. It makes use of a rule-based interpretation from the extracted first derivative of the signal. Rules are defined to classify the series of extracted first derivative. This study is significant because this does not need additional signal processors but only requires processing of signal from a scanned electrocardiograph. The only requirement that you will need to attain the output is the right definition of each wave in an ECG rhythm. Unlike other methods where you will need a significant amount of data to train analyses of signal, this study will only need rules similar to the rules followed by a human individual in reading an ECG strip to analyze P,Q,R S and T waves. If rules are properly laid, a good classification can be obtained. This solution can also be used to classify electroencephalograph (EEG) and electromyograph (EMG) signals.

In 2014, Akilandeswari and Sathya [1] used Walsh-Hadamard Transform (WHT) and Fast Fourier Transform (FFT) to extract features of ECG for early detection of arrhythmias. Feature extraction was performed by extracting segmented signals based on location of peaks.

Sao et al., [2] in their paper, used Neural network to classify abnormalities of the heart. The signal waveform from the ECG was analyzed using spectral entropy, Poincare plot and lyapunov exponent as features.

Xu and Ying [3] presents an algorithm to detect QRS complex and evaluate RR interval using Slope vector waveform (SVW). First part is the variable stage differentiation which is used to obtain the desired slope vectors for feature extraction. The second part is the non-linear amplification which is used to improve signal-to-noise ratio. The algorithm is good for signals contaminated with noise.

2. Method Used

This study used a 12-lead ECG rhythm to accommodate Myocardial Infarction. From the ECG machine, the ECG paper or strip was scanned and was subdivided into twelve sub-images which corresponded to the outputs of the ECG leads. Figure 1 below shows the pipeline of work.

Strip from ECG was digitized and pre-processed to meet condition of the system. After pre-processing the image, a continuous slope calculation was performed to get the right first derivative. Peak, starting, and ending points of the signal were identified. After performing all first derivatives, an identification was displayed in the user interface.

3. P,Q,R,S, and T Analyses

Using a 24-bit color, 8-bit grayscale (256 levels of gray) with a resolution of 1200 x 1200 dots per inch flatbed optical scanner, the ECG papers were scanned to produce a digital copy of the rhythms.

Strip from ECG

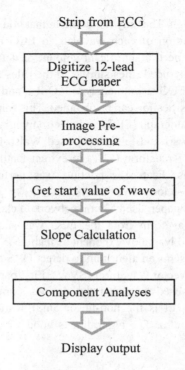

Fig. 1. Pipeline of Work

3.1. *Image Pre-processing*

Looking at Figure 2, an ECG grid is composed of red, RGB = (255,0,0) horizontal and vertical lines while the rhythm is in black, RGB = (0,0,0). This principle was used to differentiate the signal from the grid. As of the writing of this paper, the algorithm used in this study assumed that the horizontal lines perfectly lie at 0 degrees and the vertical lines are perpendicular to the horizontal lines. Figure 2 from [4] below shows the example of an ECG paper with rhythm.

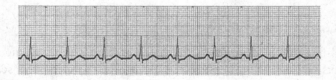

Fig. 2. An ECG Rhythm

3.2. *The ECG Paper*

Running at 25 mm/sec, the ECG paper has a finest division block of 1 mm/sec. The block is formed by a small square and lumped together to form a larger square of 5 small blocks. The width of an ECG tracing is a measure of time. The horizontal axis of the paper corresponds to time while the vertical axis corresponds to electrical voltage. Each one small square corresponds to 0.04 seconds. Five small blocks is equivalent to 0.20 seconds. The normal standardization of a 12-lead ECG is 10 mm/1mV, so 1 mm translates to 0.1 mV. Figure 3 from [5] shows the graph paper used to monitor electrical activity of the heart.

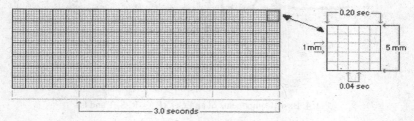

Fig. 3. The Graph Paper

3.3. *Electrocardiography*

Figure 4 from [6] below shows the individual components of an ECG signal as a result of the electrical activity of the heart. The P wave represents the first rise of the signal in the atrial depolarization. The PR interval tracks the atrial impulse from the atria through the AV node, bundle of His, and the right and left bundle branches. The QRS complex follows the P wave and represents the depolarization of the ventricles. The ST segment represents the end of ventricular conduction or depolarization and the beginning of ventricular recovery or repolarization. The T wave represents the ventricular recovery or repolarization [7].

In Figure 5 from [8], the Q wave is the first negative deflection while the R wave is the first positive deflection of ventricular depolarization. Right after R wave is the S wave, a negative deflection. QT interval represents the total time of ventricular depolarization and repolarization.

Table 1 below shows the parameters that define normal and abnormal ECG components. It addresses each of the waves, intervals and segments of an ECG in the order that they would appear. A segment in an ECG is the region between two waves while an interval includes one segment or one or more waves. This table defines the rules that will be used in this study to classify ECG rhythms. It is a collection of normal and abnormal parameters of the study. Parameters are not

164

based on a single reference but are taken from several discussions of different authors. [7][9].

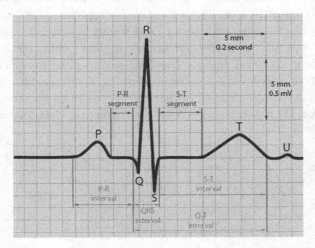

Fig. 4. Basic Components of an ECG. (P, Q, R, S, T and U)

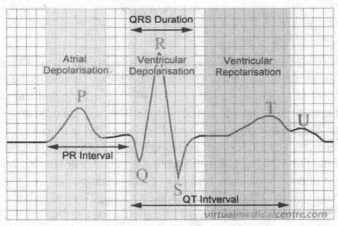

Fig. 5. Repolarization and Depolarization of Rhythm

Table 1. Parameters that Define Normal and Abnormal ECG

ECG Component	Normal Parameters	Abnormal Parameters
P wave	Duration: < 0.11 sec Amplitude: < 2.5 small squares Upright in Lead II	Inverted, Notched, Tall
PR interval	Duration: 0.12 – 20 sec	Shorter or longer than normal
PR segment	Lies in the isoelectric line	Depressed or elevated
Q wave	Duration: < 0.04 sec Amplitude: 2 small squares	Duration: >= 0.04 sec Amplitude: > 2 small squares
QRS complex	Upright in Lead II Duration: < 0.11 sec	Duration: > 0.11 sec
ST segment	In line with the PR or the TP segment (baseline)	Depressed or Elevated
T wave	< 1/8 and 2/3 of amplitude of preceding R wave	Peaked, Inverted, biphasic, notched, flat or wide forms
QT interval	< 1/2 RR interval	>1/2 RR interval

3.4. *The First Derivative*

Equation 1 with graph in Figure 6 [10] was the equation used to take the first derivative of the rhythm. The slope of a curve at a point is equal to the slope of the straight line that is tangent to the curve at that point. An array containing the slope values of each column was derived. The slope of a column was calculated by finding the difference of the average values of the next and previous columns. The result was a slope array. This array was used as an input to the component analyzer. The system starts with looking for the first positive slope, the P wave. In the absence of a P wave, a negative slope is first detected, the Q wave. It then proceeds until it reaches the T wave.

3.5. *12-Lead ECG*

The 12-lead ECG records information from 12 different electrical activities of the heart. Different leads provide different information. The six limb leads – I, II, III, augmented vector right (aV_R), augmented vector left (aV_L), and augmented vector foot (aV_F) – provide information about the heart's frontal plane. The six precordial or V leads – V_1, V_2, V_3, V_4, V_5, and V_6 provide information about the heart's horizontal plane. [7] Figure 7 from [11] below shows the 12- lead ECG Rhythm.

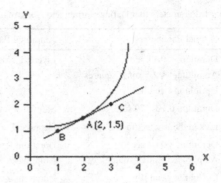

Fig. 6. Slope of a Curve at the Point of Tangency

$$slope = \frac{(y_2 - y_1)}{(x_2 - x_1)} \tag{1}$$

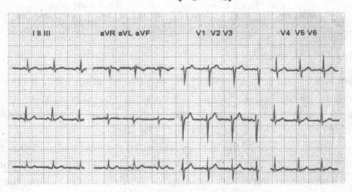

Fig. 7. Normal Sinus Rhythm Lead Strips

3.6. *Classification*

3.6.1. *Rule-based system*

This study considers only five classifications of ECG, namely, the Normal Sinus Rhythm, Sinus Bradycardia, 1st Degree AV block, Atrial Flutter and the Asystole. Other arrhythmias are not considered in this paper. Table 2 below shows the classification rules of the 5 ECG rhythms. Figure 8 from [12] below shows the rhythms.

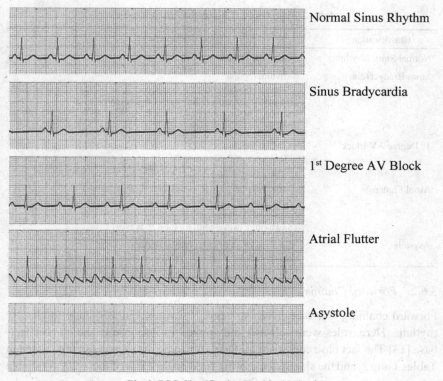

Normal Sinus Rhythm

Sinus Bradycardia

1st Degree AV Block

Atrial Flutter

Asystole

Fig. 8. ECG Classification Used in this Study

Table 2 summarizes the rules used to classify ECG rhythms. These rules were taken from [7]. A rule-based system takes the form

if <condition> then <conclusion>.

where in Backus-Naur Form grammar

condition -> ComplexSentence

ComplexSentence -> (Sentence ∧ Sentence)

|(Sentence ∨ Sentence)

|(Sentence => Sentence)

|(Sentence <=> Sentence).

Condition in this study is determined by the properties in Table 2 and conclusion is the classification of the ECG rhythm.

Table 2. Rules Used to Classify the 5 ECG Rhythms

Classification		Properties
Normal Sinus Rhythm	-	Based on Table 1
Sinus Bradycardia	-	Rhythm regular
	-	Rate <60 beats/minute
	-	Normal P wave preceding each QRS complex
	-	Normal QRS complex
	-	QT interval may be prolonged
1st Degree AV Block	-	Rhythm regular
	-	PR interval > 0.20 second
	-	P wave preceding each QRS complex; QRS complex normal
Atrial Flutter	-	Atrial rhythm regular, ventricular rhythm variable
	-	Arial rate 250 to 400 beats/minute; ventricular rate depends on degree of AV block
	-	Sawtooth P-wave configuration (F waves)
Asystole	-	No atrial or ventricular rate or rhythm
	-	No discernible P waves, QRS complexes, or T waves

3.6.2. *Forward Chaining*

Forward chaining is a data-driven strategy. It was used in this study to classify rhythms. Here, rules were selected and applied in response to the current fact-base.[13] The fact base comprises all facts known by the system as enumerated in Tables 1 and 2, and the slopes. Rules were fired on the basis of fact base. Available rules whose conditions were satisfied were fired until a conclusion was derived.

3.7. *Output*

Figures 9 and 10 show the result of applying the ruled-based ECG rhythm classification using moving first derivative of the signal. In this study, a 95% efficiency was obtained if pre-processing was not well done. This means, the horizontal strip does not lie in the 0 degree or time axis.

Twenty samples were used in this study. With proper pre-processing of the sampled data, a 100% classification accuracy was obtained. Without proper pre-processing, only 95% was obtained, meaning, not all samples were correctly identified. To correct the 5% error, image rotation was used to properly position the paper. This was assumed that the ECG paper had no lines produced by improper handling.

Efficiency computation in terms of classification performance was also based on a rule-based method. Matrices were defined as reference matrices. Here, we defined **A** as a reference matrix, **B** as the matrix obtained by the moving average, and **C** as the efficiency matrix. Using ruled-based method, **C** was updated if a rule was fired, otherwise, the next rule for **A** and **B** was fired. Euclidean distance was used to measure similarity.

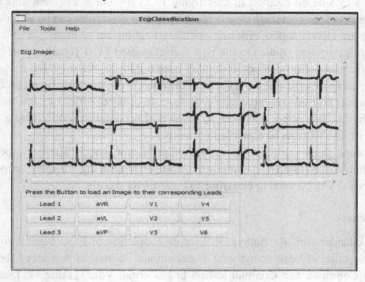

Fig. 9. 12-Lead ECG Sub-Image Rhythms Loaded to the Software

	Normal ?	Interval Duration /	QRS Duration / ms	QT Duration /ms	P Amplitude / mV	Q Amplitude / mV	R Amplitude / mV	T
Lead I	Normal	185	177	444	0.15	0.15	0.85	0.2
Lead II	Normal	185	177	444	0.15	0.15	1.1	0.2
Lead III	Normal	185	177	444	0.15	0.15	1.075	0.2
aVR	Abnormal	none	none	none	0.725	0	0	0
aVL	Abnormal	none	none	none	0.65	0	0	0
aVF	Normal	185	177	444	0.15	0.15	1.025	0.2
V1	Abnormal	none	none	none	0.775	0	0	0
V2	Abnormal	none	none	none	0.7	0	0	0
V3	Abnormal	none	none	none	0.7	0	0	0
V4	Abnormal	none	none	none	0.7	0	0	0
V5	Normal	185	177	444	0.15	0.15	1.1	0.2
V6	Normal	185	177	444	0.15	0.15	1.075	0.2

Rhythm

ECG Rhythm: Normal Sinus Rhythm

Average Values:

PRInverval -- ms: 185

QT Duration -- ms: 444   HeartRate --bpm: 60 bpm

QRS Duration -- ms: 177

Fig. 10. Classified ECG Rhythm

4. Conclusion

Using a rule-based method in classifying ECG rhythm is efficient and fast. If parameters of the signal are clearly identified, then good rules can be well defined. If rules are clearly stated, efficiency of classification can be high.

Unlike several studies in the past that classified ECG signals using outputs taken from signal processors, this study used output from a digitized image. It is hard to compare efficiency and speed of the outputs produced by signal processors and outputs produced by an image processor. In terms of efficiency in classifying arrhythmias, this paper was able to show that an output produced by a digital image of an ECG can be classified correctly.

Future study will classify all arrhythmias, not just 5. The pre-processing algorithm will be improved to minimize noise or error in digitizing the strip. Also, the method will be used to classify EEG and EMG signals.

References

1. Akilandeswari, K., Sathya, R. Feature Extraction of ECG Signals for early Detection of heart arrhythmia. (International Journal of Advanced Research in Computer and Communication Engineering. Vol. 3, Issue 12, December 2014).
2. Sao, P., Hegadi, Rajendra, and Karmakar, S. ECG Signal Analysis Using Neural Network. (International Journal of Science and Research (IJSR). ISSN(Online):2319-7064. 2013).
3. Xu, X., and Liu, Ying. ECG QRS Complex Detection Using Slope Vector (SVW) Algorithm. (Proceeding of the 26th Annual International Conference of the IEEE EMBS. San Francisco, CA, USA. September 1-5, 2004).
4. ECG Rhythms. http://www.ambulancetechnicianstudy.co.uk/rhythms.html#.V7qxVJh97IV.
5. ECG Basics. http://www.ambulancetechnicianstudy.co.uk/ecgbasics.html#.V7qpQph 97IU.
6. ECG Guide for Portable Handheld ECG EKG Users. http://www.favoriteplus.com/blog/wp-content/uploads/2013/05/ecg-2.gif.
7. ECG Interpretation Made Incredibly Easy. 3rd Ed. Lippincott Williams and Wilkins. PA, USA. (2005).
8. ECG/EKG Electrocardiogram. http://www.myvmc.com/investigations/ecg-ekg-electrocardiogram/.
9. Morris, F. et al. ABC of Clinical Electrocardiography. BMJ Books. https://www.jandur.cz/med/ABC%20of%20Clinical%20Electrocardiograph y.pdf

10. Unit 3: Determining the Slope of a Curve at the Point of Tangency. http://cls.syr.edu/mathtuneup/graphb/Unit8/Unit8a.html.
11. ECG Basics. http://www.ambulancetechnicianstudy.co.uk/rules.html#.V7wHTph9600.
12. ECG Basics. http://www.ambulancetechnicianstudy.co.uk/rhythms.html#.V7wHTph9600
13. Hopgood, A. Intelligent Systems for Engineers and Scientists. 3rd Ed. CRC Press. 2012.

Descriptive Academic Analytics System
for the College of Computer Studies of CIT University

Butch M. Cortez and Cherry Lyn C. Sta. Romana

Cebu Institute of Technology-University
Cebu City, 6000, Philippines
E-mail: cortezbutch@gmail.com, cstaromana@cit.edu

A Descriptive Academic Analytics System for the College of Computer Studies of CIT-University was developed based on data obtained from CIT University's Academic Information System. The main goal is to have a more cohesive and effective manner of presenting data that can serve as guide to academic administrators for better planning and decision making. The system includes reports on enrollment status, passing/failing rate, student performance, demographics and attrition/retention. The system presents aggregated reports visually and interactively. Users can click the components of a graph to get more detailed information. The graphical representations allow for patterns and trends to be uncovered. The system can also serve as a base for further studies on predictive and prescriptive academic analytics.

Keywords: academic analytics, descriptive analytics, educational data mining.

1. Introduction

Cebu Institute of Technology – University (CIT) is a privately-owned University located in N. Bacalso Avenue, Cebu City, Philippines. Majority of its programs are in the fields of Engineering and Technology. Enrolment population of the school ranges from 10,000++ to 12,000++. The University has 6 Colleges namely: College of Engineering and Architecture (with almost 60% of the population), College of Management, Business and Accountancy (with almost 20% of the population), College of Computer Studies (with almost 10% of the population) and the remaining 20% is shared among the College of Education, College of Arts and Sciences and College of Nursing.

The University has a liberal admission policy. Students who intend to study in CIT are given a chance to join the University. Thus, the school has a heterogeneous group of students with different knowledge, backgrounds and skill levels. To help these students with diverse backgrounds, the school has put in place, mechanisms to support the students through various forms like freshmen advising, learning enhancement program, tutorials and peer mentoring.

The overall goal of these programs is to lower down attrition rate which will therefore improve graduation rate. The problem however is how to identify students who are at risks and need support. There is a therefore a need for a close look at the profile of the students, the existing trends in attrition/graduation and success/failure rate of students. The presence of these data will guide CIT administrators for better planning and decision making. It is for these reasons that an Academic Analytics System for the College of Computer Studies of CIT University was conceptualized and explored. The system may be used as a base for the establishment institution-wide academic analytics system.

2. Academic Analytics

The term academic analytics was first used in 2005 to give a more fitting name to describe the process of applying business intelligence to academic data. It refers to the application of data mining and business intelligence techniques to data produced by academic information systems to help academic administrators in decision-making [1].

The paper [2] describes 5 steps in academic analytics. The first step in the process is to **capture** data from various information sources. The next step is to **report,** where queries; examination of information; identification of trends, patterns, and exceptions in the data are conducted. The third stage is to **predict.** In this stage, data is subjected to statistical analysis and data mining algorithms to allow the system to give predictions about what will happen in the future. Reports and predictions will guide the institution to take appropriate actions. The last stage is the **refine** stage with the over-all goal of improving the system.

These stages or steps are similar to the different types of analytics [3]. Descriptive analytics aims to describe "what happened?". Majority of analytics work are descriptive in nature. Another type is predictive analytics. In this type, the goal is to determine the possible outcome of an event from happening. In general, predictive analytics tries to answer "what can/might happen in the future?". Another stage is prescriptive analytics which use simulation algorithms to give advice on possible outcomes and answer "what should be done?".

3. Existing System

CIT University used to develop its own computer systems to manage its operations. However, integrating the data of the various systems became a challenge. Thus, in 2011, CIT subscribed to a 3rd party provider of an enterprise-wide academic management system. The modules pertaining to the academic and student information aspects of the system have been used and data have been collected for the last 5 years.

174

Even though the system can support day-to-day operations of the school, specific reports have to be done on a per-request basis. Thus, aggregate reports are not regularly provided.

4. Descriptive Academic Analytics System of CIT University

4.1. *Description and Technologies Used*

The data collected over the past years by CIT's academic information system became the main source of the Academic Analytics system that was developed.

The system is a web-based application. It was developed using mostly open-source tools. The following are the technologies used in developing the system:

- PHP – as the main scripting language,
- CodeIgniter – PHP framework implementing the Model-View-Controller architecture,
- Bootstrap and Javascript,
- MySQL – for the main database,
- Fusion charts with clickable graphs – for the data visualization,
- TCPDF php-library and php class – for generating documents in pdf format, and
- MSSQL views and queries are used in getting the data from the Academic system.

Initially, data from the College of Computer Studies was used as a base for the testing. However, the system is generic and can support data from other Colleges by changing the data source. Features of this web-based application includes enrollment status report, passed/failed percentage of subjects per class, student performance based on subjects taken, general weighted average every semester, attrition and re-enrollment report. Data are visually presented with clickable components to drilldown more information.

4.2. *Model*

Figure 1 shows the framework that was followed in the development of the study. The first part of the study collected data from the school's academic information system. These data were analyzed and data from different tables were aggregated and summarized. These data were then presented in graphical forms. The graphical representations that will be represented can uncover trends and patterns that can be used by administrators for planning decision making.

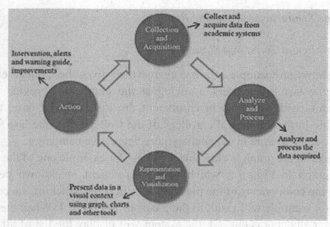

Fig. 1. Framework used for the system

4.3. *Data Types and Sources*

Table 1 shows the data types and sources. Note that the main source of the data for the moment is only the Academic Information System from the 3rd-party provider.

Table 1. Data Types and Sources

Type of data	Data	Source	Update frequency
Enrollment status	Enrollment count by college, course & year level	Academic system	Every semester
Student Performance	GWA	Academic system	Every semester
	Grades	Academic system	Every semester
	Passed/Failed percentage of subjects enrolled	Academic system	Every semester
Subjects offered	Class Size, Passed/Failed percentage of subjects offered	Academic system	Every semester
Students subject enrolled	Subject count, Units enrolled	Academic system	Every semester
Attrition/Re-enrollment	Re-enrollment count, Attrition count	Academic system	Every semester
Demographic	Age, Gender, High School attended (public/private)	Academic system	Once

4.4. Usage Scenarios and Sample Reports

4.4.1. Enrollment Trend and Status

Figure 2 shows an example of a bar chart which gives the College enrollment trend for the last 6 semesters. Looking at the graph will provide academic administrators with the trend in enrollment. In this particular case, there is a slow decline in the number of enrollees of the College over the last 5 years. It can guide administrators in conducting more aggressive campaign.

Each bar in the graph is clickable. Clicking for example one of the bars, will give the graph in Figure 3 which is the enrollment breakdown per course. Similarly, the components of the pie chart are clickable. Clicking the component for BSIT for example will result to the pie chart in Figure 4. When the pie chart for first year students is clicked, the system will display the list of all first year students under the BSIT Program.

4.4.2. Student Performance

In this module, administrators can drill-down per program, per year level to see the performance of students in terms of failure rates based on midterm and final grades. Each bar is clickable and will display the list of students per category. In the future, administrators may call the attention of these students. Moreover, automatic referral to the Dean/Department Chairs or to the Guidance Center may be done by the system.

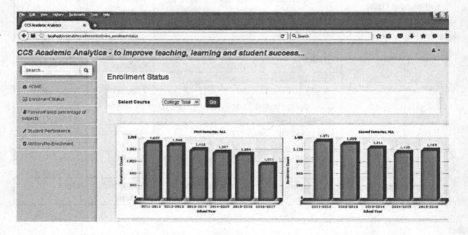

Fig. 2. College enrollment trend per semester over the last 5 years

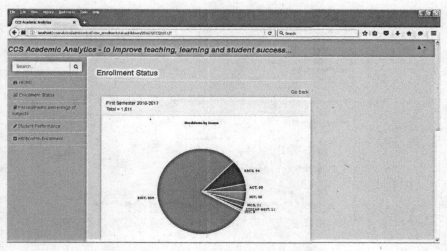

Fig. 3. College enrollment status breakdown by program

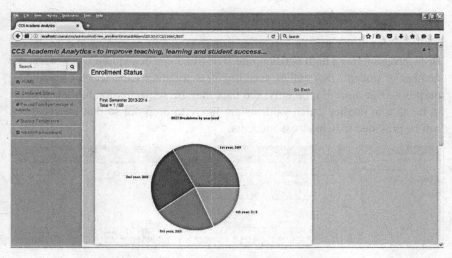

Fig. 4. BSIT program enrollment status by year level

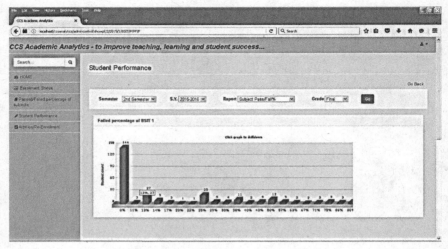

Fig. 5. Percentage of failed subjects of BSIT students

4.4.3. Attrition/Retention Status

Figure 6 shows the attrition/retention status. As can be seen from the graph, the BSIT program has a high attrition rate. The trend can be explored to forecast the number of students that will be enrolling in succeeding semesters for scheduling purposes. But more importantly, the data may be subjected for further analysis to be able to predict which students are likely to drop-out so that interventions can be provided to help at-risk students.

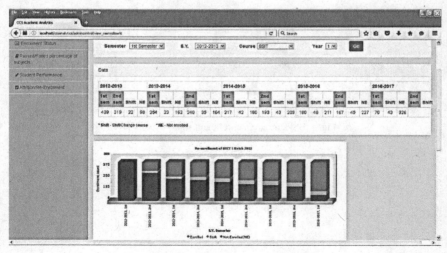

Fig. 6. Attrition/Retention Status

4.4.4. *Passing/Failing Rate per Course/Section*

The system also gives statistics on the number and percentage of students who failed in the various course offerings. An example of this is shown in Figure 7. Students in courses with the most failure rate may be given additional support and students may be advised to attend tutorial sessions or peer mentoring sessions. Faculty members handling these courses may also receive additional training and support.

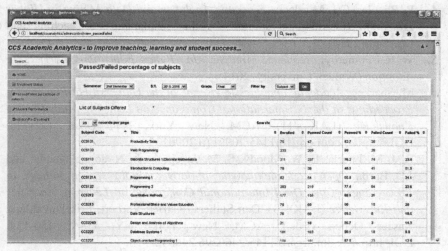

Fig. 7. Passing/Failing Rates per Course

5. Conclusions and Future Work

A descriptive academic analytics system was conceptualized and developed for the College of Computer Studies of CIT University. The various graphical reports provided by the system will allow administrators to see trends in enrolment and attrition. The reports can guide administrators in planning for necessary interventions to increase enrollment, minimize attrition, help identify "at-risk" students and improve graduation rate. However, there is a need to explore the reports, conduct more analysis so that the system may be able to predict at risk students; and forecast enrolment, attrition and graduation rates. Moreover, there is also a need to have a systematic and documented evaluation of this system for future improvement and deployment to the other Colleges of the university.

References

1. P. J. Goldstein, *Academic Analytics: The Uses of Management Information and Technology in Higher Education* (ECAR, Volume 8, 2005).
2. J. P. Campbell, D.G. Oblinger, *Academic Analytics* (EDUCAUSE, 2007).
3. *Transforming asset and facilities management with analytics* (IBM Software, 2013). http://www-01.ibm.com/common/ssi/cgi-bin/ssialias?htmlfid=TIW14162USEN
4. P. Baepler, C.J. Murdoch, *Academic Analytics and Data Mining in Higher Education* (International Journal for the Scholarship of Teaching and Learning, 2010).
5. W. L. Pomeroy, *Academic Analytics in Higher Education: Barriers to Adoption* (Walden University, 2014).
6. M. Sharkey, *Academic analytics landscape at the University of Phoenix.* In *Proceedings of the 1st International Conference on Learning Analytics and Knowledge* (LAK '11). ACM, New York, NY, USA, 122-126. DOI=http://dx.doi.org/10.1145/2090116.2090135.
7. E. J. M. Lauría, E. W. Moody, S. M. Jayaprakash, N. Jonnalagadda, and J.D. Baron. *Open academic analytics initiative: initial research findings.* In *Proceedings of the Third International Conference on Learning Analytics and Knowledge* (LAK '13), Dan Suthers, Katrien Verbert, Erik Duval, and Xavier Ochoa (Eds.). ACM, New York, NY, USA, 150-154. DOI=http://dx.doi.org/10.1145/2460296.2460325.
8. S.P. Karkhanis, S.S. Dumbre, *A Study of Application of Data Mining and Analytics in Education Domain* (International Journal of Computer Applications, 2015).

Emotion Analysis and Recognition of TAGLISHUANO Online Customer Reviews

Martin Stefanny I. Bucag and Larmie S. Feliscuzo

College of Computer Studies, Cebu Institute of Technology - University,
Cebu City, 6000 Philippines
larmie.feliscuzo@cit.edu
www.cit.edu

Consumer Reviews are increasingly important as they provide information that affect consumers' purchasing decisions and can strengthen or tarnish long-established brands. With the growing population of the internet community and the increasing number of sites that collect consumer reviews, it becomes difficult for the users, either consumers or entrepreneurs, to come up with a comprehensive view of opinions pertaining to the products of interest through manual analysis.

This study presents a hybrid approach, involving corpus-based technique and a variation of the Pointwise Mutual Information, to automatically extract semantics from informal text to produce an effective analysis of the huge volume of online consumer reviews. The resulting system is a web application based in R programming that accepts input texts that are written in either Tagalog, English, Cebuano or a combination of any of these languages. Consequently, the system recognizes Ekman's six basic emotions namely happiness, sadness, anger, disgust, surprise, and fear.

The accuracy of the resulting system was tested using 10,000 tweets that mention about two major internet providers in the country. The testing results are as follows: Happiness - 61%, Sadness - 55%, Anger - 68%, Disgust - 28%, surprise - 25%, and fear - 32%. This study further identifies that positive and negative emotions can coexists in some consumer reviews. Thus, this system proposes a more in-depth study of emotion detection that includes the extraction of keywords' tenses, relations with subject and the meaning through context.

Keywords: Emotion Analysis; Customer Review; Pointwise.

1. Introduction

Social media is one of the most dynamic developments that evolve after the Internet has been introduced. Today, online social networks have become important communication channels and have created a way of connecting people to variety of online communities. Social networking sites, such as Twitter and Facebook, provide a public platform for which people can express ideas, criticize products and exchange knowledge and beliefs. People that may never meet in the physical world but nevertheless are able to affect behaviors including purchasing decisions [1].

Online networking sites are good platform for consumers to gather information and advices. There are five domain factor identifies to explain online consumer behavior. Two of which are Consumer characteristics and Environmental influences. The first includes behavioral characteristics (looking for product information, access location, duration and frequency of usage) and experience. The latter includes social influence, peer influence and mass media, which play important roles in affecting consumers' purchasing decisions [2].

Everyday people buy things that are relevant to their needs. At the same time, they are making purchasing decisions. With the emergence and the extensive use of social networking sites, people's day-to-day decisions are affected by the information they acquire through the internet.

According to Forbes, reviews are a major factor for customers when making a final purchase decision. Research from BrightLocal has found that "73% of consumers say positive customer reviews make them trust a business more." Even more important, "79% of consumers trust online reviews as much as personal recommendations" [3].

In the Philippines, social networking is one of the most active web-based activities [4]. According to the Social, Digital & Mobile in APAC in 2014 report, the Philippines is one of the most social nations in the Asia Pacific region. The use of networking sites has become so extensive that the country has been tagged as "The Social Networking Capital of the World" [5]. A survey on more than one billion active users conducted by UM, a division of IPG Mediabrands, noted that Internet is indispensable to the Filipinos. They are very active in social media and make use of the Internet to satisfy one of core human needs of relationship that is sharing experiences and emotions [6].

With only 36% internet penetration, there is still a very wide room for further improvement that business can take advantage of. Internet penetration is expected to increase in rate up to 50% and thus expecting a larger number of users. Based on the information from Internet and Mobile Marketing Association of the Philippines (IMMAP), the earnings from advertising and ecommerce are also expected to grow to up to $179 million by the year 2016 [6]. The local businesses and entrepreneurs should take note of this growing trend towards the use of Internet for promoting their brands, products and services.

Thus, proper analysis of online consumer reviews not only provide valuable information to facilitate the purchase decisions of customers but also helps merchants to understand better the general responses of the customers for marketing campaign improvement.

With more than 40 million internet user and various social media sites, large data are produced. Thus, becoming difficult for the users to obtain a comprehensive view of opinions presented to them [7]. Consequently, it is essential and desirable to develop an efficient and effective system or technique capable of summarizing the sentiment and emotions of consumer reviews automatically.

2. Related Work

Human beings have a power to feel different kinds of emotions. Detecting emotions is a very complicated as emotions, basically, are complex. Detecting emotional state of a person by analyzing from what the person has written appear challenging but also essential. S. Shivhare and S. Khethawat emphasized that sufficient amount of work has been done regarding to speech and facial emotion recognition but text-based emotion recognition system still needs attraction of researchers [8].

The study in emotion detection started in finding the sentiment orientation. This is now called sentiment analysis and is used interchangeable with Emotion Detection. However, there is a minor difference between Sentiment Analysis and Emotion Detection. The first classifies the text into two binary state namely positive and negative. The latter uses a larger set of emotion for the division of text [9].

Pak and Paroubek proposed a solution by using distant supervision, in which their training data consisted of tweets with emoticons. They classified the tweets as objective, positive and negative. In order to collect a corpus of objective posts, they retrieved text messages from Twitter accounts of popular newspapers and magazine, such as "New York Times", "Washington Posts" etc. Their classifier is based on the multinomial Naïve Bayes classifier that uses N-gram and POS-tags as features [10].

Barbosa and team classified tweets as objective or subjective and then the subjective tweets were classified as positive or negative. The feature space used included features of tweets like retweet, hashtags, link, punctuation and exclamation marks in conjunction with features like prior polarity of words and POS of words [11].

Kumar A. and Sebastian T.M. had a study on extracting sentiment in Twitter using novel hybrid approach involving both corpus-based and dictionary-based techniques. Opinion words, combination of adjectives with the verbs and adverbs, were extracted from tweets. The corpus-based methods was used to find the semantic orientation of adjectives and the dictionary-based method to find semantic orientation of verbs and adverbs. During pre-processing phase,

URLs, hash tags, slangs and abbreviations. The overall tweet sentiment was then calculated using a linear equation which incorporated emotion intensifiers too [12].

J. Kaur and team presented a differential analysis to extract emotions from formal and informal text. Various machine learning based methods — Support Vector Machine (SVM), Naïve Bayes (NB), Decision Tree — are used to classify texts are presented in 7 International languages [13].

A great body of work exists in the field of sentiment analysis. The work done in this area includes distinguishing subjective portions in text, identifying the presence of sentiment, finding sentiment orientation and, in few cases, determining fine-grained distinctions in sentiment. Work exclusively on emotion detection is comparatively rare and lacks empirical evaluation.

S. Aman proposed a corpus-based unigram and syntactic bigram features together to provide a better combination for predicting the emotion intensity of sentences than the unigram representation alone. He performed a manual and automatic recognition of expressions based from Ekman's (1992) basic emotion categories — happiness, sadness, anger, disgust, surprise, and fear. The text under study comprises data collected from blogs, representing texts rich in emotion content and therefore suitable for this study [14].

While the works of Mihalcea and team focused on two particular emotions only, namely — happiness and sadness. They work on blog posts drawn from LiveJournal11, which are self-annotated by the blog writers with happy and sad mood labels. They perform linguistic analysis of the text in these blog posts to identify happy and sad words, phrases, and topics. They have derived happiness-factor scores for words in the corpus based on their relative frequency in happy posts. They also apply various semantic analysis techniques to identify the causes of happiness from the text. They perform temporal analysis by investigating the levels of happiness, as indicated by the linguistic indicators in text, at various times in a day and days in a week [15].

R. Burget and others used a Support Vector Machine (SVM) method with linear kernel to provide a description and evaluation of learning models of identification and classification of emotions in Czech news headlines. This work identified the presence of emotion (Anger, Disgust, Fear, Joy, Sadness, Surprise and no emotion) and classification according to the most dominant emotion present is analyzed. In case the level of resulting emotion strength did not exceed at least 20%, it was considered not to contain no emotion [16].

With the various studies reviewed, the study focused on detecting the emotions using Ekman's basic emotion category same with S. Aman and R. Burget.

3. Methodology

The problem that comes with emotion detection from text is that it is strongly dependent on the language it is written. The objective of this research is to be able to automatically recognize the dominant emotion from text that are in written in Taglishuano (Tagalog, English and Cebuano) because tweets from Cebuano or Tagalog users are written in combination of this languages. This study used a corpus-based approach to extract semantics from informal text in tweets. Figure 1 gives the architectural overview of the proposed system.

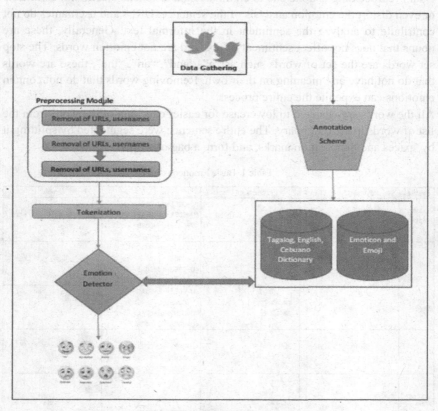

Figure 1. System Architectural Overview

The study started with harvesting of tweets to be considered as training sets. The tweets were manually tagged and the database for the emoticons and emojis are prepared together with the dictionary for the Taglishuano. Before the actual emotion is presented, a program to preprocess the tweets harvested using R programming to make it ready for the emotion detector module.

3.1. *Data Acquisition*

The study needs texts rich in emotion expression that is why tweets were gathered during an online furor in the Philippines last September 2015. It was due to a death of a college female student. The data are collected for a period of one week through a twitter API (applications programming interface).

3.2. *Preprocessing*

Data Preprocessing is done due to eliminate data or tokens that do not contribute or even distort the emotion analysis of the sentence. URLs and usernames do not contribute to analyze the sentiment in the informal text. Generally, these are nouns that does not affect sentiment of text and are not emotion words. The stop set words are the set of words such as "a", "and", "an", "the", these are words that do not have any meaning on their own. Removing words that do not contain emotions can expedite the entire process.

All the words are changed to lowercase for easier checking of the word from the list of words in the dictionary. The entire sentence were segmented by splitting it by spaces and punctuation marks, and form a bag of words.

Table 1. Basic Emoticons

Emotion	Keyboard Shortcut	emoticon	unicode	emoji
Happy	:) :-) ;) ;-) :D :P XD =-D =D =-3 =3 :-)) :-D :D 8-D 8D xd x-DxD		<U+00B8><U+00B2> <U+00B8><U+00A5> <U+00B8><U+008B> <U+00B8><U+0098>	
Sad	:(:[:-< ~:(>:[:-(:[:-c :c) :-< :< :-[:[:[:(		<U+00B8><U+00AD> <U+00B8><U+0094> <U+00B8><U+00A3> <U+00B8><U+00AB>	
Anger	>:( ]:[:-|| :@ >:(		<U+00B8><U+00A0> <U+00B8><U+0096> <U+00B1><U+008A> <U+00B8><U+00B3>	
Fear			<U+00B8><U+0093> <U+00B8><U+00B1> <U+00B8><U+00A8>	
Disgust	:/ :> :->		<U+00B8><U+008F>	
Surprise	:-o (@_@) (o_o) >:O :-O :O 8-0		<U+00B8><U+00AE> <U+00B8><U+00B0>	

3.3. *Annotation Scheme*

The primary goal behind the annotation task was to identify the emotional affinity of sentences. While most work in sentiment analysis focuses on document-level analysis, this research has focused on the sentence-level analysis for learning emotions in text. For each sentence or tweet, which is a maximum of 140 characters, the annotator is required to label the predominant emotion category in the sentence.

Research in automatic text-based emotion analysis is hampered by the unavailability of emotion-annotated data for written text. The previous works of sentiment analysis made use of existing English-based emotional lexicons, e.g., Subjectivity Wordlist, WordNet-Affect and SentiWordNet. This paper made use of WordNet-Affect for the English words. However, standardized an annotated corpora for Tagalog and Cebuano do not exist.

A. Andrei has developed a Tagalog Linguistic Inquiry and Word count (LIWC) positive and negative dictionaries based on the tweets during the Typhoon Yolanda. The researcher of this study has adopted the methodology used by Andrei since he successfully completed the dictionary. However, there were modifications as the goal of this task is to map the word into emotion category rather than just classifying as positive, negative and neutral [17].

The process of coming up with an emotion-annotated list of words in Tagalog and Cebuano are classified into three phases. The first phase is obtaining corpus of words from Twitter using specific hashtags - #PLDT, #suncellular. The second phase was verifying the translations. The list of words from the obtained corpus was through Google Translate for Filipino and then manually verified by heritage speakers with intermediate knowledge of the Tagalog and Cebuano languages. The third phase was classifying the words into emotion categories. The list of emoticons are specified in the Table 1.

3.4. *Sentiment Classification*

Given a large data set of emotion-annotated dictionary or corpus, it may seem straightforward to develop a model for emotion classification. However, it should be noted that there are sentence that may not involve any emotion. In such a case, the text should be classified as neutral.

Taking this instance into consideration, a two-step approach is used to classify the sentences. First, we categorize the input text into three sentiment polarity classes, either positive, negative or neutral. Second, the input is classified into fine-grained emotion classes.

There are additional advantages in this approach. First, it is generally known that performing fine-grained classification after coarse classification often provides good results particularly when the number of the classes is large. Second, in the context of dialog, a misunderstanding the user's emotion at the sentiment polarity level would be a disaster.

3.5. *Emotion Classification*

The goal of this step is find the dominant emotion of sentence by qualifying the semantic score of corpus-tagged words. If the sentence contain only one emoticon which matches in Table 1, then the sentence is that of emotion category. If in the sentence there is only one adjective, then the emotion annotation of the specific word is the emotion category of the sentence.

However, if the sentence contains a number of adjectives, then all the adjectives present must be considered. A variation of pointwise mutual information was adopted to measure the strength of the words.

The formula of POINTWISE MUTUAL INFORMATION

$$co\ (e.\ w) = c(e, w)^{*}\log\left(\frac{p(e, w)}{p(e) * p(w)}\right)$$

Where

$$P(e, w) = \frac{c(e, w)}{N}$$

$$P(e) = \frac{c(e)}{N}$$

$$P(w) = \frac{c(w)}{N}$$

$c(e)$ and $c(w)$ are the total occurrences of emoticon e and word w in a tagged corpus, respectively. $c(e, w)$ is total co-occurrences of e and w, and N denotes the total word occurrences. A word entry of a lexicon may contain several emotion senses.

Suppose a sentence S to be classified consists of n emotion words. The emotion of S is derived by a mapping from a set of n emotion words to m emotion categories as follows:

$$S \to \{ew1\ ,..., ewn\} \to \{c1\ ,..., cm\}$$

For each emotion word ewi, we may find several emotion senses. The steps to label a sentence S with an emotion are:

(1) Consider all senses of ewi as votes. Label S with the emotion that receives the most votes.

(2) If more than two emotions get the same number of votes, then label S with the emotion that has the maximum co.

For each adjective in the list, we calculate the score by retrieving the number of entries and the quintuple for each entry. In case of a single entry, the decision will be in favor of the emotion category with the highest score. In case of multiple entries of a term, such as different entries, we averaged the scores of each class over each entry in order to achieve some normalization. The above step will give us a quintuple for a term.

To determine the sentiment polarity of the entire comment we aggregate the score of all terms in the comment and the frequency of each class is counted. The final emotion class will be in favor of the class with the highest average among the emotion classes. The identification of emotion in TAGLISHUANO sentences is not a necessarily simple problem. To start, there is no existing emotion-annotated Tagalog and Cebuano dictionaries. The corpus used in this study are manually annotated.

We initially tested our approach to a sample set of 150 tweets containing 'PLDT' and 'suncellular' keywords. The annotators have manually checked the dominant emotion present in these sentences. Then, the file with the tweets was loaded to the system. The initial results are shown in Table 2. The accuracy of the individual classifier is measured by

$$accuracy = \frac{\text{\# of correctly labeled tweets}}{\text{\# of all the tweets in the test dataset}}$$

Table 2. Initial Testing Results

Emotion	Total # of Sentences	Correctly Identified	Accuracy (%)
Happy	15	5	33%
Sad	16	3	19%
Anger	47	13	29%
Disgust	1	0	0%
Surprise	0	0	0%
Fear	0	0	0%
No emotion	71	41	56%

Foreign researchers removed the emoticons during their preprocessing phase as they considered such as 'noise' in the texts. In the Philippines, 40% of the Internet market is comprised of 15-24 year olds who are fond of using emoticons and emojis in their online messages. With this information, the corpus is updated to consider these special characters as emotion intensifiers.

After updating the corpus, the same set of tweets used in the initial testing are re-evaluated. Table 3 shows tweets that do not contain emotion words but have emoticons or emojid.

Table 3. Sample Tweets and Emotion Classification

Tweets	First Testing	Second Testing
ung tsu? Hindi mga pldt plang kya ko :D	Neutral	Happy
12 days without internet is long enough :(:(	Neutral	Sad
PLDT!!! Anong klaseng internet yan!!! <ed><U+00A0><U+00BD><ed> <U+00B8><U+00A1>	Neutral	Anger

The third tweet shown in Table 3 includes emoji. In the actual tweet, it is presented as in Figure 2.

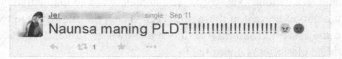

Figure 2. Sample Tweet: Emoji Present

After including emoticons and emotion-provoking emoji in the corpus, we have seen an improvement in the accuracy rate of most emotion classes. The updated testing result is shown in Table 4.

Table 4. Updated Testing Results (Emoticons considered)

Emotion	Total # of Sentences	Correctly Identified	Accuracy (%)
Happy	15	7	47%
Sad	16	3	28%
Anger	47	13	29%
Disgust	1	0	0%
Surprise	0	0	0%
Fear	0	0	0%
No emotion	71	41	61%

This result demonstrates that large training data can play an important role in emotion identification. Larger training data will lead to higher accuracy for emotion identification because it can provide a better comprehensive coverage of emotional moments in our daily lives.

During the final testing, we updated the corpus and dictionary to include more words. We also considered other possible spelling of the word. For example the word "*lagot*", can have different spellings such as *lgot* and *lagt*. We have seen improvements to the accuracy of the emotion detection. Since we used PLDT and suncellular tweets in testing, the dominant emotions are happy and anger. We, the, focused on these two emotions.

Table 5. Accuracy of the Emotions During Last Phase Testing

Emotion	24-Sept	28-Sept	29-Sept
Happy	53%	57%	60%
Anger	67%	37%	71%

From Table 5, results showed that the accuracy was increased after considering other possible spellings of words. Twitter users vary from different walks of life and it is very possible that incorrect spelling of the words exist.

4. Conclusion and Recommendation

Tweets contains a wealth of information and offers an unprecedented opportunity for researchers to create and employ theories that search and mine for sentiments and emotions. The work presented in this paper utilized a hybrid approach to classify sentiment and recognize emotions. The highest accuracy achieved was 71% with a training data containing more than 33,000 tweets.

This study has presented a higher accuracy rate for Happy and Anger emotion classes since the testing of the study focused on tweets discussing two of major internet providers in the country. However, the architecture proposed in this study is very flexible allowing it to be easily extended to classify other emotion classes by providing a reasonably-sized training set that covered required emotions.

As for future work, increasing the number of annotated words to increase number of tweets for less popular emotions especially disgust and surprise should be made. Other machine learning methods should also be employed to compare results.

Acknowledgments

Thank you for the support of our family and friends.

References

1. Evans M, Jamal A, Foxall G, (2009). Consumer Behaviour. 2nd ed. John Wiley & Sons Ltd.
2. Cheung Christy M.K., Lei Zhu, Timothy Kwong, Gloria W.W. Chan, Moez Limayem, (2003) Online Consumer Behavior: A Review and Agenda for Future Research, 16th Bled eCommerce Conference eTransformation.
3. Rampton, J. (2014). "5 Social Media Growth Hacks for Small Businesses" http://www.forbes.com/sites/johnrampton/2014/10/20/5-social-media-growth-hacks-for-small-businesses/. [accessed last July 18, 2015].
4. Goldstuck, A. (2015). "Philippines 'most social nation'". http://mg.co.za/article/2015-08-03-philippines-most-social-nation. [accessed last Sept 01, 2015].
5. Kemp, S. (2014). "Social, Digital & Mobile in APAC in 2014" http://wearesocial.net/blog/2014/01/social-digital-mobile-apac-2014/ [accessed July 10, 2015].
6. Gregorio, J. (2014). "10 Reasons Why Local Filipino Companies Should Use the Internet for Business Promotion? (Infographic)". http://digitalmarketingphilippines.com/10-reasons-why-local-filipino-companies-should-use-the-internet-for-business-promotion-infographic/. [accessed last October 21, 2016].
7. C. Yang and H. Shih. (2012). "A Rule-Based Approach For Effective Sentiment Analysis" in *Pacific Asia Conference on Information Systems (PACIS) at AIS Electronic Library (AISeL)*.
8. N. Shelke (2014). "Approaches of Emotion Detection from Text" in *International Journal of Computer* Science and Information Technology Research, pp. 123-128, April-June 2014.
9. S. Shivhare and S. Khethawat (2012). "Emotion Detection From Text", Department of CSE and IT, Maulana Azad National Institute of Technology, Bhopal, Madhya Pradesh, India.
10. A. Pak and P. Paroubek (2010). "Twitter as a Corpus for Sentiment Analysis and Opinion Mining". In Proceedings of the Seventh Conference on Language Resources and Evaluation, LREC 2010, 17-23 May 2010, Valletta, Malta.
11. L. Barbosa, J. Feng (2010). "Robust Sentiment Detection on Twitter from Biased and Noisy Data". COLING 2010: Poster Volume, pp. 36-44.
12. A. Kumar and T.M. Sebastian (2012). "Sentiment Analysis on Twitter". Department of Computer Engineering, Delhi Technological University. Delhi, India.

13. J. Kaur and J. Saini (2014). "Emotion Detection and Sentiment Analysis in Text Corpus: A Differential Study with Informal and Formal Writing Styles" in International Journal of Computer Applications, vol. 101, no. 9, Sept. 2014.

14. S. Aman (2007). "Recognizing Emotions in Text", MCS Thesis, University of Ottawa, School of Information Technology and Engineering.

15. Mihalcea, R. and Liu, H. (2006). A corpus-based approach to finding happiness, in the AAAI *Spring Symposium on Computational Approaches to Weblogs*, Stanford, California, USA.

16. R. Burget, J. Karásek and Z. Smékal (2011). "Recognition of emotions in Czech Newspaper Headlines", Dept. of Telecommunication, Brno University of Tech., Czech Republic. [accessed last October 21, 2016].

17. A. Andrei (2014). "Development and Evaluation of Tagalog Linguistic Inquiry and Word Count Dictionaries for Negative & Positive Emotion" https://www.researchgate.net/.../276917499_Developing_a_Tagalog_Linguistic_Inquiry [accessed last October 21, 2016].

Sentiment Analysis of Philippine National Elections 2016 Twitter Data

Turla, Zjan Carlo

Department of Computer Science, University of the Philippines Diliman
Quezon City 1101 Philippines
zdturla@up.edu.ph

Caro, Jaime

Department of Computer Science, University of the Philippines Diliman
Quezon City 1101 Philippines
jdlcaro@up.edu.ph

With the ubiquity of social media, news outlets have fancied reporting on the online reactions to recent events usually through simple aggregations such as number of posts. This study looks into the viability of different methods for mixed-language sentiment analysis, particularly for text extracted from Twitter, to expand the vocabulary of news reporting on social media analytics. Tweets covering the 2016 Philippine Presidential Elections were used for the training and test dataset.

Keywords: Social Media, Twitter, Sentiment Analysis.

1. Introduction

Social Networking Sites such as Twitter hold vast quantities of information that could be used to analyze the sentiment on a particular topic. Twitter, in particular, is notable for its almost stream-of-consciousness approach to blogging popularly known as microblogging. Such a format presents opportunities to study the sentiment on a particular topic.

This study will look into analyzing the sentiment of Twitter users on the 2016 Philippine Elections.

With the massive adoption of social media by the general populace and public acceptance of social media sites as fora of discourse and debate, mainstream news sites have taken to reporting on rudimentary statistical analyses of social media data. The accessibility of social media data, coupled with momentous events such as the Philippine National Elections, have ushered into an age of mainstream social media analysis news reporting.

This study will look into improving the analysis provided by mainstream news sites by providing a sentimental analysis classifier for Twitter Data that specializes in mixed-language tweets and is built for a particular topic.

2. Literature Review

For the purposes of this study, sentence level sentiment analysis[8] will be employed. As such, it might be beneficial to use subjectivity classification[9] to differentiate between objective and subjective sentences and identify which sentences are opinionated and carry a positive or negative opinion.

Bing Liu also described two types of opinions: regular opinions and comparative opinions.[8] Given that discussions in politics deal heavily in comparisons and criticisms, differentiation between the two types of opinions should prove useful.

These opinions could then be classified as having been evaluated from a rational viewpoint or an emotional viewpoint.[10]

These additional descriptors (subjective and objective, comparative and regular, emotional and rational) expand the way with which we could describe our data and could potentially help us improve our classifiers.

2.1. *Supervised Machine Learning Techniques for Sentiment Analysis*

For this study, we are focusing on two popular supervised machine learning techniques for text classification, Naive Bayes Classification and Support Vector Machines.

SVM and Naive Bayes Classifiers are popular due to their simplicity and ease of use but the trade-off is the necessity of a manually tagged training set and specificity of classifiers, classifiers trained on a specific topic may not work well on another topic. This is not a problem unique to these approaches but the reliance on a manually tagged training set brings the problem of Cross-Domain and Cross-Language Sentiment Classification to the fore.

2.2. *Using Sentiment Dictionaries for Sentiment Analysis*

Sentiment Analysis with Sentiment Dictionaries is usually performed using SentiWordNet. SentiWordNet expands on WordNet, which is a database of words organized according to their semantic relation to each other, by adding sentiment scores to the words contained within. These sentiment scores are positivity, negativity, and objectivity.[7]

2.3. *Mixed-Language Sentiment Analysis*

Previous studies regarding the use of Sentiment Analysis on Twitter Data in a Filipino context focused on natural calamitous events which the Philippines is prone to. Studies have also been made in analyzing Filipino blog comments as a marker of customer satisfaction.[2]

One of the differences brought about by the focus on a Filipino context is the presence of multiple languages. Most tweets analyzed are written in English or Filipino but there are occurrences of other regional languages. Sentiment dictionaries exist for English but currently no such reliable dictionaries are to be found for Filipino and the other languages primarily used in the Philippines.

Patacsil and Fernandez's work solved the issue by first translating all non-English text to English before analyzing the data.[2] The same problem, however, is not faced by classifiers such as a Naive Bayes classifier that primarily rely on a manually tagged training set. Classifiers that are affected by this problem are those that rely on sentiment dictionaries.

The focus on Election related tweets presents another problem. Classifiers usually work on a per-document level; in the context of Twitter, that would mean that sentimental analysis works on a per-tweet level. This presents problems for tweets that contain multiple subjects with differing sentiments attached to each, a problem that would be common in a topic such as elections where the subjects are often compared and contrasted.

2.4. *Social Media Analytics in Local Mainstream Media*

Mainstream media's analysis of social media leaves much to be desired. Much of the reported data are aggregated and analyzed merely on quantity and subjects mentioned. Some reports have included the particular topics (e.g. environment, industrialization, etc.) that tweets discuss. Sentiment analysis, on the other hand, has mostly been unnoticed and unused. The simple use of quantity in analyzing social media leaves this kind of reporting particularly vulnerable to simple manipulation of the sample.

2.5. *Our Approach*

We will be focusing our attention on the Multinomial Naive Bayes Classifier and the SVM Classifier. A manually tagged training set will be used to train the supervised machine learning classifiers.

3. Methodology

3.1. *Data Description*

Acquired data includes the post's text, user, date posted and Twitter specific information such as number of likes and retweets. Given the focus of this study, the languages present run the gamut from English, Filipino, to other languages in the Philippines.

3.2. *Data Acquisition and Pre-Processing*

The data used in this study was acquired by communicating with the Twitter API. Search queries relating to the 2016 Philippine Elections such as #halalan2016 were used.

The chosen topic to be analyzed presents further problems; we need to find a way to analyze Filipino tweets and capture multiple sentiments in a single sentence or tweet. We cannot simply ignore non-English tweets in our analysis. Other researches in applying sentiment analysis methods on a Filipino context[2] get around this problem by translating non-English words to English. Agarwal et al.[1] also translated non-English tweets for tagging and classification.

The collection of tweets are then converted into a matrix of token frequencies.

Throughout the different classification processes, we use supervised machine learning techniques, particularly Naive Bayes Classifiers and Support Vector Machines.

The data set for this study used 1500 manually tagged tweets randomly extracted from the database for training and testing.

3.3. *Subjectivity Classification*

Before analyzing the sentiment of a tweet, we are to determine whether a tweet is opinionated, that is whether it actually contains a positive or negative sentiment, this task is called subjectivity classification.[9] Note that objective sentences can still carry a positive, negative, or neutral connotation.

We compare performance between a Naive Bayes classifier and a Support Vector Machine and see their viability for subjectivity classification. Our manually tagged data set indicates whether a tweet is objective or subjective allowing us to use these supervised machine learning techniques.

3.4. *Identifying Comparative Tweets*

The same technique used for subjectivity classification is used for identifying between comparative and regular sentences.

We also propose an alternative method of identifying comparative tweets. A dictionary of terms is built containing common words in the relevant languages denoting comparisons. This dictionary is then combined with the list of relevant subjects, which in this case are the presidential candidates. Tweets are then searched for occurrences of these terms to determine whether a tweet is comparative or regular.

3.5. *Distinguishing Between Rational and Emotional Tweets*

Naive Bayes and Support Vector Machines are once again used to classify between Rational and Emotional tweets.

3.6. *Sentiment Analysis*

3.6.1. *Sentiment Analysis using Supervised Machine Learning Techniques*

For sentiment analysis, we use supervised machine learning techniques, particularly Naive Bayes and Support Vector Machines, on the manually tagged data set. For this task, we use scikit-learn's built-in Multinomial Naive Bayes function and Support Vector Machine function. We optimize the classifiers using scikit-learn's built-in Grid Search function. The Support Vector Machine classifier employs the "one-against-one" approach for multi-class classification.

3.6.2. *Improving the Classifier*

A simple modification was done to the classifier in hopes of increasing its accuracy. A simple list of hashtags with positive connotations (e.g. #Roxas2016, #Poe2016) was compiled. If a hashtag from this list is found on the text, the predicted sentiment from the classifier is ignored and a positive sentiment is assigned to the tweet.

3.7. *Analyzing Classification Results*

The following framework is presented for analyzing tweets based on their classification. This framework is based on previously defined terms:

subjectivity classification, regular and comparative tweets, emotional and rational viewpoints, and sentiment analysis.

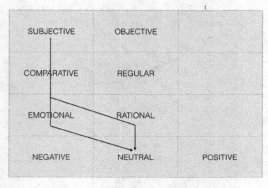

Indecision / Comparisons

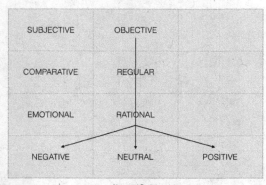

News and Quotes
Observations

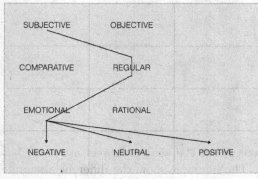

Rants / Anger   Emotional Indecisiveness   Support

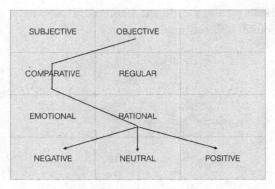

Rational Comparisons

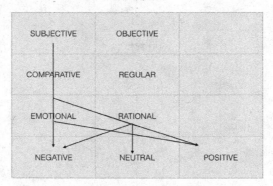

Comparative Sentences can contain a combination of all three sentiments

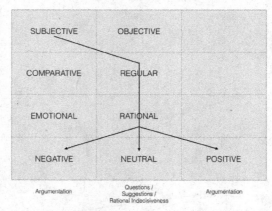

Generalizations about the analyzed tweet are made based on the classification given. The matrices show the different assumptions made with each combination.

4. Results and Analysis

Multinomial Naive Bayes and Support Vector Machines returned with almost exact performance with the SVM classifier inching out the Multinomial Naive Bayes in some classification tasks by a very small degree but not enough to call the advantage definitive.

MultinomialNB Classifier (Subjectivity Classification)

	precision	recall	f1-score
objective	0.50	0.16	0.24
subjective	0.92	0.98	0.95
average / total	0.88	0.91	0.88

Fig. 1.   Performance of Multinomial Naive Bayes Classifier on Sentiment Classification

SVM Classifier (Subjectivity Classification)

	precision	recall	f1-score
objective	1.00	0.16	0.27
subjective	0.92	1.00	0.96
average / total	0.93	0.92	0.89

Fig. 2.   Performance of SVM Classifier on Sentiment Classification

4.1. *Subjectivity Classification*

Performance from both Naive Bayes and SVM classifiers are lacklustre when it comes to Subjectivity Classification. Both display difficulty in properly classifying objective tweets though both rarely misclassify subjective tweets as objective.

MultinomialNB Classifier (Comparative Classification)

	precision	recall	f1-score
comparative	0.00	0.00	0.00
regular	0.97	1.00	0.98
average / total	0.93	0.97	0.95

Fig. 3.   Performance of Multinomial Naive Bayes Classifier on Comparative Classification

SVM Classifier (Comparative Classification)

	precision	recall	f1-score
comparative	0.00	0.00	0.00
regular	0.97	1.00	0.98
average / total	0.93	0.97	0.95

Fig. 4.   Performance of SVM Classifier on Comparative Classification

4.2. *Comparative Classification*

Both the Naive Bayes and SVM classifier fare poorly in classifying comparative tweets with both misclassifying all comparative tweets as regular.

MultinomialNB Classifier (Emotional Classification)

	precision	recall	f1-score
emotional	0.80	0.92	0.86
rational	0.43	0.22	0.29
average / total	0.72	0.76	0.73

Fig. 5.   Performance of Multinomial Naive Bayes Classifier on Emotional Classification

SVM Classifier (Emotional Classification)

	precision	recall	f1-score
emotional	0.81	0.94	0.87
rational	0.53	0.22	0.31
average / total	0.74	0.78	0.74

Fig. 6.   Performance of SVM Classifier on Emotional Classification

4.3. *Emotional Classification*

Classification between emotional and rational tweets displays generally better performance from the two classifiers. Both classifiers exhibit high precision with emotional tweets but often misclassify rational tweets as emotional but seldom misclassifying emotional tweets as rational.

MultinomialNB Classifier (Sentiment Classification)

	precision	recall	f1-score
negative	0.58	0.59	0.59
neutral	0.33	0.11	0.17
positive	0.64	0.79	0.70
average / total	0.56	0.60	0.57

Fig. 7.   Performance of Multinomial Naive Bayes Classifier on Sentiment Classification

SVM Classifier (Sentiment Classification)

	precision	recall	f1-score
negative	0.61	0.70	0.65
neutral	0.67	0.06	0.11
positive	0.62	0.75	0.68
average / total	0.62	0.61	0.57

Fig. 8. Performance of SVM Classifier on Sentiment Classification

4.4. Sentiment Classification

Both turn-in average results in classifying sentiment. SVM garners higher overall precision across the board over the three classification groups: negative, neutral, and positive. Upon analysis, it seems the SVM classifier less frequently misclassifies positive and negative tweets into the neutral category earning it a much higher precision when it comes to classifying neutral tweets.

4.5. Improving the Sentiment Classifier

Minimal improvement was observed (compare Fig. 1 to Fig. 9); the classifier exhibited a slightly decreased amount of confusion classifying between positive and neutral tweets.

MultinomialNB Classifier without Hashtag Analysis (Sentiment Classification)

	precision	recall	f1-score
negative	0.58	0.60	0.59
neutral	0.31	0.11	0.17
positive	0.64	0.78	0.70
average / total	0.56	0.60	0.57

Fig. 9. Performance of Multinomial Naive Bayes Classifier on Sentiment Classification without Hashtag Analysis

It might be the case that the features of positive and negative tweets for the collected sample are already highly distinct thus negating most of the benefits of the modification. Regardless, no decrease in performance is observed thus continued use of classification via simple identification of hashtags from a manually tagged list is suggested.

Further natural language processing techniques could be applied to the text to aid the supervised machine learning classifiers. So far, no natural language processing techniques are performed on non-hashtags tokens. Look-ups on sentiment dictionaries could help improve classification on predictions with low probability estimates.

4.6. *Sentiment Analysis of Tweet Subsets*

Words can change polarity depending on context, grouping tweets into subsets can provide the proper context for the classifier. The tweets are divided into subsets based on the framework presented. The Multinomial Naive Bayes classifier is then used to classify the tweets in the subsets.

4.6.1. *Results*

MultinomialNB Classifier (Sentiment Classification - Subjective Subset)

	precision	recall	f1-score
negative	0.67	0.6	0.63
neutral	0.29	0.03	0.05
positive	0.59	0.82	0.68
average / total	0.58	0.62	0.58

Fig. 10.   Performance of Multinomial Naive Bayes Classifier on Sentiment Classification of Subjective Tweets

MultinomialNB Classifier (Sentiment Classification - Objective Subset)

	precision	recall	f1-score
negative	0.0	0.0	0.0
neutral	0.9	0.9	0.9
positive	0.17	0.33	0.22
average / total	0.81	0.81	0.81

Fig. 11.   Performance of Multinomial Naive Bayes Classifier on Sentiment Classification of Objective Tweets

MultinomialNB Classifier (Sentiment Classification - Comparative Subset)

	precision	recall	f1-score
negative	0.43	0.38	0.4
neutral	0.0	0.0	0.0
positive	0.47	0.64	0.54
average / total	0.39	0.45	0.41

Fig. 12.   Performance of Multinomial Naive Bayes Classifier on Sentiment Classification of Comparative Tweets

MultinomialNB Classifier (Sentiment Classification - Regular Subset)

	precision	recall	f1-score
negative	0.66	0.64	0.65
neutral	0.4	0.13	0.19
positive	0.59	0.80	0.68
average / total	0.58	0.61	0.58

Fig. 13.   Performance of Multinomial Naive Bayes Classifier on Sentiment Classification of Regular Tweets

MultinomialNB Classifier (Sentiment Classification - Emotional Subset)

	precision	recall	f1-score
negative	0.65	0.67	0.66
neutral	0.0	0.0	0.0
positive	0.74	0.78	0.76
average / total	0.67	0.7	0.68

Fig. 14.   Performance of Multinomial Naive Bayes Classifier on Sentiment Classification of Emotional Tweets

MultinomialNB Classifier (Sentiment Classification - Rational Subset)

	precision	recall	f1-score
negative	0.14	0.07	0.09
neutral	0.67	0.64	0.65
positive	0.18	0.33	0.23
average / total	0.48	0.47	0.47

Fig. 15.   Performance of Multinomial Naive Bayes Classifier on Sentiment Classification of Rational Tweets

We note the marked improvement in classifier performance for the emotional and objective subsets.

5. Conclusion

A framework for classifying tweets via subjectivity, comparative value, emotionality, and sentimentality was presented. This framework can be used to expand the vocabulary of local news reporting on social media analytics.

Supervised machine learning techniques show promise in identifying the sentimental and emotional classification of tweets in our corpus gathered from the 2016 Philippine National Elections making it a viable option for quick mixed-language sentiment analysis. Improved performance could make it viable for mainstream news reporting and in-depth analysis of election trends or voter behavior.

Dividing the tweets into subsets before sentimental analysis also shows promise. However, a considerably larger data set is needed for this technique.

Future work may involve incorporating further natural language processing techniques particularly in the classification of comparative and regular tweets along with subject identification.

References

1. Agarwal, Apoorv, et al. "Sentiment analysis of twitter data." Proceedings of the Workshop on Languages in Social Media. Association for Computational Linguistics, 2011.

2. Frederick F. Patacsil, and Proceso L. Fernandez. "Blog Comments Sentence Level Sentiment Analysis for Estimating Filipino ISP Customer Satisfaction." International Conference Data Mining, Civil and Mechanical Engineering (ICDMCME'2015) Feb. 1-2, 2015 Bali (Indonesia).

3. Zelinna Cynthia Pablo, Nathaniel Oco, Ma. Divina Gracia Roldan, Charibeth Cheng & Rachel Edita Roxas. "Toward an enriched understanding of factors influencing Filipino behavior during elections through the analysis of Twitter data." Philippine Political Science Journal, 35:2, 203-224, DOI: 10.1080/01154451.2014.964794, 2014.

4. Theresa Wilson, Janyce Wiebe, and Paul Hoffmann. "Recognizing Contextual Polarity in Phrase-Level Sentiment Analysis." Proceedings of Human Language Technology Conference and Conference on Empirical Methods in Natural Language Processing (HLT/EMNLP), pages 347–354, Vancouver, October 2005.

5. Efthymios Kouloumpis, Theresa Wilson, and Johanna Moore. "Twitter Sentiment Analysis: The Good the Bad and the OMG!." Proceedings of the Fifth International AAAI Conference on Weblogs and Social Media.

6. Joachims, Thorsten. "Text categorization with support vector machines: Learning with many relevant features." European conference on machine learning. Springer Berlin Heidelberg, 1998.

7. Baccianella, Stefano, Andrea Esuli, and Fabrizio Sebastiani. "SentiWordNet 3.0: An Enhanced Lexical Resource for Sentiment Analysis and Opinion Mining." LREC. Vol. 10. 2010.

8. Liu, Bing. "Sentiment analysis and opinion mining." Synthesis lectures on human language technologies 5.1 (2012): 1-167.

9. Wiebe, Janyce M., Rebecca F. Bruce, and Thomas P. O'Hara. "Development and use of a gold-standard data set for subjectivity classifications." Proceedings of the 37th annual meeting of the Association for Computational Linguistics on Computational Linguistics. Association for Computational Linguistics, 1999.
10. Chaudhuri, Arjun. Emotion and reason in consumer behavior. Routledge, 2006.
11. Troussas, Christos, et al. "Sentiment analysis of Facebook statuses using Naive Bayes classifier for language learning." Information, Intelligence, Systems and Applications (IISA), 2013 Fourth International Conference on. IEEE, 2013.

Designing a Context-Based English Synonym Database

Jannie Marie C. Baclayon and Robert R. Roxas

Department of Computer Science, University of the Philippines Cebu,
Gorordo Ave., Lahug, Cebu City, 6000, Philippines
E-mail: jcbaclayon@up.edu.ph and robert.roxas@up.edu.ph
http://upcebu.edu.ph/

This paper presents a context-based synonym database that could aid human or machine to find the appropriate synonyms of words based on their use in the sentence. The database is similar to WordNet in structure with additional fields for important information like: the number of syllables, pronunciation of the last syllable, and possible context words. The data are stored in a relational database which can be accessed via SQLite and Java. Manual evaluation showed that the database was able to return correct synonyms with a 79.81% average accuracy.

Keywords: Context-based; synonym database; context words; rhyming tool.

1. Introduction

Poetry has always been a part of the culture and history of any country. It is a bridge between ourselves and the poet and between ourselves and others. It speaks so often of our common human condition and experiences[1]. Poetry makes use of language that conveys emotion and meaning in a way different from ordinary prose. It uses devices such as rhyme, repetition, imagery, and word association to achieve musical and extraordinary effects.

One of the devices being explored in this study is the rhyme. Rhyme represents the correspondence of final sounds of words, starting with the rightmost stressed vowel. Hence two words rhyme if their final stressed vowels and all following phonemes are identical[2]. Rhythm in poetry has always been prevalent for a long time. The earliest poets used strict figurative expression and formal organization such as those of parallelism, meter, rhyme, and alliteration[3]. Rhyme schemes as a mnemonic device also helps them memorize and recite long poems[4].

G.D. Birkhoff measured the beauty of a poem based solely on phonemic features, such as alliterations and assonance, rhymes, and musical vowels[5]. Many poems, however, often have no definite rhyme scheme and meter constraints at all. Although creativity is still valued, having a rhyme scheme adds interest to the reader or listener, whether young or old. Children thrive on the rhythm of a word or the flow of a stanza first, before understanding the poem later[1].

In an attempt to edit and add rhyme to poems, there is a need to consult a dictionary and thesaurus to determine the proper words to add in the poem. These tools, however, also have their limitations. One of the existing and recurrent problems in almost all languages is the problem of word sense disambiguation (WSD). WSD is defined as the task of automatically assigning the most appropriate meaning to a an ambiguous word within a given context[6]. Many words can be expressed in a different meaning. This is called polysemy. Traditional approaches to WSD rest on the assumption that there exists a single, unambiguous communicative intention underlying every word in a document[7]. In other words, the correct sense of a polysemous word can be selected based on the context where it occurs. Through this context, the proper synonyms of a certain word can be found.

2. Review of Related Literature

An instrument by Ciobanu and Dinu[8] can provide rhyming words for a given input word and offers other features as well, such as detection of words without rhymes and clustering words based on syllable number. Such instrument made use of syllable counters and provided syllabification based on pronunciation using knowledge about stressed vowels and syllabification. But their instrument did not care about the semantics. We cannot just replace a word at the end of the line with any word that can rhyme with the previous or succeeding line without considering the meaning of the word that will replace a non-rhyming word. It is because it will definitely change the original meaning as intended by the poet if the rhyming word has a different meaning than the non-rhyming word to be replaced.

One problem that needs to be addressed here is the WSD problem. It is a difficult task, and despite the fact that it has been the focus of much research over the years, state-of-the-art systems are still often not good enough for real-world applications[9]. To address the disambiguation problem, some database depended only on the familiar meaning and a frequency rating, which was based on a sense-annotated version of some corpus. This method deemed to be not feasible since a word may have a big frequency rating at the time of writing, but in the next years it may change.

Ghazvininejad and Knight's study[10] produced a tool for rhyming pairs, whose phonemes were only identical from the last stressed syllable onward. Its discards the consonant preceding the nucleus of the last syllable, which could be a great factor in producing a good rhyme. Their tool generated rhyming pairs like "notified" and "nationwide" which were similar because they recorded the phoneme $AY\ D$ only. One improvement would be to include the consonant before the nucleus as basis for determining rhymes for polysyllabic words. An example of this would be that the rhyming word for "notified" must be "petrified," and not "nationwide."

This study presents a database that contains important fields for syllabification based on pronunciation and stress as well as the pronunciation of the last syllable to determine rhymes. Instead of asking for a word, this study asks the user for an input phrase or sentence to determine in which context a word was used so that it could retrieve synonyms that also rhyme with the headword. This study proposes a solution of using collocations as basis for context words to determine the appropriate sense of a word. Collocations are easy to be familiar with and are often placed together in a given context. Using context words to disambiguate a polysemous word would be an easier way to determine the sense of a word.

3. Methodology

To create the database, this work made use of existing dictionaries and added extra features which were helpful in finding the correct synonyms and rhyming the lines of a poem, such as 1) syllable count of a word useful if we maintain the meter of the line, 2) pronunciation of the last syllable of the word useful for determining rhyming pairs, and 3) possible context words for a word which can have multiple meanings. This study used natural language processing tools to come up with the improvised synonym database.

3.1. *Implementation*

This study made use of two Java programs to perform different tasks. The first Java program served as the user interface to be able to add entries into the database. The second Java program served as the tool to query the database and read input from a text file that contained random lines of poems. This program performed the preprocessing part first then produced an output file. From the input file, it parsed each phrase, and retrieved the last word of the phrase. The program will query the WORDS, SENSES, and SYNONYMS table for the synonyms of the last word. Finally, the program will replace the last word of each line with its synonym and write them into a separate file.

3.2. *Database*

The structural design of the database was modeled from WordNet's[a] database since it is free and readily accessible. The database contained nouns, verbs, and adjectives grouped into sets of synonyms, which made it an ideal basis for the synonym database. The synonym database followed the same word-sense relationship in WordNet. It consisted of the WORDS, SENSES, and SYNONYMS table. The WORDS table consisted of 4 fields `word_id`, `word`, `last_syllable` (pronunciation of the word's last syllable only), and `num_syllables` (number of syllables). The SENSES table housed all the definitions and the context words. Each row in the SENSES table contained a `sense_id`, a `definition`, and `context_words`. The definitions were taken from Merriam-Webster online dictionary[b]. What connected the two tables was the SYNONYMS table. The SYNONYMS table contained a unique `synonym_id`, a `sense_id`, and a `word_id`. The entries in the SYNONYMS table were referred to as "word-sense pairs" because each pairing of a `word_id` with a `sense_id` was one complete meaning or "sense" of a word. Therefore, the words which had the same meaning were grouped together by having its `word_id`'s mapped to the same `sense_id`. SQLite was used to store the synonym database and Java was used to add, edit, and delete entries in the database.

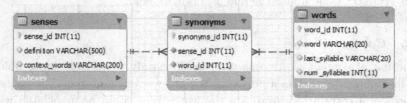

Fig. 1.   Entity relationship diagram.

Figure 1 shows the entity relationship diagram of the synonym database which was modeled after the word-sense relationship of WordNet's database.

---

[a] https://wordnet.princeton.edu/
[b] www.m-w.com/cgi-bin/dictionary

3.3. *Rhyme*

Ghazvininejad and Knight[10] made use of the CMU[c] pronunciation dictionary to determine whether a pair of words rhymed. A pair of words rhymed if their last stressed syllable's phonemes are identical. The dictionary used 39 phonemes, which were based on the ARPAbet[d] symbol set developed for speech recognition and was the standard for English pronunciation. It output the phoneme sequence of a word and its stress pattern through the use of the digits 0, 1, and 2 as stress indicators: zero for no stress, 1 for primary stress, and 2 for secondary stress. For polysyllabic words, only the phoneme of the last syllable was added to the database to determine rhymes. The consonant preceding the stressed vowel of the last syllable was included to ensure that rhyming pairs strictly have the same last syllable. For monosyllabic words, however, the phoneme starting only with the last stressed vowel onward was recorded.

3.4. *Syllable Count*

The CMU Pronunciation Dictionary was also used to count the number of syllables in a word. Although the dictionary did not include in its data the exact number of syllables in a word, this work made use of a simple Java function to count the number of stress indicators contained in a word's stress pattern to serve as the syllable count. The stress indicators were placed after a syllabic vowel, and each stressed syllabic vowel would count as one syllable. The word's syllable count was automatically inserted into the WORDS table under the `num_syllables` field.

3.5. *Context Words*

The use of context words was used in this study to address the problem of disambiguation when a polysemous word was encountered. The context words of a certain headword are the words that could be associated with the headword based on a given context. For example, the noun *"bank"* could have 2 senses: a financial institution and a place by a river or canal. The context words for the first sense of *"bank"* would be *"money," "cash," "deposit,"* and *"account."* The context words for the second sense of *"bank"* would be *"river," "water,"* and *"along."* The context words were placed

---

[c]http://www.speech.cs.cmu.edu/cgi-bin/cmudict
[d]https://en.wikipedia.org/wiki/Arpabet

in the SENSES table which were mapped to a word in the WORDS table through the SYNONYMS table.

This study made use of collocations to serve as a guide only to determine the context words for some polysemous words. In corpus linguistics, a collocation is a sequence of words or terms that are placed together in a predictable pattern [11] and are often used together in a given context. Examples of collocations are "*crystal clear*" and "*wishing well*." Some collocations used in this study were taken from the Online OXFORD Collocation Dictionary[e]. The dictionary contained over 150,000 collocations for nearly 9,000 headwords and was based on 100 million word British National Corpus.

3.6. *Adding Entries to the Database*

The website Just English[f] was browsed for synonyms of 96 common English words to be manually inserted in the database. Some synonyms were also taken from Merriam-Webster Dictionary and Thesaurus[g]. To access the database, a Java program was implemented to serve as the user interface for manipulating the data. Only an authorized user would be able to access the database. The program would let the user fill out a form for the corresponding fields in the WORDS, SENSES, and SYNONYMS table. The user would fill out a word, its last syllable (taken from CMU Pronunciation Dictionary), its definition, and its possible context words. Upon saving, the program would be the one to map the word and definition in the SYNONYMS table. The program could also let the user delete, edit, and view each entry in the database.

3.7. *Synonymity*

To retrieve the synonyms of a word given an input phrase, this study made use of another Java program to do the file handling and querying of the database. Given the input phrase, only the last word would be retrieved by the Java program. First, the WORDS table would be queried for the `word_id` of the word. Next, the SYNONYMS table would be queried for the `word_id` with its corresponding `sense_id`. If it returned more than 1 row, which means that the word has more than one sense, the program

---

[e]http://oxforddictionary.so8848.com/

[f]http://justenglish.me/2014/04/18/synonyms-for-the-96-most-commonly-used-words-in-english/

[g]http://www.merriam-webster.com/thesaurus

would check the `context_words` field in the SENSES table to check whether or not the input sentence contained one or two of the context words and would return the appropriate `sense_id`. But if it only returned 1 row as a result, meaning the word only had one meaning, the program would proceed directly to query the SYNONYMS table, check for the `word_id` and its `sense_id`, then return all `word_ids` that shared the same `sense_id` with the headword. The program would retrieve the synonym and edit the original phrase, substituting its original last word by its synonym. The program will then display the output in a separate file.

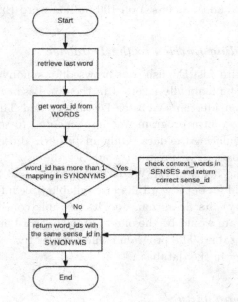

Fig. 2.   The flow chart for retrieving synonyms by the Java program.

Figure 2 shows the flow chart of how the Java program would query the synonym database given an input phrase or sentence and return the correct synonyms through the use of context words to disambiguate.

4. Evaluation

A manual evaluation was conducted in this study to measure the accuracy of the database in retrieving the correct synonyms. The output file was divided into six equal sections to be evaluated by different persons. Six respondents were asked to manually give a score for each output depending on how semantically related it is with the input. They were asked to give a score between 0.0 to 1.0 as to how likely they would substitute that output sentence with the input sentence without changing the meaning, with 1.0 being the most likely.

As for the demographics of the respondents, five of them were BS in Computer Science students and one of them was a BA in Communication graduate. The six respondents were composed of four females and two males. As for their qualifications, their inclination and love for poetry and writing were the basis for choosing them. Only six respondents were asked to give their scores because this was just an initial test considering that the synonym database had limited entries yet.

Figure 3 shows an example of the output and the ratings given by the respondents. The first line in the group of sentences is the input, that is, line without a score. The other lines are the options presented by the system, which were rated by the respondents. Their scores are shown at the end of every option presented by the system.

5. Results and Discussions

The data gathered from *justenglish*[h] and Merriam-Websters yielded 501 entries into the WORDS table of the database. Some synonyms from *justenglish* were vague so the Merriam-Websters online thesaurus was consulted to find more synonyms. The database was able to disambiguate more than 10 polysemous words in the English vocabulary by using context words. The relationship between the three tables in the database was easy to trace because the words and senses were mapped in a single table. The `definition` column of the SENSE table proved to have no definite purpose yet in the program as of this time. It just served as a reference to make the database look like a dictionary.

Results from the manual evaluation showed that the average accuracy of the returned synonyms was 79.81%. This was satisfactory since the database was able to reach an almost 80% accuracy for the correct synonyms returned. Six persons were asked to manually score each output phrase from 0 to 1, then the average of all the scores was computed, and then multiplied by 100 to get the percentage. The probability of getting a 100% accuracy was low since there were a number of phrases that got a score of 0.5 and below. Another reason was that some words had similar meanings,

---

[h]http://justenglish.me/2014/04/18/synonyms-for-the-96-most-commonly-used-words-in-english/

Test Sentence and Output Sentences	Scores
And the sadness I didn't mean to start	
And the sadness I didn't mean to begin -	0.7
And the sadness I didn't mean to open -	0.5
And the sadness I didn't mean to launch -	0.5
And the sadness I didn't mean to initiate -	0.7
And the sadness I didn't mean to commence -	0.5
And the sadness I didn't mean to originate -	0.5
And the sadness I didn't mean to form -	0.5
And the sadness I didn't mean to establish -	0.5
And the sadness I didn't mean to set up -	0.5
I tried to think	
I tried to conceive -	1.0
I tried to consider -	0.9
I tried to feel -	0.3
I tried to reckon -	0.3
I tried to suppose -	0.7
I tried to believe -	0.7
I came up twice and cried	
I came up twice and bawled -	1.0
I came up twice and sobbed -	1.0
I came up twice and weeped -	1.0
If that water hadn't a-been so cold	
If that water hadn't a-been so chilly -	1.0
If that water hadn't a-been so freezing -	0.5
If that water hadn't a-been so frigid -	0.5
If that water hadn't a-been so icy -	1.0
If that water hadn't a-been so numbing -	0.5
If that water hadn't a-been so wintry -	0.3
Someone who will not condemn or judge	
Someone who will not condemn or decide -	1.0
Someone who will not condemn or determine -	1.0
Someone who will not condemn or settle -	0.9
Someone who will not condemn or deliberate -	1.0

Fig. 3. Scores given by the respondents.

but when used in a poetic sense, it became confusing and sounded weird. Moreover, there could only be at most 3 words which were appropriate to replace the last word, which meant that some words could have lower scores than the others. Also, different people were asked to manually score and each person had different preferences over words, which makes the results lower than expected.

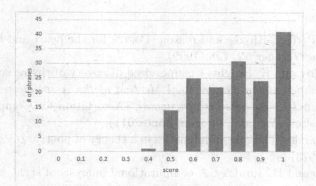

Fig. 4.   Comparison of scores.

Figure 4 shows a visual representation of the number of phrases given a corresponding score. The figure shows that almost all of the returned phrases yielded a score above the 0.5 threshold. Most of the scores given to each phrase ranged between 0.4 to 1.0, which showed that a great number of phrases were not given a perfect score. The distribution of the scores of each phrase was varied which was the reason why a 100% accuracy could not be achieved. The number of phrases that were given a score of 0.6 to 0.9 were almost the same so the average accuracy stayed near 80%. Still, the result was satisfactory since there were no phrases that were given a score below 0.4.

6. Conclusions and Future Works

The study on designing a context-based English synonym database was presented. The results showed that the database, given a line from a poem, could produce the correct synonyms based on context. The additional fields in the database, like the last syllable pronunciation and the syllable count, could help in retrieving the rhymes of a word while sticking to a meter constraint as well. The use of collocations as basis for context words was a good choice since collocations are words that always appear together given a context. This greatly minimizes the problem of disambiguating polysemous words given a context.

The database still has limitations that should be improved. The accuracy of the database could be improved by searching for more words which are commonly used in poetry, not just in prose. The system also needs to filled with more entries, and eventually more respondents should be asked to test the accuracy of the system.

References

1. K. A. Perfect, Rhyme and reason: Poetry for the heart and head, *The Reading Teacher* **52**, 728 (1999).
2. S. Reddy and K. Knight, Unsupervised discovery of rhyme schemes, in *Proceedings of the 49th Annual Meeting of the Association for Computational Linguistics: (shortpapers)*, (Association for Computational Linguistics, Portland, Oregon, June 2011).
3. P. Kiparsky, The role of linguistics in a theory of poetry, *Daedalus* **102**, 231 (1973).
4. J. Kao and D. Jurafsky, A computational analysis of style, affect, and imagery in contemporary poetry *Proceedings of the Workshop on Computational Linguistics for Literature* (Association for Computational Linguistics, Montréal, Canada, June 2012).
5. I. Peterson, A measure of beauty https://www.sciencenews.org/article/measure-beauty/ (May, 2004), [Online; accessed 24-October-2015].
6. R. Mihalcea, Using wikipedia for automatic word sense disambiguation, in *Proceedings of NAACL HLT 2007*, (Association for Computational Linguistics, Rochester, NY, April 2007).
7. T. Miller and I. Gurevych, Automatic disambiguation of english puns, in *Proceedings of the 53rd Annual Meeting of the Association for Computational Linguistics and the 7th International Joint Conference on Natural Language Processing*, (Association for Computational Linguistics, Beijing, China, July 2015).
8. A. M. Ciobanu and L. P. Dinu, On the romanian rhyme detection, in *Proceedings of COLING 2012: Demonstration Papers*, (Association for Computational Linguistics, Mumbai, Dec. 2012).
9. L. Li, B. Roth and C. Sporleder, Topic models forword sense disambiguation and token-based idiom detection, in *Proceedings of the 48th Annual Meeting of the Association for Computational Linguistics*, (Association for Computational Linguistics, Uppsala, Sweden, July 2010).
10. M. Ghazvininejad and K. Knight, How to memorize a random 60-bit string, in *Human Language Technologies: The 2015 Annual Conference of the North American Chapter of the ACL*, (Association for Computational Linguistics, Denver, Colorado, June 2015).
11. J. Conzett, *Teaching Collocation: Further Developments in the Lexical Approach* (Thomson Heinle Language Teaching, 2000).

A Study on Self-Organizing Maps and K-Means Clustering on a Music Genre Dataset

A. Azcarraga and F. K. Flores

Computer Technology, De La Salle University,
Manila, NCR, Philippines
arnie.azcarraga@delasalle.ph and fritz.flores@dlsu.edu.ph
www.dlsu.edu.ph

Understanding the relationship of the different music genres have been a research pursued by many. A common approach for it is through clustering. Data within a cluster are more closely related to each other as opposed to data on other clusters. Through the use of SOM, clustering could be easily represented since SOM force clustering on a 2 dimensional plane, however the drawback to this is that SOM take a lot of time to calculate and learn. Another method to cluster is through the use of K-Means, which is computationally much faster than SOM, however more than 3 clusters would make the K-Means a little bit harder to visualize in terms of plotting them due the fact that the K also represents the number of dimensions. Though some studies have already provided means to handle visualization of multi-cluster or multi-dimensional planes, a table is usually still used to determine their relationships. This study focuses on understanding the difference of SOM and K-Means as well as to try to implement in determining the relationships of music genres.

Keywords: Self-Organizing Maps, K-Means Clustering, Music Genre, Classification.

1. Introduction

In the field of Neural Networks, computer learning is subdivided into mainly two methods; supervised learning and unsupervised learning. In supervised learning, the information fed to the algorithm or program must have a corresponding label in order to allow the program to determine if the learning value is correct or not through a resulting value or error. The other mode of learning is unsupervised learning, where a dataset would be fed to a computer and the computer would output a form of clustering, showign the relationship of the data contained in the dataset.

An example of clustering through unsupervised learning is Self-Organizing Maps, which is a method of clustering created by Professor Kohonen. This method of unsupervised learning creates a topographical map, containing relationships between the data connected to it. Whereas clusters that are closely related with each other are more related as opposed to clusters that are far away. SOMs also represent clustering, usually though a labeled 2 dimensional plane.

Another form of clustering through unsupervised learning is through the use of K-Means. This is a type of clustering where the number of clusters is given to the discretion of the user. It must be noted however that there is an optimal number of clusters. However each cluster would allow an understanding based on the relationship of each of the node in the cluster.

The drawback of using K-Means is that, even though the program is simple, unlike SOM, K-Means typically is harder to visualize with more than 3 clusters. However there are already mathematical techniques in place that would allow visualization of multi-dimensional planes from K-Means. The study would focus of implementing SOMs and K-Means as well as to check their differences and how each one is to be used and applied.

For this study, the Music Genre Dataset would be used. This is a dataset that comes from the 3D SOM research by Sean Manalili and Prof. Arnulfo Azcàrraga. The dataset contains 69 music features from 1000 music files. The 1000 music files are subdivided based on their categories; which are blues, classical, country, disco, hiphop, jazz, metal, pop, reggae, and rock. Each genre contains 100 different music files. Music Miner and jAudio were used to extract features such as MFCC, Spectral Centroid, Spectral Flux, and others from these music files.

2. K-Means Clustering

2.1. *Introduction*

The process of K-Means Clustering is different from SOM in a way that K-Means are represented by K-Dimensions as opposed to SOM, which is typically represented as a 2D format. However, one thing to take note is that to run SOM, it is much longer for the values to be trained and learned one by one as opposed to do clustering by K-Means.

There are also multiple programs that readily provide a method to do K-Means, one of which is RapidMiner. For this study, the implementation of K-Means that was used, was that of RapidMiner's. This is mainly because for SOM, most libraries are much harder to modify, and there are very few implementations of SOM, which are openly available, but since there have already been so many implementations of SOM, not all are open or widely used as opposed to the algorithm used by K-Means.

The algorithm of K-Means focuses on either selecting a random or predefined point in a K-sized dimensional space. For each iteration, each of the nodes is to be dragged closer to the nearest cluster centroid until such a time that there is a more defined separation between each cluster. This in turn determined on which cluster a node is group into.

2.2. Music Genre Dataset

Table 1. Cluster Distribution using K-Means for the Music Dataset with 2 Clusters and 4 Clusters

Genre	C0	C1	Genre	C0	C1	C2	C3
Blues	3.04%	16.77%	Blues	3.88%	20.73%	2.50%	4.05%
Classical	0.81%	18.93%	Classical	0.49%	2.89%	1.67%	48.55%
Country	1.01%	18.74%	Country	0.00%	22.31%	0.00%	8.67%
Disco	14.60%	5.52%	Disco	16.99%	5.25%	15.00%	5.20%
Hiphop	19.07%	1.18%	Hiphop	33.98%	5.25%	4.17%	0.00%
Jazz	1.83%	17.95%	Jazz	1.94%	15.49%	0.83%	20.23%
Metal	17.44%	2.76%	Metal	2.91%	3.94%	31.67%	1.73%
Pop	14.40%	5.72%	Pop	9.71%	7.61%	16.25%	6.94%
Reggae	15.42%	4.73%	Reggae	28.64%	9.97%	1.25%	0.00%
Rock	12.37%	7.69%	Rock	1.46%	6.56%	26.67%	4.62%
	K-Means with 2 Clusters			K-Means with 4 Clusters			

For the first implementation of the K-Means a K = 2 is used. This would mean that the dataset is subdivided into 2 clusters. Based on the output, it can be observed that more or less the total amount of samples per cluster is quite even on about 500 for each cluster. Upon closer examination of the Music Genres that were classified, Disco, Hiphop, Metal, Pop, Reggae, and Rock mostly belong to Cluster-0 while Blues, Classical, Country, and Jazz, as well as a few from the other genres are part of Cluster-1. Through a slight observation, it is seen that the Music Genres on Cluster-0 are more on the noisy or beaty music while those on Cluster 1 are more on the soothing and gradually changing types of music.

For the second implementation of the K-Means, a K = 4 value is used. This is done in order to determine the possible clustering of the music genres when there are to be 4 clusters. Based on the results of the clustering, C0 contains high amounts of Hiphop and Reggae with a little bit of Disco and Pop, C1 contains Blues, Country, and Jazz. For C2, Metal and Rock are generally the highest on these values. However there are small traces of Disco and Pop, lastly for C3 it is mostly populated with Classical and a little bit of Jazz.

It may be observed from C0 that the music genres on that cluster are more on beaty types of music. The genres on C1 may be understood as the more of the types of music that has emphasis on the music being played as well as the emotion being depicted by the music. For C2 the relationship of Rock, Metal, and a bit of Pop and Disco continues to show the wilder and more noisy types of genres. The last cluster, C3 focuses on the soothing instrumental music of

Classical genre and a little bit of Jazz. It may already be observable from the past two tests, that which each different number of clusters used for K-Means, each cluster would still have a corresponding relationship or connection with that of their data, regardless of those data, having a different label.

Table 2. Cluster Distribution using K-Means for the Music Dataset with 6 Clusters

Genre	C0	C1	C2	C3	C4	C5
Blues	1.95%	7.21%	2.90%	4.17%	21.97%	3.57%
Classical	1.95%	1.80%	0.72%	54.17%	4.34%	0.00%
Country	0.49%	0.00%	0.00%	8.33%	25.14%	0.00%
Disco	6.83%	7.21%	6.52%	4.17%	4.62%	83.93%
Hiphop	2.44%	27.93%	35.51%	0.00%	3.47%	5.36%
Jazz	0.98%	5.41%	2.17%	13.89%	19.65%	1.79%
Metal	37.07%	3.60%	5.07%	2.08%	2.89%	0.00%
Pop	13.66%	4.50%	28.26%	7.64%	4.91%	0.00%
Reggae	0.98%	39.64%	18.12%	0.00%	7.80%	3.57%
Rock	33.66%	2.70%	0.72%	5.56%	5.20%	1.79%

For the third implementation, where K = 6, it is initially observable that some clusters have a higher count as compared to others. For instance C4, which is the group that contains the Blues, Country, and Jazz, has a significantly high number as opposed to the C5, which is dominated by Disco music. It may also be observed that the C4 has a similar set of genres with the C1 of the second implementation of K-Means of the study where K = 4, as well as this implementation of C0 and the previous one's C2. It may already be inferred from here that there is a similarity in the relationship between those two fields even with such a small value for K. The other clusters such as C1, which is similar to the C0 of the previous implementation, also shows that Hiphop music has a similarity with Reggae music. C5 is also dominated by Disco music as well as C3 is dominated by classical music.

Table 3. Cluster Distribution using K-Means for the Music Dataset with 8 Clusters

Genre	C0	C1	C2	C3	C4	C5	C6	C7
Blues	3.68%	2.25%	2.27%	3.98%	31.34%	1.53%	2.15%	11.40%
Classical	2.21%	65.17%	0.00%	0.57%	1.84%	0.76%	18.28%	14.04%
Country	3.68%	6.74%	0.00%	0.00%	29.03%	0.00%	15.05%	10.53%
Disco	11.76%	5.62%	88.64%	9.66%	1.38%	6.11%	8.60%	3.51%
Hiphop	9.56%	0.00%	4.55%	36.93%	5.07%	3.82%	1.08%	2.63%
Jazz	6.62%	7.87%	0.00%	0.57%	11.52%	0.00%	49.46%	10.53%
Metal	17.65%	3.37%	0.00%	3.98%	0.92%	41.22%	0.00%	8.77%
Pop	19.85%	3.37%	0.00%	9.66%	5.53%	14.50%	0.00%	19.30%
Reggae	11.03%	0.00%	2.27%	32.95%	9.22%	0.76%	2.15%	2.63%
Rock	13.97%	5.62%	2.27%	1.70%	4.15%	31.30%	3.23%	16.67%

The fourth implementation now considers using K = 8 in order to determine the other possible clustering relations of the dataset. C1 determines a highly Classical cluster, same with C2 which determines a Disco based cluster, C3 continues to be a cluster of Hiphop and Reggae. For the cluster of C4, initially the related genres of Blues, Country, and Jazz is now changed in this implementation. This is because for C4, the amount of Jazz has decreased, and now Jazz has its own cluster on C6. C5 continues to be the cluster of Metal and Rock, however C7 is a combination of various genres. Perhaps it could be inferred that in this case, the music on the C7 cluster are the hybrid music.

Table 4. Cluster Distribution using K-Means for the Music Dataset with 10 Clusters

Genre	C0	C1	C2	C3	C4	C5	C6	C7	C8	C9
Blues	0.00%	2.67%	1.61%	4.03%	1.03%	32.09%	4.38%	4.55%	0.00%	16.87%
Classical	2.30%	70.67%	0.00%	0.67%	1.03%	1.86%	2.19%	4.55%	26.03%	19.28%
Country	5.75%	8.00%	0.00%	0.00%	0.00%	31.63%	0.00%	0.00%	10.96%	15.66%
Disco	22.99%	4.00%	64.52%	2.68%	9.28%	0.93%	5.11%	45.45%	6.85%	0.00%
Hiphop	2.30%	0.00%	6.45%	44.30%	1.03%	5.58%	9.49%	0.00%	0.00%	2.41%
Jazz	5.75%	6.67%	0.00%	1.34%	0.00%	12.56%	3.65%	27.27%	50.68%	15.66%
Metal	18.39%	1.33%	11.29%	1.34%	32.99%	0.47%	26.28%	4.55%	0.00%	4.82%
Pop	5.75%	2.67%	6.45%	8.72%	13.40%	3.72%	27.01%	9.09%	1.37%	18.07%
Reggae	9.20%	0.00%	9.68%	35.57%	0.00%	8.84%	8.03%	0.00%	1.37%	2.41%
Rock	27.59%	4.00%	0.00%	1.34%	41.24%	2.33%	13.87%	4.55%	2.74%	4.82%

Lastly, the fifth and last test would be when K = 10, this is because it is under a premise that all music in the dataset are categorized into 10 genres, which would mean that there should be a significant difference in the features of composition depending on the genre that they may belong to. Here, it may be observed that there are clusters with a smaller amount of samples as opposed to other with more than a hundred or hundreds of samples. For instance C7 and C9 are the more hybrid types of music. C0 may be seen as types of music which fit in with the beaty music of Disco, Rock, and Metal. Pop Rock and Pop Metal genres may be closely related to C4 in this case. Blues, Country, and a hint of Jazz, continue to be clustered on C5s.

However, even though there are clusters with hybrid contents, there are still clusters which maintain to be somewhat pure to a genre. Examples of which are C1, which continues to be a Classical cluster, C2 would be a Disco cluster. This would mean that music which stay true to their genre have a higher change to be part of the original cluster while music which has properties of other genres are more or less included in the other more hybrid types of clusters.

3. Self-Organizing Maps

3.1. *Introduction*

Self-Organizing Maps or better known as SOMs are used to determine the relationships of abstract data through the representation of topographic maps according to the research of Ritter and Kohonen. These abstract maps are more commonly represented on a 2 dimensional plane, however there are researches that use a 3 dimensional plane. The relationships of the abstract data are determined based on the mathematical relationships of each value or feature on the map. It is to be noted that SOMs, which are authored by Kohonen already have numerous variations, one approach that is used by this study focuses on one of its simpler versions.

The process of 2 dimensional SOMs used by the study, starts with initializing a rectangular or hexagonal grid or map of fixed length, with a node evenly spaces between each other. A node in this study, is a representation of an entity with a set number of attributes, features, or weights. These features contain a mathematical value that determine the degree of presence a feature has for that node. During the initial state of the map, the features of each node are completely randomized, nonetheless must be within the value of 0 and 1. It is to be noted that these features are to be understood in such a way that the smallest value be 0, representing a complete lack or inexistence of the said feature, and the highest value be 1 stating that there is a complete presence and existence of that feature on the node. Since during the initial phase of the map, all the features of all nodes are randomized, there are no relationships that relate the adjacent nodes as of the moment.

After setting up the environment, the next step is to include a data set, which is the set of data to be clustered by determining the relationship of each of its entries. This is because the map is to be compared with a dataset containing a list of different data samples, with each one having its own set of features and labels for the process of learning. The features in the dataset is similar to that of the nodes in the map wherein its value ranges from 0 to 1 where 0 means that the feature is completely inexistent and a value of 1 would mean that the feature is completely existent to the specific data entry.

An example of which is a data sample with a feature value of 0.8, this would mean that the said sample, more likely has a closer relation to possessing that feature or that the said feature is evident to that sample as opposed to having a value of 0.2 where it is evident that the said feature is barely seen or observable in that specific sample.

This would go on for all the features of all samples in the data. However in the case that certain samples have completely no relationship with the said feature, a value of −1 is used; this is to designate that regardless of the value of that specific feature, it does not pose any significance in identifying the properties of the said sample. For this type of SOM, a value of −1 for a particular feature is disregarded when doing calculations.

As stated earlier, the dataset would contain features as well as a label for each one. This is to allow clustering or grouping of the values. An example of a dataset could be a set of colors, wherein its features would be the feature value of Red, Green, and Blue, while the label would be the color family with its designated color name. This is because the SOM would be clustering data based on their relationships, and with a label, the clusters could easily be identified.

After initializing the map and selecting a dataset, the process of training is done. Training takes about four (4) steps for each iteration. The first step is to select a random sample from the dataset, this is to ensure that there is a fair selection to all of the samples in that set. In order to ensure a fairer selection process, it is highly recommended that the samples on the dataset should be at an equal quantity with all the other samples. This is to say that if there are 100 samples of a specific label or group, there should also be 100 samples for each and all of the other labels or groups. Giving a dataset with unequal samples might result in a more biased form of selection of nodes.

The second step of the learning process is to compare the randomly selected sample from the dataset to all of the nodes in the map. This is because we would like to determine the node with the closest relationship or distance to the randomly selected sample, to be designated as the Best Matching Unit (BMU) or the Winning Node. The relationship or distance between the nodes and the randomly selected sample may be obtained through numerous methods, however for this study the algorithm to be used is the Euclidean Distance, which would be discussed in the latter part of the study.

The third step is to determine the wining neighborhood, which is the set of nodes whose centroid is the Best Matching Unit, and where all the nodes in the winning neighborhood would learn and adjust their weights or features closer to that of the randomly selected sample. The nodes inside the winning neighborhood is determined based on a fixed distance between the BMU and the nodes. Nodes which are within the neighborhood distance to the BMU would adjust their weights while nodes further to the BMU would not be affected during that iteration. The purpose of this is to allow the nodes in the winning neighborhood to have a closer relationship to the selected sample by a factor which is called the learning rate.

The fourth step is to update the gain parameter used on the learning rate as well as to modify the neighborhood size. These parameters are to be modified in a way that they decrease overtime. There are multiple methods to decrease them, but for simplicity, this study uses a linearly decreasing method. This is because for the initial stages of learning, which is also called Global Ordering, we would want the entire map to be able to learn and adjust in a course manner. After such a time the gain parameter would reach a plateau and the neighborhood size would reach a degree of 1, wherein the neighbor nodes are now the directly adjacent nodes of the BMU, in which case, the learning process would still continue but in such a way that the adjustment would be for finer tuning.

After modifying the parameter and neighborhood size, the process of learning would start over again by selecting another random sample from the dataset. This gives chance to the other samples in the dataset to have an area in the SOM map. Then the cycle continues. It is to be noted that during the early phases of the SOM learning process, it may be observed that the entire map would be drastically changing from one after the other, however after some time, the bits of changes and differences between each node would be seen as the neighborhood size decreases as well as the gain parameter.

With the four steps of learning, the initial map is to be trained over and over for its Global Ordering, then continued to be trained for fine tuning until such a time that it would now possess certain topographic connection between each other based on its features. This would mean that nodes or entries in the map which are closer, have a relatively closer set of feature values as opposed to nodes which are far from each other.

After which two processes could be done; either to label the nodes or to upload the dataset to the nodes. In the process of labeling, each node is to be compared to all of the data samples in order to determine the sample with the closest relation to the node, the winning sample would be the one whose label would be designated on the node. This would go on until all the nodes in the SOM map would be filled with labels which are closest to the nodes. After completion of the labeling process, the entire labeled map would now provide a visual representation on the relationships of the dataset.

One has to understand the since Self Organizing Maps are a classification of Unsupervised Learning and Clustering, it does not have an exact correct answer, but rather present a clustering based on a mathematical relationship between samples or values on a certain extent. Factors such as type of map, sample size and granularity contained in a dataset, size of the entire SOM map, gain parameter and neighborhood size for the learning, and others may greatly affect the result of the SOM.

3.2. *Algorithm*

There are generally five (5) algorithms that would be used in the SOM of the study namely; the Euclidean Distance, Best Matching Unit or Winning Node determination, learning and adjustment of weights in the winning neighborhood, update the gain parameter of the learning rate, and decrease or decay of the neighborhood distance.

The first algorithm used is the Euclidean Distance. According to the research of Singla and Karambir, the Euclidean distance is the ordinary distance between two (2) points in a plane. This algorithm is used in the study to determine or measure the distance between two mathematical values. It must be noted that for determining the distance of two features or weights, other algorithms may be used, such as the Manhattan Distance, however for this study, Euclidean Distance would be used, this is because the algorithm is easily scalable even to a n dimensional space.

$$\sqrt{(x - y)^2}$$

(1)

The Euclidean Distance formula suggests that the distance between two variables x and y is measure by obtaining their difference, squaring them, and finally obtaining its square root.

The second algorithm used is determining the Best Matching Unit or Winning Node, w_c, from the map, M, this is in terms of distance between each node to the randomly selected sample, x, in the dataset. Each feature of the selected sample is to be compared with each of the corresponding weights of each node and summed in order to get the total distance between each node to the selected sample. The Best Matching Unit, w_c, is the node with whose distance is the smallest compared with all the other nodes in the map for a certain time t.

$$M(x^t, w_c^t) = min_{i=1,N}[M(x^t, w_i^t)]$$

(2)

It has to be noted that for every iteration during the learning process, the selected sample is most likely different from the previously selected sample, due to it being randomly selected from the dataset for every iteration. This would mean that the winning node is also most likely different from the winning node of the previous iteration. Therefore it could be observed that for every iteration, there is a randomly selected BMU from the entire map, evening out the feature values of the map.

For the case of the tests used in the study, a square map with 16 rows by 16 columns would be used. This would total 256 nodes with each one containing a set number of weights or features based on the dataset to be used.

$$w_{ij}^{t+1} = w_{ij}^t + \alpha(t)(x_j^t - w_{ij}^t) \tag{3}$$

The third algorithm used by the study is the learning and adjustment of weights in the winning neighborhood. The value of w_i signifies that the process is done for $i=1$ to N where N is the number of nodes inside the winning neighborhood and w designated a node in the winning neighborhood. The value of j determines the respective weight or feature between each node from the winning neighborhood to its corresponding feature in the selected sample. In the case that the particular weight of the node is higher than that of the selected sample, then that weight of the node would decrease, but if the weight was lower than that of the selected sample, then it would increase.

What the algorithm does is to sum the previous value for each of the weights of each node with the difference between the value of the feature of the selected sample and the corresponding weight of that node, multiplied by a gain parameter α. In effect, the weights of the nodes would go closer to the value of that of the selected sample. It is to be noted that without a gain parameter, all nodes in that neighborhood would have the same values for all weights to that of the randomly selected sample, this is similar to having a gain parameter of 1. If the gain parameter is at least less than 1, then there would be a slight fractional difference, however in the case that the gain parameter would be 0.1, then each node would get closer to the selected sample, but only by a bit.

$$\alpha(t) = \alpha_i - \left(\frac{\alpha_i - \alpha_n}{t_g}\right)t \quad ; \text{when } t < t_g$$
$$\alpha(t) = \alpha_n \quad\quad\quad\quad\quad ; \text{when } t \geq t_g \tag{4}$$

The fourth algorithm is to update the gain parameter of the learning rate, in which this study would use a linear decreasing function. The variable $\alpha(t)$ designates the gain parameter of time t, wherein the value of the gain parameter is different based on the time. Since a linear decrease is also done, it is understood that the value of $\alpha(t-1)$ is slightly greater than that of $\alpha(t)$. In this equation α_i is the highest learning point while α_n is the lowest learning point for the gain parameter. For the purposes of this study the highest learning point used would be 0.9 while the lowest learning point would be 0.1, this is because a gain parameter of 1 would mean that all nodes which would learn would now have the same values as that of the selected sample but a value of 0.9 allows a slight retention of their previous values, while a learning point of 0 would mean that there is no learning or change happening but a value of 0.1 would mean that there is at least a slight learning or change from its previous value.

It can be observed that the algorithm is also split into two (2) parts, the top part is the formula to be used while the learning iteration is still at its Global Ordering t_g, designated by time t is less than the Global Ordering time t_g. This would mean that the gain parameter would be decreasing linearly until such a time that the Global Ordering time is completed. Once finished, the gain parameter would stay at a constant value denoted by w, which is the value of 0.1 used in the study. This is to take into account the fine tuning phase of the SOM.

$$d = \frac{\max(t)}{\max(r) - 1}$$

$$r(t) = \left\lfloor \max(r) - \frac{t}{d} \right\rfloor$$

(5)

Lastly, the fifth algorithm used in the study for SOM is the decrease or decay of the neighborhood distance. For the simplicity of the algorithm and the purposes of the study, a gradual decay or floor-based linear decay function is used as opposed to an exponential function. The decay algorithm used is divided into two (2) parts, the rate of decay and the neighborhood radius size. For the first part, the value of d is the rate of decay, which is obtained by dividing the total learning time with the highest radius subtracted by 1 and getting its floor value, in order to determine an evenly split value for a certain number of iterations as it goes from the highest radius value to 2 for the Global Ordering. This is because once Global Ordering is completed, the radius for the fine tuning phase of the SOM would be 1, which would mean that the directly adjacent nodes of the winning node are the ones that comprise the neighborhood.

For the purposes of the study, the initial radius of that would be used would be the highest between the number of rows and the number of columns of the map used by the SOM. This would mean that for the first parts of the learning process, all the nodes would be learning and changing their weights. However as time passes, the radius would gradually decrease overtime until such a time that only the adjacent nodes belong in the neighborhood. As stated in the previous paragraph, this is used to provide a fine tuning to the values in the map.

230

3.3. *Implementation*

In this implementation, the Music Genre Dataset would also be used. Compared to the Animal SOM, whose features are based on a yes or no, a dataset similar to the Music Genre, each music may not stick to a pure genre but a combination of two or more genres. Also there is a certain granularity in terms of feature values as opposed to the simple yes and no used on the Animal SOM.

B	Blues	H	Hiphop	Re	Reggae
Cl	Classical	J	Jazz	Ro	Rock
Co	Country	M	Metal		
D	Disco	P	Pop		

Fig. 1. Music Genre Dataset Legend

The parameters used for the Music Genre SOM are a map with 16 rows and 16 columns, a Global Ordering time of up to 10,000 iterations, a fine tuning time of up to 20,000 iterations, an initial neighborhood radius of 16, a gain parameter of 0.9 for the highest and a 0.1 for the lowest.

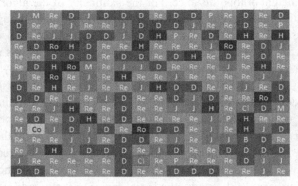

Fig. 2. Labeled Music Genre SOM Map at Time 0

During the start of the SOM, the map would be initialized to a random value for each weight of the nodes. This is why there are not much relationships between as of the moment. However it may be seen evidently that there are majorly scattered values of Disco, Jazz and Reggae throughout the map as opposed to the other values. This may be caused due to the fact that the values for Jazz, Disco, and Reggae are closer to the mean or average of the node features as opposed to the other values. During the first iterations of the test, the learning rate is close to 1 and the radius affects the whole map, this would mean that regardless of the randomization of the map during the initialization phase, everything would be influenced by the first few iterations by a lot, allowing the entire map to change drastically. This would mean that using an algorithm with a high learning rate and a radius that spans the entire map, the initialization of the map would have almost none, if not, have no effect on the outcome or result of the trained SOM map.

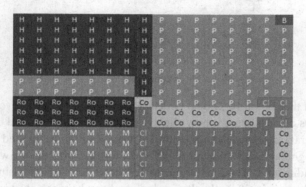

Fig. 3. Labeled Music Genre SOM Map at Time 6,000

The 6,000th iteration for the Music Genre SOM, shows slightly more varying results as opposed to the 2,000th iterations, on whose reasons are due to the parameters are decreasing bit by bit. It may now be observed that a significant number of Pop, Hiphop, Jazz, Metal, and Rock music have emerged. A slight number of Classical, Country, and single Blues also appears in this iteration. This would most likely mean that the Country, Classical, and Blues section might have been the earlier selected sample labels as opposed to those other more dominant labels, which most likely have been the more recent samples, while others such as Reggae, which was seen during the time 0 in Fig. 2, might have been overlapped by the other genres due to having a high learning rate as well as radius at this point.

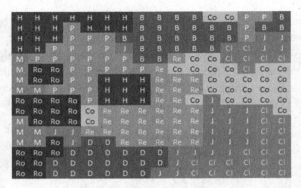

Fig. 4. Labeled Music Genre SOM Map at Time 10,000

Then at the end of the Global Ordering phase of the SOM, the topographical relationships of each genre is now slightly more evident as opposed to that of the previous iterations. However a fine tuning stage is still to be applied wherein the map would go through 10,000 more iterations for fine adjustments with a gain of 0.1 and a radius of 1. The fine tuning phase allows for slight adjustments on the nodes which may significantly alter nodes which are between cluster borders.

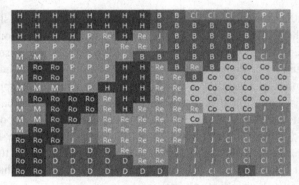

Fig. 5. Labeled Music Genre SOM Map at Time 20,000

Finally after completing both the Global Ordering phase and the fine adjustment phase, it could be observed that there are still areas in the map wherein there might be misplaces nodes of a particular genre. Examples of which are the separated Jazz, Reggae, Classical, Pop, Rock, Disco, and others from their main clusters. These outlying nodes are not errors, but are actually very important, parts of the map. This is because they are the nodes which are a hybrid of other genres as opposed to what they generally are.

In order to properly determine if the Music Genre SOM is correct, another test is done. During this stage the nodes have newly been initialized and the values are randomized. For this test, the other iterations would also be skipped since they more or less similar to that of the first test.

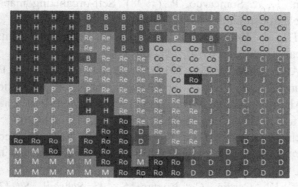

Fig. 6.   Labeled Music Genre SOM Map Test 2 at Time 20,000

Fig. 6 shows the end result of the second test of the Music Genre Dataset. It is observable that similar to the first test, there are certain nodes which are separated from their main clusters due to that fact that they are hybrid values, which have traits of their adjacent clusters but are still generally part of a different genre.

For both tests, it could be observed that there is a connection between Country music to Blues, Reggae, and Jazz. Metal and Rock are almost always beside one another. Pop is also seen to have traits of both Rock and Hiphop, with a slight Reggae. Disco is also still close to Classical, Jazz, Rock, and a slight Reggae. Overall the SOM proves the topographical relationship of these nodes, regardless how many tests are run.

References

1. Azcarraga, A., Caronongan, A., Setiono, R., & Manalili, S. (2016). Validating the Stable Clustering of Songs in a Structured 3D SOM.
2. Alsabti, K., Ranka, S., & Singh, V. (1997). An efficient k-means clustering algorithm.
3. Huysmans, J., Baesens, B., Vanthienen, J., & Van Gestel, T. (2006). Failure prediction with self organizing maps. Expert Systems with Applications, 30(3), 479-487.
4. Kangas, J. A., Kohonen, T. K., & Laaksonen, J. T. (1990). Variants of self-organizing maps. Neural Networks, IEEE Transactions on, 1(1), 93-99.

5. Kanungo, T., Mount, D. M., Netanyahu, N. S., Piatko, C. D., Silverman, R., & Wu, A. Y. (2002). An efficient k-means clustering algorithm: Analysis and implementation. Pattern Analysis and Machine Intelligence, IEEE Transactions on, 24(7), 881-892.

6. Kohonen, T., & Somervuo, P. (1998). Self-organizing maps of symbol strings. Neurocomputing, 21(1), 19-30.

7. Ritter, H., & Kohonen, T. (1989). Self-organizing semantic maps. Biological cybernetics, 61(4), 241-254.

8. Singla, A., & Karambir, M. (2012). Comparative Analysis & Evaluation of Euclidean Distance Function and Manhattan Distance Function Using K-means Algorithm. International Journal of Advanced Research in Computer Science and Software Engineering (IJARSSE), 2(7), 298-300.

9. Steinbach, M., Karypis, G., & Kumar, V. (2000, August). A comparison of document clustering techniques. In KDD workshop on text mining (Vol. 400, No. 1, pp. 525-526).

10. Wagstaff, K., Cardie, C., Rogers, S., & Schrödl, S. (2001, June). Constrained k-means clustering with background knowledge. In ICML (Vol. 1, pp. 577-584).

Music-emotion Recognition Based on Wearable Dry-electrode Electroencephalogram

Patraporn Senachakr

Department of Computer Engineering, Faculty of Engineering,
Chulalongkorn University, Bangkok 10330, Thailand
E-mail: patraporn.se@student.chula.ac.th

Nattapong Thammasan

Graduate school of Information Science and Technology,
Osaka University, Osaka 565-0871, Japan
E-mail: nattapong@ai.sanken.osaka-u.ac.jp

Ken-ichi Fukui and Masayuki Numao

The Institute of Scientific and Industrial Research,
Osaka University, Osaka 567-0047, Japan
E-mail: {fukui,numao}@ai.sanken.osaka-u.ac.jp

Despite the success of previous research in emotion recognition using electroencephalogram (EEG), the traditional EEG devices used in those research had limited practicability to be employed in a naturalistic and real-world situation. Accordingly, a new wearable EEG mounted with dry electrodes has been recently developed, yet the feasibility to use it for emotion detection has not been confirmed. In this work, we present a preliminary study of emotion recognition in music listening using the new EEG device. Spectral features were extracted from the selected six electrodes (Fp1, Fp2, C1, C2, T3, and T4) of the EEG and the support vector machine was employed to classify binary classes of arousal and valence. Our empirical results demonstrate the promise of using the new EEG to recognize emotional states of a human during music listening.

Keywords: Dry-electrode Electroencephalogram, Wearable sensor, Emotion classification, Music emotion.

1. Introduction

Emotion detection has gained the attentions of researchers for several decades. A variety of methods has been proposed to automatically estimate emotional state of human[1]. Recently, physiological signals have been actively utilized to construct emotion recognition system. Among these attempts, an electroencephalogram (EEG), a noninvasive tool to measure brainwaves, is one of the most dominant tools owing to its excellent temporal resolution and potential to provide the clue of emotion processing inside human brain. Consequently, recent years have witnessed a great number of attempts to estimate emotional states using EEG[2,3].

Despite the success in the laboratory setting, there still exists a big gap between research of EEG-based emotion detection and practical application in real world. Several EEG devices used in previous emotion recognition research[4-6] were proper to be utilized for medical diagnosis as the devices connected to computers via wired connectors resulting in the limited mobility of users. A newly developed wireless EEG used in another work[7,8] still relied on conductive gel or saline solution rendering annoyingly long time in EEG setting. The limitation of the currently existing EEG devices led to the shift toward the development of wearable EEG devices on which dry electrodes were mounted[9]. The novel device has been targeted to provide comparable outcome with the traditional devices in terms of signal-to-noise ratio, signal stability, and usability. Despite its potentials, the applicability of the new EEG device to estimate emotional state has not been confirmed yet.

In this work, we present a preliminary study of emotion recognition using a wearable dry-electrode EEG device. The device has eight active electrodes and communicates with terminal computer via Bluetooth communication. While emotion can be evoked by various types of stimuli, we opted to use musical excerpts as the stimuli based on the reason that emotion detection in music listening could potentially enable various types of interesting application, e.g., EEG-based music recommendation, multimedia tagging, and automatic music composition[10]. While emotion can be represented in numerous ways, we employed arousal-valence model[11], which is an actively exploited dimensional model to represent emotion in affective computing (Figure 1); arousal indicates the level of excitement in one dimension, while valence represents the level of emotion positivity on the other orthogonal dimension.

2. Experiment

2.1. *Subjects and devices*

Two male subjects (Thai nationality, 26 and 29 years of age) having normal mental health were recruited to participate in our experiment. The

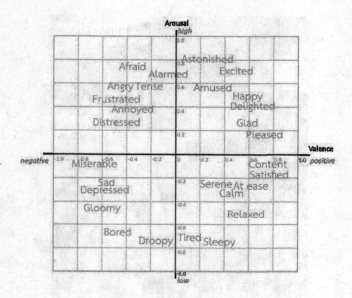

Fig. 1.   Arousal-valence space

EEG used in this research is a wireless EEG headset developed by imec[a]. Eight electrodes, namely Fp1, Fp2, C1, C2, T3, T4, O1, and O2 in accordance with the 10-20 international system, were mounted on the headset. The headset's two reference electrodes were contacting mastoids, while two ground electrodes were touching the scalp nearby the positions of F7 and F8 electrodes in the 10-20 international system. Nevertheless, O1 and O2 electrodes could not perfectly contact the scalp of any subject because of the unfit design of the headset, the signals from those two electrodes were, therefore, discarded in our study. Headphones were used to present musical stimuli to the subjects; one subject used experimental insert earphones[b], whereas the other subject used a headphone with noise-canceling function[c]. In addition, a wireless electrocardiogram patch and a wrist-worn watch capable of recording galvanic skin response were also set to collect supplementary information for further investigation. A snapshot of the experiment is shown in Figure 2.

[a]https://www.holstcentre.com/innovation-areas/wearable-health-solutions/
[b]ER1
http://www.etymotic.com/auditory-research/insert-earphones-for-research/er1.html
[c]QuietComfort3 http://worldwide.bose.com/productsupport/en_us/web/qc3/page.html

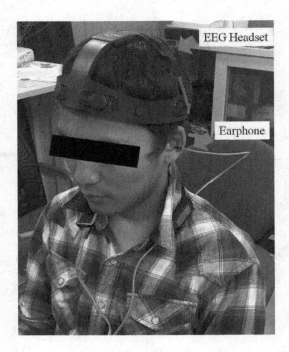

Fig. 2. A subject during undergoing experiment

2.2. *Musical stimuli*

The music collection used as stimuli was comprised of 49 MIDI musical excerpts having duration of 37.53 seconds on average. The considerably high number of the songs in this collection were intensively used in previous research aiming to construct automatic music composition system[12]. In the collection, 25 songs had major tonality, whereas the other 24 songs had minor tonality. The song titles are summarized in Table 1.

2.3. *Experimental protocol*

Our experiments were conducted in an experimental room using our developed software implemented in Java and the software of EEG headset. Each subject was asked to sit on a comfortable seat, and a brief guideline to the experiments was given. Musical stimuli were presented to subjects as sounds synthesized by the Java Sound API's MIDI package[d]. During

---

[d]http://docs.oracle.com/javase/7/docs/technotes/guides/sound/

Table 1. List of the songs used in the experiment

Tonality	Song titles
Major	Twinkle Twinkle Little Star, She Loves You, Radio Taiso Daiichi, Robinson, Ginga Tetsudo 999, Niji, Don'na Toki Mo, Jupiter, I was born to love you, Hitomiwotojite, Ano Subarashi Ai Wo Mo Ichi Do, Hey Jude, Ama-chan Opening Theme, Sambo, Baroque Hoedown, Mamma Mia, Sekaini Hitotsudake No Hana, Yesterday Once More, Okina Furudokei, Neko Funjatta, Choo Choo TRAIN, Let It Go, Sing, Auld Lang Syne, I Need to Be In Love
Minor	Aporo (Apollo), Beat It, Rabusutori Wa Totsuzen ni, The Final Countdown, Klaviersonate Nr.14 cis_moll Op.272 Moonlight, Poker Face, Christmas Carol No koro Ni Ha, Haru Yo Koi, SAKURA, Wataruseken Wa Oni Bakari Opening Theme, The Imperial March (Darth Vader's Theme), Garamond Song, Sakura Sakura, Romantic Ga Tomaranai, From The Swan Lake Scene, Gekko (Moonlight), Thriller, CAT'S EYE, Kimi Wo Nosete, Merry Christmas Mr. Lawrence, Bittersweet Samba, Mononokehime, Mission Impossible Theme, Jonetsu Dai Riku

listening to each song, each subject was asked to close his eyes and minimize his body movement to reduce the effect of unrelated artifacts. At the end of each song presentation, each subject was instructed to annotate the emotion felt while listening to the song by clicking at a corresponding point in arousal-valence space displayed on the monitor screen. Horizontal axis represented valence level ranging from -1 (extremely negative) to 1 (extremely positive), and vertical axis represented arousal level ranging from -1 (lowest) to 1 (highest). Each subject was encouraged to take a brief rest until being ready to proceed to the next song session.

2.4. *Feature extraction and emotion classification*

The acquired EEG signals were associated with the timing of musical stimuli presentation via timestamps. The EEG data only between the start and the end of each song presentation were utilized. To extract informative features from the EEG signals in each session, we applied the fast Fourier transform technique to convert EEG data originally in the time domain into the frequency domain using Scilab[e]. Five spectral features, namely delta (1–3 Hz), theta (4–7 Hz), alpha (8–12 Hz), beta (13–30 Hz), and gamma (31–50 Hz), were obtained by averaging spectral powers within the

---

[e]http://www.scilab.org/

corresponding frequency band range for each electrode channel. Inspired by the successful results in the literature[13], additional differential asymmetry feature was also added to the original feature set; the feature was calculated by subtracting a feature from the left hemisphere electrode's signal by the feature extracted from the signal produced by its symmetric electrode in the right hemisphere, e.g., Fp1-alpha – Fp2-alpha. Accordingly, we obtained 45 features in total from all electrodes. To obtain a higher amount of data from each session, a non-overlapping sliding window with the size of two seconds was applied. The extracted features were then labeled by the associated arousal and valence level.

For the sake of simplicity, we converted emotion recognition into the binary classification of arousal (low vs. high) and valence (negative vs. positive) using the signs of numerical arousal and valence values. We then applied support vector machine with the Pearson VII kernel function (PUK) kernel to classify arousal and valence classes. The SVM was implemented using WEKA library[14].

3. Results

To reflect the performance of the subject-dependent emotion recognition model, a stratified 10-fold cross-validation was applied. Table 2 shows the accuracy, precision, and recall of arousal and valence classification for each subject. The associated majority class, which refers the percentage of instances in majority class in the total instance, was also shown. Focusing on the accuracy, the performance of emotion classification in Subject 1 was greatly higher than majority class classification. In Subject 2, however, the model could recognize arousal slightly better than majority class classification but failed to outperform majority class classification in valence recognition. Generally, the results demonstrate the potential of constructing emotion recognition model to classify binary classes of arousal and valence.

Table 2.   Results of emotion classification

Subject	Classification	Accuracy	Precision	Recall	Majority class	
1	Arousal	69.30%	0.719	0.787	low	59.07%
	Valence	76.42%	0.755	0.791	negative	50.61%
2	Arousal	54.13%	0.537	0.554	high	50.33%
	Valence	74.46%	0.746	0.854	negative	74.67%

Note: [a] Precision and recall are for high arousal and positive valence classes.

4. Discussion

The aim of this work is to examine the feasibility of using the newly developed EEG device to recognize emotional states in music listening task. Although the preliminary results demonstrated the promise of the new EEG device, several issues leave room for discussion.

As the device was the product of ongoing research, the stability in device usage was occasionally unsatisfied. For instance, the EEG signal quality highly relied on how well the electrodes contact the subject's scalp and mastoids, hence the unintentional disconnection between electrodes and the scalp could sometimes reduce the signal quality. In addition, the metal electrodes and imperfect head-shape matching could cause slight pain and discomfort as reported by the participating subjects. Even though the subjects were encouraged to take a short break when feeling uncomfortable, the disparity in EEG setting in the different epoch could have a certain effect on the acquired EEG signals. However, these limitations will be expectedly alleviated in the future as the EEG device is currently being actively developed toward more reliable and comfortable device, especially in long-duration usage.

It is noticeable that the generalization of this work seems limited. There were merely two subjects participating in the experiment. Recruiting more subjects, taking several subjectivity factors (e.g., age, gender, music familiarity[15]) into consideration could potentially be helpful in generalizing our results, and these are already included into our future works.

5. Conclusion

In summary, this work demonstrates the feasibility of using a newly developed wearable EEG mounted with eight dry electrodes to recognize human emotion during music listening. Binary classes of arousal and valence could be recognized by classifying spectral features extracted from six EEG electrodes using support vector machine. The improvement in the next generation of the EEG device could expectedly further enhance the performance of emotion recognition model with the aim to practically use EEG to recognize emotional states in the naturalistic and real-world situation.

Acknowledgment

This research is partially supported by the Center of Innovation Program from Japan Science and Technology Agency (JST), JSPS KAKENHI Grant

Number 25540101, and the Management Expenses Grants for National Universities Corporations from the Ministry of Education, Culture, Sports, Science and Technology of Japan (MEXT).

References

1. A. Konar and A. Chakraborty, *Emotion Recognition: A Pattern Analysis Approach* (Wiley, 2014).
2. R. Jenke, A. Peer and M. Buss, Feature extraction and selection for emotion recognition from EEG, *IEEE Trans. Affect. Comput.* **5**, 327 (2014).
3. M.-K. Kim, M. Kim, E. Oh and S.-P. Kim, A review on the computational methods for emotional state estimation from the human EEG, *Comp. Math. Methods in Medicine* **2013** (2013).
4. S. Koelstra, C. Muhl, M. Soleymani, J.-S. Lee, A. Yazdani, T. Ebrahimi, T. Pun, A. Nijholt and I. Patras, DEAP: A database for emotion analysis using physiological signals, *IEEE Trans. Affect. Comput.* **3**, 18 (2012).
5. W.-L. Zheng and B.-L. Lu, Investigating critical frequency bands and channels for EEG-based emotion recognition with deep neural networks, *IEEE Trans. Autonomous Mental Development* **7**, 162 (2015).
6. N. Thammasan, K. Moriyama, K. Fukui and M. Numao, Continuous music-emotion recognition based on electroencephalogram, *IEICE Trans. Inform. Syst.* **E99-D**, 1234 (2016).
7. O. Sourina, Y. Liu and M. K. Nguyen, Real-time EEG-based emotion recognition for music therapy, *J. Multimodal. User. In.* **5**, 27 (2012).
8. N. Jatupaiboon, S. Pan-ngum and P. Israsena, Real-time EEG-based happiness detection system, *The Scientific World Journal* **2013** (2013).
9. V. Mihajlovic, B. Grundlehner, R. Vullers and J. Penders, Wearable, wireless EEG solutions in daily life applications: What are we missing?, *IEEE Journal of Biomedical and Health Informatics* **19**, 6 (2015).
10. Y.-H. Yang and H. H. Chen, *Music Emotion Recognition* (CRC Press, Boca Raton, FL, USA, 2011).
11. J. A. Russell, A circumplex model of affect, *J. Pers. Soc. Psychol.* **39**, 1161 (1980).
12. N. Otani, S. Shirakawa and M. Numao, Symbiotic evolution to generate chord progression consisting of four parts for a music composition system, in *Proc. 13th Pacific Rim International Conference on Artificial Intelligence*, 2014.

13. Y.-P. Lin, C.-H. Wang, T.-P. Jung, T.-L. Wu, S.-K. Jeng, J.-R. Duann and J.-H. Chen, EEG-based emotion recognition in music listening, *IEEE Trans. Biomedical Engineering* **57**, 1798 (2010).

14. M. Hall, E. Frank, G. Holmes, B. Pfahringer, P. Reutemann and I. H. Witten, The weka data mining software: An update, *SIGKDD Explor. NewsL.* **11**, 10 (2009).

15. N. Thammasan, K. Moriyama, K. Fukui and M. Numao, Familiarity effects in EEG-based emotion recognition, *Brain Informatics*, 1 (2016).

Author Index

Alcalde, J. G., 59
Alferez, K. P., 44
Arellano, A. E. C., 160
Azcarraga, A., 219

Baclayon, J. M. C., 208
Bucag, M. S. I., 181

Caro, J., 194
Cempron, J. P., 70
Chua, G., 59
Chua, J. A., 83
Cortez, B. M., 172

de Leon, R. P., 132
Demabildo, I. M., 59

Famador, S. M. W., 160
Feliscuzo, L. S., 181
Feria, R., 132
Flores, F. K., 106, 219
Fukui, K., 235

Gemba, F., 120
Go-Soco, J. P., 83
Gonzales, J. B., 70

Hagihara, S., 14
Hanakawa, N., 120
Hayakawa, Y., 70

Ilao, J., 106
Iwasaki, Y., 14

Joko, H., 28

Morano, I. S., 83

Nagayama, K., 1
Nazario, M., 132
Nishizaki, S., 28
Numao, M., 235

Ong, A. V., 83
Ong, M. A., 59

Pacilan, J. D., 44
Pelayo, C. A., 160
Pequiras, K. D., 83

Romana, C. L. C. S., 172
Roxas, R. R., 94, 208

Salinas, C., 70
Sawada, K., 1
Senachakr, P., 235
Shimakawa, M., 14
Solamo, Ma. R., 132
Suzuki, K., 1

Thammasan, N., 235
Tominaga, H., 120
Turla, Z. C., 194

Uriarte, B. D. C., 94
Uy, R. L., 59, 70

Watanabe, T., 1

Yonezaki, N., 14

Printed in the United States
by Bookmasters

Printed in the United States
By Bookmasters